Soul Journeys

Also by Rosalind A. McKnight
Cosmic Journeys

Soul Journeys

My Guided Tours through the Afterlife

Rosalind A. McKnight

HAMPTON ROADS
PUBLISHING COMPANY, INC.

Hampton Roads Publishing Company, Inc.
1125 Stoney Ridge Road
Charlottesville, VA 22902

434-296-2772
fax: 434-296-5096
e-mail: hrpc@hrpub.com
www.hrpub.com

If you are unable to order this book from your local
bookseller, you may order directly from the publisher.
Call 1-800-766-8009, toll-free.

Library of Congress Cataloging-in-Publication Data

McKnight, Rosalind A.
  Soul journeys : my guided tours through the afterlife / Rosalind A.
McKnight.
      p. cm.
  ISBN 1-57174-413-4 (pbk. : alk. paper)
  1. Future life. 2. Spiritualism. I. Title.
  BF1311.F8M35 2005
  133.9'01'3--dc22

                          2004019444

10 9 8 7 6 5 4 3 2 1
Printed on acid-free paper in the United States

Dedicated to
Spirit . . . the All That Is

Contents

V. New Beginnings

Acknowledgment

I want to thank God
and
my Friends on the other side for
all they have done in preparing this manuscript:
for planning it in the no-time realm,
for dispatching it into the Earth plane through
my mind via my computer,
and for joyously guiding me through many
dimensions beyond the Earth to
experience its contents.

Introduction

This book is about life—and only life! It is written to dispel the fear of death, which many, many people have.

I wrote a poem in my teenage years about death and I ended with "Death is merely a word created by humans to describe something they do not understand." We have a fear of the unknown. Death is an unknown that causes us to fear becoming extinct once we cease breathing. What meaning would there be in a life that became extinct once it ceased to be? Very little—because, as humans, we love to have something to look forward to.

So if we knew exactly what happens to us after we depart our temporary existence here on this awesome planet, we would live a more meaningful life filled with joy and anticipation of the most exciting and incredible journey we will ever take. And life would consist of what we often see on bumper stickers: NO FEAR . . .

How do we find out what the next world is like? Simple . . . Ask someone who lives there and record what is said. Better yet, let that "someone" take you on a tour of their world.

This is exactly what I have done. And let me say that this book has nothing to do with religion or religious beliefs. If you decide to take a trip to France, you can line up a tour with a travel agent from that country. That has nothing to do with religion. Taking a tour of the dimensions beyond the Earth likewise has nothing to do with religion.

But it does have to do with the soul and spirit, which is a vital part of who we are. Have you ever had someone ask you: "Do you believe you have a spirit or soul?" I'm sure you have been asked this because most people have at some point in their lives. I read a poll once taken on that question and around 89 percent of the people polled answered yes.

But that is incorrect because the real answer is that we do not *have* a spirit or soul, we *are* a spirit with a soul that is currently having a human experience.

So this book is written for everyone who is having a human experience—young or old, male or female, religious or nonreligious, black or white. It is written for everyone from all walks of life because everyone on this planet *is* a spirit with a soul.

How was I able to meet someone from the world beyond and ask them for details of what life is like over there? Well, I had a visitation from a radiant spirit who offered to take me on a tour of the afterlife. Of course I said yes because I have always had an inquisitive mind and I love to travel. This book is about the very exciting tours that we took together.

I'm sure you are wondering what our means of travel was. The answer again is simple—spirit! She is a spirit who is out of her physical body and I am a spirit with a physical body just as you are. But spirits are of a more refined substance than the physical body so are free to travel when and where they please. Every spirit on planet Earth, including you, travels at night when the body sleeps. So she came for me and guided me on exciting tours of the afterlife.

Your next question may be, "How do you learn to take these tours and consciously record what you experience?"

I just happened to stumble upon a situation in the early 1970s where a gentleman by the name of Robert Monroe was doing research in human consciousness. He was using a process called Hemi-Sync, which safely alters brain-wave patterns, helping individuals to experience deeper levels of self-discovery and expanded awareness. This assisted me in having communication with and visits to other energy systems and realities. The motto of the Monroe Institute, which developed as a result of his research is "I am more than my physical body."

I participated for 11 years as an Explorer in Mr. Monroe's laboratory at Whistlefield in Afton, Virginia. My book entitled *Cosmic Journeys* is a record of many of my unusual and exciting experiences, which took place in the lab.

Since I had extensive experience in exploring other realities, I was well prepared and equipped to take Radiant Lady (as I call her) up on her offer to explore further into the many dimensions of the afterlife.

Soul Journeys is a record of those experiences. Enjoy!

PART I

The Journeys Begin

1 Meeting My Tour Guide

I pulled up in front of my parents' house on Eichelberger Avenue in Dayton, Ohio. It had been a long day. I turned off the engine and laid my head back to recharge before getting out of the car. I began having images of what Eichelberger Avenue was like when I was a child growing up there. I wondered what it would have been like to live in this house when it was first built in the late 1800s. Two major landmarks from the past stood out clearly in my mind: the old nightclub and the windmill.

A nightclub had been built within "hollering" distance of our farmhouse. It seemed strange that an elegant nightclub would have been located out on farmland. But it was built in the days of prohibition when people were not permitted to buy or drink alcohol. (The Eighteenth Amendment to the Constitution made alcohol illegal from 1920 to 1933.) It was probably a speakeasy, where a member would go to the door and give a password before getting into the club.

In fact, there was a section in the floor of our old house that was used to conceal the prohibited spirits. As kids we used to open the hinged door and peek down to see if we could see any of the "spirits"! But Dad spoiled our fun and threw cold water on our imaginations by sanding the trapdoor and nailing it down.

The center of the old nightclub was the dance floor. The large cement slab had no doubt been covered with nice wood until the great fire sometime in the 1930s. A half-acre of rubble, with many nooks and crannies, left a lot to the imagination. But the dance floor in the burned-down nightclub became the central attraction for us children, where skating on its smooth surface brought hours of joy to our feet, as the Charleston must have done for the nightclub revelers in the 1920s and early '30s.

As a regular ritual, the neighborhood kids who frequented our "clubhouse" used to dig endlessly through the rubble around our skating rink, always hoping to find that "something more." As children, we had an inner certainty that there was much more there than our eyes could see, and we were going to dig until we found it. I remember using little sticks to dig for hours at a time. I knew intuitively that if I dug enough, I would uncover the magic of life that is hidden from sight.

And sure enough, one of my first major lessons about the Laws of the Universe was discovered at our sacred open-air clubhouse where so many delicious childhood memories were made. The following incident describes very simply the Law of Karma—that what we do to others, good or bad, returns to us in kind.

As children we had created our "pee spots" in the weeds beside our circular rink. As my little friend, Lilly Ann, was squatting down one day, and I was squatting down behind her, I got the idea that it would be a very funny joke if I would rub poison ivy on her exposed bottom. So I grabbed a handful of some poison ivy growing beside me, and said, "Lilly Ann, there's a spider crawling on you!"—and I rubbed the ivy on her buttocks, as if I was knocking off the spider. She was freaked out at the thought of a spider crawling on her bottom, and she jumped up screaming, pulling her panties up as she ran. I had a good laugh over the incident.

I had plenty of time to laugh, however, when I had a few itchy, miserable days at home from school. I was covered with poison ivy from top to bottom—"bottom" because I too had to pull my panties up as I dropped the poison ivy and ran laughing behind Lilly Ann.

The Law of Karma, "What you sow, so shall you reap"—or "the poison ivy you rub on someone will get on you"—was a major lesson for me. I never even considered the possibility of the ivy affecting me. Later, Lilly Ann didn't mention anything to me about having poison ivy, and consoled me when she saw my eyes almost swollen shut. And my hurt ego never allowed me to expose my fiendish scheme.

(Thus I learned early in life, through my poison ivy prank, that energy boomerangs: that when you send it out, it comes back to knock you down a notch, or bump you up to a higher level of living—or both!)

The other landmark, which still stood in our yard when we moved there in 1939, was a windmill. I had such an adventuresome spirit, even at the age of five, that I thought nothing of climbing to the top of the windmill to see what was out there that I couldn't see from the ground. If I couldn't find that "something more" that I was looking for by digging, surely I could find it by looking toward the horizon as far as my eyes could see. But my dad put a stop to my airborne activities by taking down the windmill.

As I sat in my car reminiscing, I realized that the digging and climbing of my early childhood have continued into my adult life as a restless searching for the truths that lie beyond what the physical eye can see and the hand can touch. I had a continual urge to dig for answers to my questions not only in my "backyard," but also around the world—and finally within myself, where the real answers are to be found. I sat there with a deep feeling of satisfaction for the work I was doing with young people. But at the same time, I felt a nagging sensation that there was something more that I needed to find out.

I had been working almost four years with teenagers. I had no special training for this work other than a bachelor's degree from Manchester College in Indiana. Having no idea what I was going to do with my life after college, I had signed up for a double major in Peace Studies and Sociology, hoping that one or the other would one day help me to get a good job. And here I learned another very important lesson in life—that loving to be with young people, and loving them unconditionally, was a special formula that went far beyond any academic degree that one might have.

The thought kept coming to me, however, that I needed to go on for a master's degree to help me develop greater skills in working with these young people. But the larger truth was that I needed a change, needed to move into a new phase of growth. Thus it wasn't my salary that led me to leave my position as district youth fieldworker for the Church of the Brethren at $2,000 a year, minimal though that pay was.

Once when visiting one of our churches on a Sunday morning, I settled back to enjoy some time off from my responsibilities by listening to the minister's sermon. When he got up for the sermon, he said, "We're really happy to have our youth fieldworker with us today. She is going to gift us by preaching the sermon. Rosie, could you please come on up to the pulpit?"

Luckily, I had just given a three-point talk to a group of churchwomen a few days earlier, and I quickly retrieved the three points from my memory as I walked to the pulpit. As it turned out, they were impressed with my "sermon"—and I was relieved to have had an ace up my sleeve to save me from passing out on the spot! This experience gave me my first inkling that I needed to consider working on a master of divinity degree.

As I sat relaxing in my car, I felt an overwhelming feeling of joy and appreciation for what my parents were doing for me. Having raised eight kids, they were never in a position to pay for any of my years of education. But they compensated for that by giving me free room and board any time I wanted to come home to stay for any period of time. So even on my $2,000-a-year income, I was able to save several thousand dollars by rooming at home. That money would give me a good financial foundation for going on to graduate school.

Needing to get my tired bones to bed, I got out of the car and headed down the sidewalk to the house. It was only a little after nine P.M. and the lights were out in the house. The one reprieve my mother and father had from raising eight kids was going to bed early (which may have helped perpetuate our clan). Mom was 42 and I was 13 when the twins, Larry and Linda, were born. Now that they were in their teens, we all got extra perks through my job. I got to be with Linda and Larry more and they met a lot of new friends through regional and national youth events we attended together.

The most memorable experience for all three of us was our trip to the National Youth Conference at Estes Park, Colorado. Our denomination's national office, located in Illinois, leased an entire train to transport the young people of the central and eastern United States to the conference. The idea was to keep the young people together and safe, but the train ride resulted in an incident that could very easily have sent some of us into the next dimension! I'm sure that all of our guardian angels were attentively gathered on the roof of the train, since they were probably warned ahead of time that they had an important task to perform.

And this is where I learned another lesson about life, which I will call the "Disconnect Principle."

I was just ready to step into the train car that Larry and Linda were in to see what fun they were up to when suddenly I heard a strange metallic sound that caused me to pull my foot back from the ledge leading to their car. The rush of wind that embraced me when I closed the door behind me caused me to hold on to a metal railing for dear life as I watched in horror as Larry and Linda's car disconnected before my eyes and sped ahead of my car at triple speed. The young people in their car began screaming and clutching one another as their speed quadrupled. With nothing in front of me to block my view, I watched "The Little Train that Could and Finally Did" become a mere dot on the horizon as my car and ten or so more behind it glided to a halt.

By the time the engineer was able to control his runaway engine it took a good while for him to back up and reconnect with us. I felt like someone right out of an old-time cowboy movie—with a horse running beside a train and someone motioning for the rider to jump on! When I finally got reconnected with my very frightened brother and sister, it was a great relief. And I was very thankful to our guardian angels for keeping us out of harm's way.

This episode taught me another lesson about life: that at any time we can instantly—yes, I mean *instantly*—become disconnected from people and things that we dearly love, sometimes being reconnected . . . and sometimes not. And thus this Disconnect Principle helped me to learn to live in the moment, and to be more thankful for what I had.

My youth-worker job suited me well because my adventuresome spirit was always ready to be challenged. I was in my late twenties, and working with teens was the fuel that kept my spirit recharged. My father, being from the Southern tradition that emphasized the importance of marriage and children for a successful life, began viewing himself as a failure, having a daughter who was an "old maid."

Dad was a bit confused, since in my large high school (about 260 in my graduating class) I had been very popular and very active on the dating circuit. I had been invited into the best sorority, voted a Homecoming Queen attendant, and received the distinction of being the first female president of the tenth grade class at Fairview High. I dated lots of guys; once when I had two dates in one day, Dad reprimanded me, saying that my dating life was getting a little out of hand.

Now, however, he let me know in no uncertain terms that he expected me to concentrate on finding a mate instead of seeking more education and new experiences like a business degree, a job in Europe, a college degree, and now youth work. He sat me down and gave me "the marriage/children lecture." All my older brothers and sisters were now married and raising children. I was happy for them—and for me because I looked at it as a way of having the pressure taken off me to follow suit.

I knew that my mother was silently cheering me on to achieve the things she was not able to achieve in life. In fact, I'm sure she was living vicariously through me since, after graduating from high school, she went right into the marriage and family role that her parents expected of her.

Mom had always dreamed of writing a book since writing was her greatest gift, beyond being an incredible mother and household executive. (Now that I am writing my second book, I'm sure that she is still vicariously living through me, and cheering me on from the "other side.")

Dad, being a farmworker in his early life, only finished the sixth grade and I think was somewhat intimidated by my desire to further my education and seek unusual experiences beyond my family boundaries. So instead of encouraging me in my endeavors, he was always challenging me. I never liked to "take telling," as he used to say. His telling me what to do with my life only made me more determined to do the opposite. I guessed that my insurgent desire to get a master's degree would probably send him into orbit—which it did!

It was indeed time to still my mind with sleep. I tiptoed upstairs to my room. I didn't even bother turning on the light. A faint glow from the street-light shone into the room as I stepped out of my clothes, leaving them on the floor because I was too exhausted to hang them up. I grabbed my night-gown out of the dresser, put it on, and crawled into my warm, cozy bed. Going to sleep and dreaming has always been one of my favorite things.

As I closed my eyes and started down into dreamland, I experienced the strangest thing that had ever happened to me in my life thus far. . . .

Just as I started drifting down into another state of consciousness, I had a stricken feeling that in the darkness of the room someone was watching me. Immediately as that thought crossed my mind, my eyes popped open—and there looking down at me was the most beautiful woman I have ever seen. Light radiated all around her, and she had a vibrant, shimmering appearance. She was dressed in a brilliant blue gown and it flowed as she moved slowly backward, and disappeared!

My shock and surprise were probably the contributing factors that moved her radiant form away from me as she faded into the darkness of the room. You can imagine that I was now wide-awake, and I felt goose bumps rise up all over my body. My heart was beating hard as I lay there trying to put this experience into a category in my mind that might make sense out of what had just happened. It didn't fit into any slot other than "ghost."

I had heard ghost stories most of my life. My father, being from the mountains of Tennessee, carried on an oral tradition of telling amazing stories from his past. One of the main entertainments for my brothers and sisters, me, and the neighborhood children was to rest on the front porch on a summer evening after playing kick-the-can or hide-and-seek, and listen to my father's spine-tingling ghost stories.

But I knew intuitively that this was not a typical ghost. It left me with no feeling of fear. I lay there, wide-awake, seemingly for hours, with a feeling of awe. Something very important had happened, but I didn't know what.

As I replayed the experience over and over in my mind, it dawned on me that I was so overwhelmed by the radiance of the lady that I didn't notice her facial features. If I had thought to scrutinize her face, I might have recognized someone I knew, now on the Other Side, who was dropping in for a visit. I had never had such a visitation from a deceased acquaintance, nor expected such a thing to happen.

I must have fallen asleep with these thoughts because when I awoke, it was light. But the experience of the radiant lady was still on my mind. I lay there still in a state of awe and wonderment. Then I heard my mother coming up the stairs, and I called her into my room. We had always been very close, and I could tell her anything.

"Mom, I have to tell you what happened to me as I was going to sleep last night," I said, as she sat down at the foot of my bed.

"What happened?" she asked in a concerned manner.

"Well, Mom, you might think I have gone off the deep end if I tell you," I said, as I momentarily contemplated keeping it to myself. I could tell by the look on Mom's face, however, that I was obliged at this point to tell her because I had aroused her curiosity and concern.

"Mom, I saw the figure of a radiant lady."

"You mean, you *dreamed* of a radiant lady?"

"No, she was actually beside my bed, looking down at me. I had an eerie feeling that someone was watching me in the darkness, so I opened my eyes."

"Did she say anything to you?" Mom inquired.

"No, I don't recall her saying anything," I responded with something of a quiver in my voice. "I opened my eyes, and recall thinking that she was so stunningly beautiful, like no one I had ever seen before. Then she floated backward and disappeared."

"Do you have any feeling who she could be?" Mom asked.

"I . . . I didn't catch her features," I stuttered, as an unusual thought entered my mind. "She had a glow around her that made her really stand out in the dark room. She was very much alive, radiant and . . . and . . . you know what, Mom?" I asked.

"What?"

"I just had a strong sensation that she is a part of *me.* That a beautiful part of me was leaving my body or something, and floating off into the darkness. But how could that be? I don't even know why I think she was a part of me. Now, that does sound crazy, doesn't it?"

Mom, a very wise and spiritual person, didn't question my analysis of my experience. "Well," she said, "remember the time I woke up and saw your sister Pauline's spirit at the foot of my bed? Her spirit came to tell me that she had tuberculosis. So I had her checked by the doctor the following week, and indeed she did have tuberculosis. We were able to catch it before it became serious."

"Yes! I also remember that you said that my spirit appeared to you while I was in Europe in great emotional turmoil. I don't remember coming to the foot of your bed in spirit, but you said I did, so I believe you. And that's why you and Dad sent for me to come home. I was so depressed that I even attempted suicide. . . . Even crazier, Mom, remember how you saw our dog, Speck, that we had for so many years? You said after he died he appeared to you on the floor beside your bed where he used to lie."

"Yes, Rosalind," Mom replied. (My family always used my given name and not Rosie, as all my friends call me.) "Speck appeared to me a short time after dying to let me know by his wagging tail and familiar bark that he was very much alive and happy in another world. He also sent me a mental impression that your grandmother, who lived in our house when he was alive, was there to meet him. And, even stranger, he looked like he did when he was a young pup. He didn't show any signs of old age. His little spirit body was very radiant, and very much alive. He appeared, barked, wagged his tail—and then was gone. He never appeared to me again."

I laughed to myself as I thought of our little dog, Speck, checking in to say goodbye before going on to Doggie Heaven. And I realized I shouldn't give another thought to Mom thinking I was crazy for seeing a radiant lady in the dark.

"Wow, Mom," I mused. "You've seen spirits before. What do you think I saw last night?"

"I can't tell you, Rosalind," she replied thoughtfully. "Only you can know that."

"But do you think it's possible that I saw a part of myself?" I asked, puzzled. "And if I did, what would that part be doing looking down at me, and then floating away?"

"Anything is possible with God, Rosalind. If you think the lady was an aspect of yourself, it might just be. I don't doubt that you actually experienced something very unusual. Perhaps someday the lady will return and tell you who she is, and why she appeared to you," Mom replied in a quietly confident voice.

"Mom, I'll tell you what: since you are experienced with 'spirit appearances' I'll take your suggestion to heart and know that if this experience was important then the 'Radiant Lady,' as I'll call her, will appear again. I'll just tuck it away and go on with my life, until the time that she might make another visit and let me know the meaning of her appearances."

"That's the best approach," Mom answered as she stood up. "I was coming upstairs to see if you were awake and tell you to come on down for breakfast," she said and started back down the stairs.

"I'm fully awake now! And really hungry."

I grabbed my clothes off the floor, jumped into them, and quickly followed the smell of bacon and eggs down the stairs to the kitchen.

∞

I had completely forgotten about Radiant Lady. She had faded from my mind like she faded away in my room that night 40 years earlier.

I was lounging on my living room couch at my nine-acre "estate" (as I like to call my home after living in a mobile-home park in Virginia for two decades). It was such a wonderful new phase of my life, gifted to me by the writing of my first book, *Cosmic Journeys.* I always feel so content being out in the country with my animals—something like Heaven must be. I call my place "Heavenly Acres."

It had been foggy and rainy all day, and then turned out to be what I call one of those "Brigadoon" evenings: misty, mystical, and leaving me with a feeling of déjà vu.

I felt all evening as if I was in a timeless dimension, with not a care in the world, but with an anticipation of something about to happen. Like the legendary Scottish village of Brigadoon that suddenly appears out of nowhere every one hundred years, I had a feeling that something from my distant past was going to come alive on this magical evening of great expectations.

As I lay stretched out on my couch with my legs dangling over the end, I became so relaxed that I must have drifted down into the alpha brain-wave state because images of some of the recurring dreams I had been having over the past six months began to surface. As I ruminated over these particular dreams, I began to get a somewhat empty, unsettled feeling in the pit of my stomach that I always have when I wake up from these recurring dreams. It is always a dream that makes me feel that something in my life is unfinished. I am often in college repeating courses that I have taken before. Sometimes I find myself starting all over again in the same college.

I know intuitively that the dream is trying to get my attention, to tell me something. But I don't have a clue as to what it is. I always pray daily for help with all that I know I need, and even what I don't know I need. I do believe that if we ask, we will receive. I also believe in giving praise and thanksgiving daily for my many blessings.

As my recurrent dream images popped up, I asked for help in knowing what my subconscious mind, my Inner Self-Helper or Higher Self, was trying to tell me. I prayed over and over in my mind, "Please, dear God, help me. Thank you. Help me. Thank you."

Suddenly, I heard the voice of a woman speaking, just as clearly as a voice on the telephone. The voice said, "Rosalind, go to your computer and prepare yourself to write."

I jumped up, opened up my word processor, and typed the following message very rapidly as it came to me.

"Rosalind, this is Radiant Lady. I know that you remember me because I made a great impact on you once in your earlier life on planet Earth. I came to you to impress my image and energy upon you, so that when the time was right we would begin our mission that we planned before you were born.

"Yes, I am coming alive from your past. Your perception of this magical evening is indeed correct.

"Your dream is telling you that you do have something unfinished. Your work is yet unfinished. It has to be accomplished before you leave this planet. It is very important work, and there are many from our dimension who are going to help you to accomplish it.

"I want you to know that you are a wonderful light in our dimension. You visit with us often in your dream state. We work with you and teach you. You will soon be able to keep one foot on the Earth and one foot in Heaven, so to speak.

"As we begin our work together, you will gain a greater understanding of who I am, and why we have chosen to accomplish this important mission together.

"I will guide you through experiences of very exciting journeys. We will travel into many dimensions beyond the Earth as you record these experiences. You have much experience since you have done this for many years as an Explorer in a laboratory setting. You have a special gift. You were easily able to record experiences verbally as they were happening. And now you will record them through your fingertips as they are happening. It is the same energy process.

"It is time for souls upon the Earth to be reawakened to the knowledge of their true Home, from whence they came and to which they will return. And you are one who made a contract before you were born to help in this reawakening.

"There are many wonderful souls you will meet in the planes of existence that you will be visiting. You will meet nonphysical energies from many different dimensions, including family, friends, guides, teachers, and angels, who will all share their personal experiences of the worlds in which they exist.

"I am your tour guide.

"When you are ready to experience and record these Soul Journeys, I am ready to help you and guide you through them.

"I send light, love, and joy to you as you prepare for this life-changing adventure into other dimensions. When you are ready for each journey, your thoughts of readiness will manifest instantaneously in my energy field. Our energy fields are connected in a very special way. Your very thought of readiness sets off a silent signal in my energy field, and I am there immediately as your dedicated tour guide, with wonderment and joyful expectations of what we will experience together as a team."

Then the voice stopped—and all was silent.

2 Thought: Our Platform for Communication

I was ready for my first tour, and eager to learn how Radiant Lady would handle the details of our trips.

It is the nature of tour guides to be very organized, planning the tour agenda thoroughly. I know this because I've had some experience being a tour guide myself.

I love to travel so much that after David (McKnight) and I were married and moved to Mount Solon, Virginia, I organized three tours abroad mainly out of a desire to help us see more of the world at almost no cost.

Yes, I finally got married, but not until age 35. David was 33. Dad was so happy and relieved, even though we didn't produce any grandchildren. But the fact that he and David had the same May 4 birthday made up for it: Dad realized that finding someone just like him takes a little more time!

An unusual mind was something they had in common. Dad could remember the details of anything, and David had graduated magna cum laude from Harvard. He and David became very good buddies, which was clear at Dad's funeral when David spent a long time with Dad's body at the open casket, silently talking with him upon his departure from planet Earth.

The memory of Dad's open casket reminded me of an open-casket incident in my early childhood. Then it was the tradition to have a wake during which the body lay in an open casket at home for a period of three days, and people would sit mourning and visit for extended periods.

Thus my mother's father lay at his wake for three nights and days in the grand living room of their homestead in Harrodsburg, Kentucky, where I was born. The old pump organ was the major feature of that room until Grandpa's casket competed with it for space.

One night four of us kids (my younger brother Ronnie, two cousins, and I) just couldn't go to sleep in the room directly above the casket. So we decided to sneak down and see if Grandpa was "a-wake" yet. We clutched one another in a little group as we snuck down the spiral staircase and sat nervously in a clump across the room from the body. We kids thought that Grandpa's body was placed there in the house because at some point he was supposed to "wake up" and return to life.

Then one of my cousins said, "There, did you see that? Did you see his hand move?"

And we all fell over each other trying to get out of the room before Grandpa crawled out of the casket. We knew he was right behind us as we jumped into the same bed and hid under the covers. Now I realize that his spirit was probably right there behind us laughing uproariously because Grandpa loved children. It's good that he did because he and my grandma had 11 of them.

I have since learned that some souls stay around Earth for about three days before they go on into their next life. And some even observe their own funerals, with their guides standing by their side, perhaps to learn one last important lesson before taking flight to the next stage of their Eternal Tour.

Getting back to the travel tours I planned, we didn't have any trouble signing people up for them. David was an instructor at our local community college and we both taught evening courses in adult education, so we were both in contact with many adults. I started a home-based business called "Creative Living Institute," sponsoring seminars, classes, and tours, and a lot of folks were eager to participate in the activities I planned for education and growth. When I decide to do something, I go for it. So I set up my first tour abroad so that David and I would get an all-expenses-paid trip.

My first tour came together very quickly after I read a fascinating article about a spiritual community in Findhorn, Scotland. The residents of Findhorn communicated with Nature Spirits, who in turn helped them to raise very large vegetables and beautiful flower gardens. This community was new and was getting a lot of publicity and we became the first of many tour groups they hosted. They affectionately called us "the wonderful Virginians"—rightfully so, since we really were quite a wonderful group of adventuresome souls.

But getting to Findhorn was something else, and introduced me to my third life lesson, called the "Chaos Principle": there is an order and pattern in everything; and when it seems to fall apart, it's simply coming together at a higher level. Though this theory is not of my creation, it has certainly applied in my life at many stages of my spiritual growth here on this planet.

Our tour group to Findhorn was made up of 33 adults. One couple, Gladys and Joe, were from Mount Solon, the farming community where we lived, and they had never been farther away from their home than a hundred miles.

I was so excited to be running my first tour, and on our trip to Dulles Airport, outside Washington, D.C., I worked hard to impress my little group with my professional expertise by walking up and down the aisle of our bus checking to make sure everyone had valid, updated passports. I knew my passport was fine, for it was still valid from an earlier trip to Europe, and the passport stated that it was good for ten years.

We entered the terminal, and I was beside myself with pride as I led the group around like a mother hen with her chicks. I made sure they all got checked in before me. David led the group to the place where we were to board the plane. We were scheduled to fly on one of Pan Am's new 707s, with its upstairs lounge for first-class passengers. And the plane was booked to capacity.

I breathed a deep sigh of relief when the last of my group went through the doors to the point for boarding the plane. I hadn't had much sleep the night before and the pressures of the day were starting to wear on me. I pushed my passport across the counter into the hands of a dignified, grey-haired agent.

He looked at it and then looked at me and said, "I'm sorry, Mrs. McKnight, but this passport has expired."

I shot right back, "Oh, no, it indicates on the passport that it is good for ten years. It *is* valid."

He called in another man from a back room who looked at it and said it was valid. Since the two of them disagreed, they excused themselves and went to the back room to consult with a third party.

They came back out with a look on their faces that I didn't want to see. "Mrs. McKnight," said the grey-haired gentleman, "This is an invalid passport. A new law has created a five-year validation period on passports, which makes yours invalid."

I was shocked and humiliated as I looked back over my shoulder, glad that I had sent my "chicks" on ahead of me.

I said, "But I have to get on that plane with my tour group. I'm the tour guide."

The man in charge replied, "If we let you on that plane with an expired passport, Mrs. McKnight, we will be in trouble, and when you arrive in Great Britain, they will send you right back to the U.S. We have the same flight going out tomorrow afternoon. We can book you on that flight, and you can go into D.C. early tomorrow morning to get a new passport."

My knees were like rubber, and I thought I was going to pass out. Then I regained my composure long enough to say, "Please, let me talk to my husband to give him the material needed to lead the tour. I need to give him the tickets for the hotel when they arrive in Edinburgh."

With that explanation, he reluctantly agreed to let me go to the boarding area to talk with David.

Everyone was excited as they moved up to have their tickets checked before boarding the plane. David loves to be around friends, and was especially high over the opportunity to be with 33 of his student friends for two weeks without having to teach a class.

I grabbed his arm, interrupting his conversation with one of the tour members, and told him I couldn't board the plane, and that he would have to take over leading the tour. He was terrified at the thought of having to guide the tour until I caught up with the group. He didn't know the details of the tour, and had no clue as to what to do in leading the group.

He instinctively grabbed my arm and said, "Get in front of me. You are getting on this plane! They will never know the difference." He pulled me in front of him and grabbed the back of my jacket, pushing me along toward the last ticket booth before boarding. The tour members who heard what was happening supported his idea so they crowded around me hoping to make me indiscernible to the "powers that be," the ticket takers.

As David and I reached the ticket booth before boarding the plane, there loomed in front of me like a giant the grey-haired agent, with an angry look on his face. He exclaimed, "Mrs. McKnight, I am very disappointed in you, trying to sneak onto the plane like this."

Then he motioned to two security guards and barked a command for them to remove me from the line. The burly guards came on each side of me and literally picked me up by the arms, pulling me away from David's clutch and quickly moving me away from the group, as they continued to board the plane.

Here I was leading my first tour abroad, and I was being treated like a criminal. The two guards held onto my arms until the door leading to the plane closed, and then released me. It was the most humiliating thing I had ever experienced.

The terminal was now as empty as I felt inside. Luckily for me, our neighbors, Gladys and Joe, had relatives there to see them off. Having taken in the whole embarrassing scenario, they quietly walked up to me and offered to take me home for the night.

When I walked back into the terminal the next day, rested, with new passport in hand, the first person I encountered was the grey-haired ticket-taker who looked up at me and started saying again, like a broken record, "Mrs. McKnight, I'm very disap—"

I interrupted him and said, "Please, please accept my apology. I'm very sorry for what happened. My husband, David, was so shocked at being suddenly asked to lead our tour with no preparation that he became irrational and pulled me into the line in front of him. And I was still in so much shock about not having a valid passport that I didn't have the presence of mind to resist. Please accept my apology. You have a right to be disappointed in me."

He was writing out my new ticket as I was apologizing, and then quickly held it up under my nose and said, "Compliments of Pan Am, we're sending you first class."

I was sure that I was going to end up sitting either in the luggage area or in the bathroom. I looked up at him, speechless, and was only able to say "Thank you" before he smiled and walked away.

According to the Chaos Principle, "When everything falls apart, it is coming together at a higher level." And just as quickly as everything fell apart for me, it literally came together at a much higher level: I needed the rest and I wasn't missed on the first tour day, which was designated as a free day to see Edinburgh. Besides that, my first-class travel experience was incredible, allowing me to miss the cattle-car conditions of my tour members. I got up once and walked back into the economy-class section thinking, "Oh my goodness, these poor souls! It must be very uncomfortable in those small seats."

The tour was a great success for everyone involved. When I landed back at Dulles, I passed my grey-haired angel, who acknowledged me with a wave and a smile.

∞

When I was finally able to quiet my mind, as I sat at my computer with a blank screen in front of me and my hands on the keyboard, I thought, "My hands are all aboard, and I'm ready to travel. . . ."

Then I heard the words clearly in my mind:

"Hello. This is Radiant Lady checking in. I am working with a team from this side, and we instruct you to always start out by writing the words you hear in your mind, or a description of the images you see in your mind's eye.

"Always do this and do not question it.

"Just know that these thoughts and images are being directed to you from an energetic field that has recorded your life since you arrived at your first destination—planet Earth. And, of course this field has recorded your Spirit Journeys from their inception in the Mind of God, which is the ultimate source of the All That Is.

"Thoughts are a living substance. So in our level we call this energetic field your 'Life Imprint,' which comes from your Akashic Record. 'Akasha' is a term we use for the ether or energetic field that is projected from The Source. You need not understand how it works—only that it does work. We are all living cells in the Mind of God. Therefore, every thought we have is recorded in this Living Substance that is in the All That Is.

"Because you had agreed to work with us even before you were born, you have given us permission to go into your magnetic records of the past, present, and future, and play them back to you to help facilitate and even jump-start your guided tours. If you question the mechanics of how these thought energies could be projected into your energy system by us, just remember that with God all things are possible.

"So therefore we will be projecting images, thoughts, and specific experiences from your spiritual database, and would like for you to record this magnetic information as you perceive it."

There was a pause, and Radiant Lady projected to me in her very clear and somewhat monotone voice, "We are ready to send if you are ready to receive...."

"Yes, yes, I am ready to receive," I replied in my mind, with a feeling of, "I sure hope my receptors and transmitters are in good working order!"

"Yes, they are, Rosalind," Radiant Lady responded. "We have been testing out your receiving and transmitting capacities over many years of Earth time, and now they are in perfect order."

"Oh, I didn't realize you would pick up on my doubts," I thought, somewhat sheepishly.

"Rosalind, just be aware that your doubts cause your transmitters to clog and shut down. Having faith and trust in the process is what keeps them clear. But we do know now that you finally and absolutely believe in the magnificence of the afterlife."

"You are right, Radiant Lady. For many years when I was actually picking up information from your dimension, I didn't really believe the information was accurate, because I didn't have confidence in and love for myself. I just thought I was imagining it."

"Yes, we know. However, imagination is pure thought with a picture associated with it. Your doubts are thoughts, alive and electric in nature. When you concentrate on your doubts, they will expand and stagnate with other energies. Just thinking about your doubts gives them power. What you concentrate on truly expands because of the magnetic nature of thoughts. So we will just concentrate on the expansion of your light and joyous energies. Just remember that everything you think goes somewhere, and these thoughts will eventually be sent out in solidified thought-forms to the whole planet via the book that many of us in other dimensions are helping you to bring together."

"Wow, let's continue, Radiant Lady. I'm ready and excited."

"And, yes, Rosalind, just know that I, as your tour guide, will not abandon you or send you on ahead of me. Your passport into the afterlife dimensions is valid. We are very organized on this project. (For the first time, I sensed Radiant Lady laughing.) We actually are not 'dead' here. A sense of humor is a cherished trait in our dimension. Just know that these journeys will, in most cases, be fun—that is, until we tour the lower dimension. . . .

"So, we are ready."

∞

As I sat and waited for something to happen, I began to see an image clearly in my mind. It was an image of David and me sitting by the bedside of a man from the Staunton, Virginia, area. He used to be one of our students and I remembered his first name as being Tom.

Tom had just come out of surgery. He gave us a smile as he opened his eyes and saw us. I grabbed his hand and squeezed it as David patted him on the arm.

"We're really glad to have you back with us, Tom," David said.

"I knew that I was going to survive this operation," Tom said with a twinkle in his eyes.

"How is that, Tom?" I asked.

"Well, I'm glad you are here so that I can tell you what happened to me while I was under anesthesia. I don't think the doctors would believe me if I told them what happened. And it was as real as sitting here talking to you.

"I found myself flying rapidly among the stars. Suddenly, I came upon a disc hanging out there in space, just like planet Earth."

"Wow!" I exclaimed.

"Well, I knew that the disc had something to do with me, so I stopped long enough to examine it. I actually hated to stop because it was really fun flying through space."

"What did you find?" David asked.

"I found one slot missing in the disk, and at a knowing level I was aware that it represented an operation that I had as a child."

"That's interesting," David responded.

"Then I saw another slot carved out of the disk," Tom continued. "It was a fresh cut, and I knew it represented my present operation."

"So what did it indicate about this operation?" I asked.

"I knew from the shape of the slot that I would survive the operation because it was exactly like the slot representing the other operation. I just knew that I would come out alive and head back to my life on planet Earth."

"That's absolutely fascinating, Tom. Then what happened?" I asked.

"Well, I opened my eyes and saw two angels standing in front of me," Tom said with a smile on his face.

"You really saw two angels?" I asked

"I sure did. I'm looking right at them as I speak!"

David and I both laughed, and took it as a great compliment.

"I am really glad that you two angels are here to hear my story," Tom continued, "because it helps to verify what happened and makes it more credible, since I am just coming out of the anesthesia and wouldn't have time to make all this up."

"We absolutely believe that what happened to you is true, Tom," David replied. "It must have been a Life Imprint from your Akashic Record that you saw."

"That's what I assumed," Tom chuckled. "You just talked about that in class recently, and here I go and experience it firsthand."

"Well, we're very glad you've come back to tell us the story," David said in a sincere, animated tone.

"Welcome back to planet Earth," I said as I squeezed Tom's hand again.

∞

The image of us at Tom's bedside disappeared and now Radiant Lady and her team were moving the story ahead in time. I saw David and me at a party with Tom and his wife. It seemed to be at least five years after the hospital incident. Tom looked good.

I went over to Tom and said to him, "Tom, I have never forgotten what you told us about having a personal look at your Akashic Records."

Tom looked at me very strangely.

I tried to dispel his quizzical look by saying, "You know, Tom, when you told us about being in contact with your Akashic Records in outer space during your operation a few years ago."

"I don't remember what you are talking about," Tom replied. "What did I tell you?"

So David and I repeated his story, realizing it was good he had shared it as he was coming out of the anesthesia. His brain was probably still in a deep alpha state. Once he got back to a normal waking beta state, he simply forgot the experience, just as most people forget their dreams after waking up. It was fun to tell Tom's story to him because he was so excited to hear it, and thankful that he had told us both. Then the energy of our experience with Tom faded.

∞

Next, Radiant Lady explained to me that the experiences of life-review memories while still attached to the physical body often unfold in unique ways, as they did with Tom.

She continued by saying that when human beings near death, cells in their bodies cooperate to flash images of their entire life across their minds in seconds.

∞

I sat there absolutely fascinated by the way I was receiving information. It was coming to me so rapidly.

Yesterday I finished the first chapter, and then was very hungry. So I took a notepad and decided to go into our little town of Madison Heights to a local restaurant, get some good old "down home" cooking, and see if I could get some dictation from Radiant Lady even in that crowded environment.

The information in the first part of this chapter came to me so quickly that I had trouble eating because of writing. After the restaurant cleared out, my attractive waitress, named Alice, walked over to me and asked, "Are you writing a book?"

"Yes," I replied.

"I knew you were," she said, "because you were writing so fast."

"Well, I'm just writing it down as they dictate it to me from another dimension," I replied.

This thought didn't seem to faze Alice, and she replied, "Well, good luck on the book. I want to read it someday."

She never asked what the book was about, but did ask if I had written a book before. I told her that I had, and that a story about my first book, *Cosmic Journeys,* appeared in our local Lynchburg paper.

"I'll look for a write-up about your new book," Alice replied with a twinkle in her eye.

As I paid my bill to Alice, I said, "Well, I have to get home to my word processor. The dictation is coming so fast that I can't keep up with it."

"I understand," Alice responded. "I'm really glad to see you writing your book on my shift, and I'll certainly look for it."

"I'll let you know when it is published," I said.

"Great, come anytime," she replied as she closed the cash register.

As I got in my car and shut the door, I thought about the new TV show called *Joan of Arcadia,* in which God talks to Joan through different people, giving her assignments and encouragement. I thought to myself, "You know, Rosie, God just talked to you through Alice to give you thumbs-up and encouragement on your book."

∽

So there I was, the day after my chat with Alice. "Okay, guys, what next?" I thought, my fingers geared up to record on my computer.

I heard in my mind, "Sit quietly. We are going to transport you to the Hall of Records."

"Hello, Radiant Lady," I replied in thought. "Can I ask you some questions before we begin?"

"We appreciate questions. We are here to help you in whatever you want to know."

"Now, you don't have time on the other side, do you?"

"No, we don't."

"And do you have to eat?"

"No, we don't."

"Do you have to sleep?"

"No, we don't."

"And you don't have jobs to earn money to survive?"

"No, we don't."

"Do you have houses and buildings where you are?"

"Yes, we do," she replied. "And that is where I was planning to transport you or rather, I should say, where you will transport yourself."

"So do you have forms of transportation over there?"

"Yes, but transportation is very different from yours on planet Earth. We travel by thought. We just think where we would like to be and are there instantly. In this dimension we have the ability to be in two spaces at once. My mental body is with you but my spirit body is perceived by those around me to be in this dimension. That is the same with you. Your body is sitting at your computer but when you are in our dimension, your soul/spirit body is perceived as being here."

"That's amazing," I said.

"In the physical world your bodies have brains through which the mind works. It is a two-step process: you think, and then act on your thoughts. But in the spirit world, our light spirit bodies—our real bodies—*are* our brains. Thought and act are a one-step process. Thinking is at once translated into action."

"So, Radiant Lady, is that how you are going to transport me?"

"No, Rosalind, you are going to transport yourself."

"So, how do I transport myself?" I asked in desperation. "My brain can't transport my body!"

"You know how to transport yourself here, Rosalind, because you are traveling via the brain inherent in your soul/spirit body. You have done it many times in your sleep when your soul and spirit are freed from your body. Also, you have traveled here many times through your Explorations while at the Earth lab that you worked in for many years."

"Oh, you mean in the Monroe laboratory when I worked as an Explorer with Robert Monroe?"

"Of course, Rosalind. You might not remember the journeys you take during your dream state, but you certainly should remember the journeys you took while at the Monroe lab."

"Well, I remember some of them. But it has been a long time since I took them. Every time I read *Cosmic Journeys*, I think 'Wow, that is amazing. I don't remember doing that. . . .'"

"That is exactly the way with life. We have so many thoughts and experiences that we don't always consciously remember everything. So just relax and I'll scan one of your 'Life Imprint' journeys here when you visited the Hall of Records. That way you can just move into the energy and be here instantly."

"Okay, I'll try. . . ."

"We never use the word 'try,' Rosalind. In the thought process, you either do it, or you don't. There is never an in-between state called 'trying.'"

"Okay, I'll *do* it!"

Upon saying precisely that I would do it, I sensed my energies changing. I found myself in a building quite different from any building we have here on planet Earth. It had great pillars, and many steps leading up to it. I was sitting on a marble bench that had a glow that our Earth benches don't have.

I turned and looked beside me—and there she was. She looked just like I had seen her in my bedroom that night long ago. For the first time, I noticed her face. So much love and joy radiated from her eyes.

"Hello, in person—or should I say in Spirit?—Radiant Lady. Everything about this building has the same kind of glow that you have."

"Welcome to the Hall of Records, Rosalind. Yes, and you even have a glow yourself because you are in your soul/spirit body. While on Earth, your spirit is encased in your soul body as well as in your physical body."

"Wow, I didn't know I was carrying so many bodies around," I exclaimed.

"Well, you are not 'carrying' the bodies. Rather, your spirit is *wearing* the bodies."

"So there is a difference?"

"Yes, quite a difference. You make it sound like it is a laborious thing to wear these bodies."

"Well, Radiant Lady, the energies of planet Earth are so intense and dense that often it really does get to be tiring to carry the weight of our bodies around," I said.

"That is why you have sleep in your dimension."

"About our physical bodies: we have to feed them, rest them, keep them healthy, keep them beautiful, keep them from harm, keep them active, keep them from getting fat, keep them from getting diseases. In fact, most of our Earth lives are consumed with concentration on our bodies."

"But Rosalind, you are not in your Earth body now. Don't you feel the difference?"

"Well, as a matter of fact, I do. I feel a lot lighter."

"That's because you are here only in your soul/spirit bodies, and have left your other body in the dense dimension of Earth."

"You are right. And I need to leave these dense thoughts back with my physical body."

"Everything in this dimension is harmonious. Can you imagine, Rosalind, living in an environment where there is only love?"

"It's very hard for me to imagine, but just being here makes me feel different. I feel lighter, brighter, and energized. As I absorb the atmosphere, I feel love radiating all around me."

"You *are* lighter and brighter, Rosalind—just as you are most of the time on Earth when you express your light, love, and joy. Your spirit is radiating through your soul body and you appear to others here to be just like me."

"I do? They can see me? And you mean that I look like a Radiant Rosalind?"

"Certainly, because you are out of your very dense physical body."

"Let me test that," I thought. "I notice that the beings here are in all types of attire. But here come two spirits in flowing robes, sort of what I expected to see over here—robes and angels with wings. I'm going to speak to them, and see if they see me."

"Let me give you one of your first lessons, Rosalind. You don't even have to speak. They have already heard you. They are smiling and coming toward you because they have received your thoughts about them."

"Well, I'm sure glad I didn't think anything negative."

"Actually, Rosalind, negativity is not even possible in this dimension. Those beings with a lot of negative energy get screened out of this dimension. Your soul/spirit body goes directly to the level with which your energies vibrate. Your soul/spirit bodies are electromagnetic, and upon physical death you go where the density of your energies automatically places you."

"Hello, friend from planet Earth. Welcome to the Hall of Records," I heard, as the thoughts of one of the energy beings entered my mind.

"Thank you. I am amazed that you can see and hear me," I thought back to them. "Wow, this is fun sending thoughts instead of talking verbally."

"Your light and thoughts came into our energy fields very clearly," the second gentleman replied. "We work here in the Hall of Records, and would love to show you around and answer any questions that you may have."

"Yes, I have a question. You said that you work here. I didn't think that you had to work in this dimension."

"We don't have to. But if we want to, we can," he replied. "Just like on planet Earth, we have choices. And there is a lot of work to do here, but it is different from on Earth where most people have to work to survive. Here, you could say that we survive to work. There is no time here, however, thus no pressure on us to perform or compete. 'Service' is the term we like to use for the ways in which we help people. Most all who live in this dimension are involved in some type of service. Come with me. I will show you what the Hall of Records is all about."

Immediately as he thought this, I moved from the brilliant marble bench I was sitting on into a room with rolls and rolls of scrolls. They were impeccably lucid and organized, and I was in awe looking at what seemed like thousands of them.

"The scrolls are in the billions," my competent new friend informed me.

"What are these scrolls for?" I asked, just as the name Raymar came to me. "Your name is Raymar?" I inquired. "I'm not sure how I know your name."

"I sent it to you through thought. I thought it was time I introduced myself to you. And my friend here who serves with me is named Atasha. I go by the nickname Ray, and he likes to be called Tash."

"Well, in that case, my name is Rosalind, but you can call me Rosie if you would like."

"We like the rhythm of Rosalind," both Ray and Tash thought at the same time. "So we will call you that."

"Did you notice your rapid change in environment?" asked Ray.

"I sure did," I replied. "How in the world did we get here?"

"Well, you need to change that to 'How in heaven's name did we get here?'"

We all laughed. Radiant Lady was right there beside me as she promised she would always be.

"We were transported by the thought of moving to this magnificent room where your records are kept," Ray replied in thought.

"My personal records?"

"Yes," answered Ray. "You can think of them as the imprints of your life. We like to call them your 'Life Imprint' records."

I was still a bit confused. I thought, "But how did I move here with you when I didn't even know where you were going?"

"Your soul/spirit body was in the middle of our energy, and we expanded our thoughts to move you along with us. I sent out the thought to Radiance and Tash to expand their energies to move you with us on our 'thought escalator.' And they did, so here we are."

"So here we are. But where is here?" I asked.

"The Scroll Chamber is where we are, and here we can retrieve your scroll of Life Imprint discs and scan your complete spiritual history from the time you were conceived in the Mind of God to right now," Ray mentally remarked.

"That makes me a little uncomfortable," I thought. "I'm not sure I want people to look into my files and learn everything about me. I'm not proud of everything I have done. Is this something like what we call on Earth an 'FBI file' on someone?"

"It is a file," projected Ray to my mind. "And everyone who has ever been created has one. But there is no judgment involved. It is just a record of the absolute, pure history of a spirit. Also, here in the Hall of Records the history of planet Earth is recorded. Earth historians who come here love to step in the Memory Chamber and experience history the way it really is."

"Are you saying that I can step into this Chamber and experience my life, and other lifetimes, just as if they are happening now?"

"Absolutely. You can view your lives like a hologram. Each one plays in brilliant color right in front of you, and with stereo—or better yet, astral—sound. You can also experience your Akashic records just through sound. Or you can merge into the energies of your past, present, and future and be right there in your experiences, just like they are happening now—because they are, since in God's reality there is no time, only the Eternal Now."

"So while I'm here, can I peek into my future as well?" I thought excitedly.

"Your future is still fluid because the options you choose as you experience yourself in the time zone can vary considerably," Ray explained to me. "But in fact, it is an option for you to do that, if you wish."

As I pictured myself looking into my future, it made me a little nervous, and I thought, "No, I'll just stay with my past. I have too much to absorb being in this dimension. And it's clear that we can't get away from ourselves no matter where we go."

"That's what the life of the spirit is all about—knowing and growing," replied Tash. "There is never an end to your spiritual growth. You get some 'rest stops' in the higher dimensions before going back to Earth where your main growth takes place. Many come here to this building to study their records when they feel it is time to go back to Earth. They do that when they feel it is time to do some more clearing, so that they can continue to evolve up the spiritual ladder back into the pure essence of God from whence they came. Spiritual growth takes place faster on planet Earth because of the frictional nature of the energy."

"Compared to the energies of planet Earth, where we are right now seems to be the pure essence of God," I mused.

"The pure essence of God is always within us and around us," Ray replied. "But because of our slower vibratory levels, we are not able to perceive the energies of God in their fullness. We cannot be fully back in God's pure presence until our energy levels are rarified and match the purity thereof. There are many Spiritual Beings that reside with God, and they occasionally appear at our level to teach us. And several masters have appeared on planet Earth to teach spiritual lessons, as you well know.

"Our purpose is to continually grow spiritually until we get back into the awareness of the pure presence of God. God's presence is a part of our innate being, and is always within us in the form of Spirit, the true Reality. It is a matter of us opening up to a greater awareness of this Presence, that has been and always will be a part of our spirit."

"Well, I'm almost afraid to look or hear or merge with my records for fear of running head on into my 'stuff,'" I thought.

"There is no judgment in the mind and heart of God," Tash responded. "The only judge that you confront when you experience your spiritual records is *you!*"

"Fear and judgment are the biggest things we have to contend with on planet Earth."

"Getting beyond fear is the main step in moving into the pure Love realm," replied Ray. "Fear and Love do not blend, so I think what is happening for you right now is that you are picking up information about yourself from your scroll, which I am now holding in my hand."

"Can I see what it looks like?"

He unrolled the scroll far enough so that I could view the writing inside. It was an incredibly beautiful script that I couldn't interpret.

"What is this language?" I inquired.

"The scrolls are written in Aramaic, which is the universal language used in the spirit worlds," was Ray's immediate answer.

"But how can I read it if I don't understand it?"

"Well, let me show you," Ray said, as he unrolled the scroll farther. "Run your eyes down the manuscript."

I ran my eyes down the scroll, and as I did I started hearing words translated into English. "It's talking to me," I exclaimed excitedly.

"There is instant translation in your mind as your eyes examine the scroll."

"But how does my information get into my scroll?"

"That's simple," replied Tash.

"As you think, your thought is connected to the pure mind of God, which is, in turn, unlimited energy. It can reproduce in many different forms; in this case, your mental energy bounces off the pure God energy and reproduces in the form of script. In simple terms, it writes itself," said Ray with a twinkle in his eyes.

"This explains the power of prayers," he continued, "which are thoughts with strong emotion attached to them. Prayer thoughts go into the pure God energy and are dispersed out to angels who, in turn, take on the task of answering them. Know that your thoughts and prayers never fall on deaf ears. This universal thought process is like a master computer that never crashes. It is perfect because it is the mind of God. Strong emotion should be attached to any request you have, or to anything you desire."

"I have always heard that 'thoughts are things.' It is awesome, the power that has been given to us by God to think." I found myself becoming uncomfortable thinking.

"Let's forward to the present moment on your scroll, and you can see the experiences that are taking place right now automatically appearing on your scroll."

"Amazing! It looks like someone is writing an e-mail message about my life," I thought, my eyes practically popping out as I watched.

"Well, someone is," Tash interjected. "Namely, God, because life itself is God's way of communicating with us. We were created in the image of God, and thus we are connected at our core to this energy of the All That Is. God is the Ultimate Creator, and we, in turn, are the creators of our own destiny.

That is the nature of the free will that God gave to us when we were sculpted out of the Pure Essence of the God Energy."

Ray continued guiding me through the Hall of Records. "If you step into the rooms with the blue lights, you receive holographic visions of what is in the scrolls. So you can experience your Life Imprints from the Akashic records through sound, sight, and even experience."

"Back on planet Earth there are people who have the ability to regress us back into past lifetimes," I remarked. "So does the information received from those sessions come from the Life Imprints of our Akashic records?"

"Absolutely," replied Ray.

Tash jumped in with another important thought. "There is another Hall greater and even more magnificent than the one we are in. It is called the Hall of Wisdom, and it is where newly arriving souls actually enter into this dimension. If you recall when you visited the capitol of your nation, you walked into a great hall with marble pillars and ceilings."

"Yes, I do remember it," I replied.

Tash continued with animated enthusiasm: "So you remember how awesome it was as you stood in the center looking up and all around?"

"Yes, it was breathtaking."

"Well, if you magnify that hall a million times, you can only begin to perceive the magnitude of the Hall of Wisdom. And in the bosom of the great Hall is what we call a Scanning Machine. It is set into a large dome that has a blue crystalline surface where you view the events of your life before your eyes like a three-dimensional hologram. All around it are luminescent marble benches where those souls newly born into this dimension sit to view their past before entering into a very thorough orientation process. We will take you there in another session to watch a newborn soul enter this dimension. You have your 'birthday' in the spirit world just as you have your birthday when you arrive on planet Earth."

"Oh, wow," I thought. "This is such an awesome tour—and it's only my first one."

"As we told you earlier, your records are actually with you while you are in your physical body. Your brain and body change when you come over to this dimension."

"How do they change?"

"For one thing we don't need reproductive or digestive organs in this dimension," Tash interjected into my mind.

"You mean no sex and no food?" I immediately asked. "People addicted to sex and food might think they are entering Hell if they can't have those particular needs fulfilled."

"First, if they carry negative, earth-addictive energies with them when they die," Tash replied, "like addictions to alcohol, drugs, cigarettes, sex, or even food, they can temporarily screen themselves out of the higher-vibration energy levels because of their need to feed their addictions. Some souls will actually hang around planet Earth to try to feed their addictions by entering into the energies of addicted Earth people's bodies. This creates a form of spirit possession. Thus it is important to overcome your addictions before you die."

Radiant Lady picked up her tour-guide duties by gently interjecting the mental comment that it was time to leave the Hall of Records.

"As you are well aware, Rosalind, our purpose for bringing you here is to orient you to the ways in which communication will take place."

"It was very helpful," I thought. "I see clearly that I will have sound, sight, and experiences, like I am having now. I am very impressed. And will follow directions to the T. It is sometimes hard for me to do that, but I know I will receive a lot of help from 'above,' so to speak!"

"Yes, Rosalind, your lessons here at the Hall of Records are over for now. So we will project you back to the Earth level and will look forward to our next encounter."

"Thank you so much for the lessons, Ray, Tash, and Radiant Lady. I am eager to find out where we will go next."

And then the sounds and sights faded.

∞

A couple of hours had passed since I sat down at my computer ready to receive and transcribe. I was *so* hot. I had to take off my sweater. When I sat down, I had had a blanket around me because I was so cold. So my energy body really heated up during this enlightening tour.

I had to go to bed. I had to recharge so that I could go to work tomorrow to earn money to pay for all the things I needed to survive on this planet. To think that Heaven is a place where we can do what we want, when we want to, sounded good to me. Especially to sleep in—but you don't even have to sleep! It's hard to imagine a place where you don't have to work, do dishes, scrub toilets, make beds, cook food, wash cars, and so on. Actually, the idea of such a place offered me a great ray of hope.

I was pretty much of an expert about life in the Earth dimension because I had been on Earth for quite a few years. Life on planet Earth really is a challenge most of the time, as you who are reading this book would agree. (Unless you are reading it from the other dimension, and in that case you don't even have to buy the book.)

When things got tough on this challenging planet, however, I always thought, "What will this matter one hundred years from now?"

Then I felt good when I answered, "It won't really matter."

But now I realized that every thought and everything we do really *does* matter.

Whew! I must rest my Earth brain. Good night.

3 Behind the Mystery of Death and Birth

I was so excited. I decided I wanted to start this third chapter in the Barnes & Noble bookstore in my home base of Lynchburg, Virginia.

I walked into Barnes & Noble and stopped by the best-seller section that my eyes fell on as I entered the store. I clearly visualized *Soul Journeys* sitting on a table by itself right in front of all the other bestsellers, with a big sign stating:

"LOCAL AUTHOR, ROSALIND MCKNIGHT, ON THE BEST-SELLER LIST."

Wow! I clearly felt the excitement of being on the best-seller list. Thinking about what my friends Radiant Lady, Ray, and Tash had taught me about the power of every thought with powerful emotions attached to them, I felt that I was almost manifesting the copies right on the spot.

I also believed strongly in the power of affirmations, and on my morning walks I repeated over and over to the rhythm of my steps, "Millions and millions of people buy my *Soul Journeys* book. . . . I give millions and millions of dollars to help the cats and dogs who need our care." (So if you are enjoying this book, please tell at least ten people about it, and you, in turn, will do a great deal to help the animals of the planet along with me and my wonderful publishing company, who could also use an extra financial boost in these very challenging times.)

Actually, reading this book is doing a great deal to help the people on this planet to get a different perspective of what life is *really* all about as opposed to life on a planet that is so filled with fear, anger, hostility, and all the lower emotions. So just send an e-mail to everyone on your address list and tell them to *buy* a copy of *Soul Journeys.* Be sure not to loan your copy because you'll never get it back. This is the kind of book that you will read over and over. Tell your friends to buy their own copy, and also to buy copies to give as gifts. (Radiant Lady, I'm sure, has encouraged me to give you this message.)

After walking around in the store for a while and picking up the amazing energy from the trillions of thoughts in the books, I sat down at a little round table. I put my writing pad down to save my spot while I went to the coffee shop section to get my usual English Morning tea and a cinnamon scone.

I had read the biography of a best-selling author who wrote her books in a coffee shop in England that was owned by her cousin. That intrigued me because I love to sit in this particular coffee shop surrounded by such incredible energy while sipping my tea and writing. So I thought that patterning after such best-selling energy might just rub off on me. Oops, the coffee shop just made an announcement that we should only stay an hour when the shop is busy. Oh, well, my thoughts are so powerful that what I sent out will work! It only takes a few minutes to have our thoughts manifest in action in this realm of existence. So I don't have to stay here very long. I just have to keep the thought in mind, and picture it as if it has already happened.

Actually, I was also testing my tour guide to see if she was really right there when I was ready to write. Well, since I just sent out the message, I needed to follow instructions. I needed to relax and see what Akashic memory they were going to project to me this day. Here goes . . .

∞

Hmmm. There was an interesting image forming in my mind.

I was in my car, and just had a tire blow out. I was on my way to Washington, D.C., where I was to give an evening lecture on "Death & Dying" at a local community college on the outskirts of the city. Drat it—I was already pinched for time and here I had a blowout.

I pulled my car off the highway as best I could. Luckily, I was coming into a small town, so at least I wasn't stranded way out in the country. Being in the problem-solving mode, I looked over and noticed a house sitting back in the trees. I had my heels on, so I had to walk very carefully up the narrow walkway. I knocked on the door and received no answer. All I needed was to find a phone to call a local wrecker to come out and change my tire.

I walked back to the rear of my car, and in desperation spontaneously stuck my right thumb in the air as a small convertible approached me. As soon as I did, the sports car braked and pulled right up behind my car. (Good record for my first time at hitchhiking.)

I opened the passenger's door and looked into the brilliant blue eyes of the most gorgeous man I had ever seen.

"Can I help you?" he asked.

"You certainly can," I replied. "I have a flat tire and wonder if you can drive me to a local garage in town. I need to find someone who can come back and fix my tire."

"Sure, jump in," he said in an enthusiastic tone as I slid into the passenger seat, discounting everything I had ever been taught about not taking rides with strangers.

As his cool little sports car rolled back onto the highway, he asked, "Where are you heading?"

"I teach a course on death and dying at our local community college in Lynchburg, and I'm on my way to lecture on the subject at a community college outside D.C."

He got a very strange look on his face and replied, "What? You mean you teach a course about death? I've never heard of such a thing."

"I certainly do," I replied.

"I can hardly believe that you would teach a course about death," he continued. "Incredible!"

"Well, it's a very popular subject today because it's a course that everyone is going to have to take, along with the required lab work," I said, with a slightly caustic tone in my voice.

Then he seemed to lighten up. "I need to take that course," he replied with something of a twinkle in his bright blue eyes. "I fly for the Blue Angels, and my other pilot friends and I face death every time we do our air show. We think about the possibility of death every time we go up, but we never talk about it."

"Most people prefer not to think or talk about death," I rejoined. "I had a younger brother who was killed on Interstate 81 a few years ago. He and his new bride of five months were coming down to Virginia from Indiana to spend Thanksgiving with me and my ex-husband."

"I'm sorry to hear that," he replied.

"They didn't show up at noon when they were supposed to arrive. There had been a big snowstorm, so we knew that it might have caused some delay. But when they didn't show up by five P.M. and we hadn't heard from them, we knew that something was wrong.

"David, my ex-husband, answered the phone when it rang. He talked briefly and then handed the phone to me, saying 'It's Linda. . . .'

"When I said hello, Linda said that Larry was dead. I held onto the phone as I fell to the floor, feeling sick all over and like I had been hit in the solar plexus with something.

"'Oh God, oh God, oh God,' I cried, as I shook all over. 'Are you okay, Linda?'

"'Not really,' she said, 'I'm in the hospital in Winchester, Virginia, and am very bruised.'

"'We'll get there as quickly as we can,' I told her—which we did."

"So you took a course in death and dying to deal with your brother's death?" the handsome gentleman asked.

"No, there were no such courses at the time, that I knew of," I replied. "I started researching everything I could find on the subject to help me deal with his death. And I was amazed to learn how much material was out there. I ended up convincing the community college to let me teach a credit course on the subject. It became a required course for the respiratory therapy students."

"Well, my Blue Angel pilot friends and I need to take a course like that to deal with our fear of death," my new friend replied.

"I can't believe that you fly those jets in formation on a regular basis, and have a fear of death."

"At least I don't have a fear of flying," he chuckled, glancing over at me. "I imagine most people have more of a fear of dying than a fear of death. No one wants to suffer, or be crippled for life."

"Yes, and we deal with all that in the course," I said, with a bit more animation. "Everyone agrees that they have more fear of dying than of death.

And when asked how they would prefer to die, nearly everyone wants to die in their sleep."

"Well, I guess that dying in a plane crash wouldn't be such a bad way to die," the Blue Angel replied, "because I would at least die doing something I love."

"Yeah, I tell my students that I love storms and lightning so much that being struck by lightning wouldn't be a bad way to die! However, if I survived and was crippled for life, that's a different story. I guess we're all cowards at heart."

We pulled into a station in town as my handsome blue-eyed Angel asked how my sister-in-law was doing.

"Well, the most amazing thing happened," I said. "They discovered that Linda was two weeks pregnant. Becky was born eight and a half months later. They had a dog, Frenchie, who had jumped out of the car and gotten away when the state trooper opened the door. Frenchie was lost for two weeks. He finally showed up at someone's house and was returned to Linda. So, Linda, Becky, and Frenchie are doing fine."

The gentleman reached his hand over to shake mine as I started to open the door to get out.

"I'm Bob," he said. "I was so fascinated by you being a death and dying teacher that I forgot to introduce myself."

"Hey, Mr. Blue Angel, I'm glad our paths have crossed for this few minutes in time. I'm Rosie," I said, enjoying his handshake.

I arrived at my destination just in time.

Even to this day, every time I think about my Blue Angel experience, I feel my heart smiling as I think how nice it was to be picked up by an "angel" driving a little sports car.

Well, obviously Radiant Lady had found me. I had so completely gone back into the mental record of my Blue Angel experience that I almost forgot where I was until I looked up and saw myself surrounded by Barnes & Noble's books.

"I guess I've been in here long enough to leave a lasting impression on the universe to move *Soul Journeys* into the best-seller section when it has finally manifested onto the Earth plane," I said to myself. "I need to get home and back to my computer, to see where Radiant Lady is going to take me from here."

∞

I was back home. Some time had passed. I work better in late evening. In fact, between six at night and six in the morning is when my mind is the clearest, so I was back at my computer, following instructions by relaxing. I was waiting to see or hear what was going to happen next. . . .

"Greetings, Rosalind," a voice resonated in my head.

"Hello, Radiant Lady," I responded.

"Are you ready for your next exciting journey?"

"I couldn't be more ready."

"We talked to you about the power of your mind, and showed you how thoughts and images are recorded by taking you directly to the Hall of Records. So guess what the topic is this time?"

"I would guess that because of the scenario from my life that I experienced while in Barnes & Noble today, it is probably about death."

"Well, yes and no," she said. "It's really about life, since there is no death. Showing that there is no death is the main reason for these journeys. We want people on planet Earth to know for sure that there is no death, that 'death' is just a word they have created to explain something they know nothing about. Well, I take that statement back. Everyone on planet Earth, at a spiritual level, knows there is no death."

"How is that?" I asked.

"Well, because they have all put on a body, taken it off; put on a body, taken it off; put on a body, taken it off many, many, many times."

"You mean going back and forth from Earth to the real world of spirit?" I asked.

"Yes. So today, we are going to show you the truth behind the magic door of 'death.' Again, we ask you to relax and report the images we project to you. You are doing a great job of following instructions."

∞

I was getting relaxed. I saw an image of . . . Hmmm, an image of . . . I was behind the wheel of a car. I looked down at my hands and they were masculine hands. "Oh, Radiant Lady must be taking me into one of the Life Imprints of my brother Larry," I thought. I looked over to my right, and there was Linda, my sister-in-law, dozing. I was imprinted over Larry's body. I could see out of his eyes. We looked out the window and the snow was very deep. I was just passing the I-81 sign and an arrow that indicated the turn that would take us into Martinsburg, West Virginia. Larry was thinking about stopping, but saw a sign indicating that the Virginia state line was just 30 miles farther and decided to keep going. Winchester, the first town in Virginia, would be a good place to take a break.

There was only one lane of traffic on I-81 because of the deep snow. He saw the Martinsburg exit up ahead with a semi truck parked under the bridge. He realized that it was not a good place for the truck to park, and being a driver's education teacher himself, he was going to be very careful as he passed the truck, with just one lane open. But just as he was thinking that, a car came onto I-81 from an entrance just behind the truck. The car was coming right at him and wasn't slowing because of the snow. Larry threw on his brakes to miss the oncoming car. He missed the car, but skidded sideways right into the truck. Larry's driver's side hit the back of the truck. That was the last thing he remembered. . . .

He opened his eyes and saw the beautiful face of a young lady looking down at him. She smiled at him, and he said, "Wow, I must be in Heaven. . . . you look like an angel."

The young lady replied, "You *are* in Heaven. But I'm not an angel. My name is Becky, and I am your daughter."

"I would love to have you as my daughter," Larry replied. "But I don't have a daughter. I just have Linda, my wife. We've only been married five months. . . . Linda? Where is Linda? Where am I? I remember her sleeping in the seat beside me. The last thing I remember, I had thrown on the brakes and my Jimmy skidded into the parked truck. Oh, my God—I'm dead. . . ."

"No, you're not dead. Do you feel dead, Dad?" Becky asked.

"No, I don't feel dead at all. But you seem so serious about me being your Dad."

"Yes, I am serious, and you *are* my Dad. But you're coming, and I'm going," said Becky. "You and my mother, Linda, just conceived me two weeks ago in Earth time."

"That is good news . . . and bad news. I've always wanted a wife and a child—and now that I have them, I've abandoned them," Larry said sadly. "But why am I lying here on this beautiful couch, feeling very much alive?"

"When you arrived, the counselors and spirit therapists in charge of your orientation to this dimension put you on the couch and into a sleep state temporarily," Becky said.

"Why did they do that?" Larry asked.

Becky reached over and put her hand on her father's forehead and said, "They put you into a resting state because you died of a blow on the head. Do you remember having any pain?"

"Not at all," Larry replied.

"I didn't think so," responded Becky. "I was right there to observe what happened. Your body was pretty torn up. The thing that killed you was what you loved most about your GMC Jimmy. You bought the one where you can take the roof off. With all the work you were doing with the Boy Scouts, you finally had a vehicle that would be great for your camping trips.

"Since there was no hard roof, the frame on your side of your SUV went right into your left temple. Then the rescue squad had to use a blowtorch to get you out of the vehicle because your hip and lower body were completely smashed. You actually lived for a couple of hours after arriving at the hospital, but your brain and the left side of your body were so damaged that you could never have lived a normal life."

"Oh, I loved my Jimmy so much. It's hard to believe that I would tear it up like that. And hurting my body like I did . . . it happened so quickly. It takes a long time for a life to be created and mature, even for a car to be built. And then within seconds it is all destroyed. . . . But Linda is so much more important. How did she survive the accident?" Larry asked.

"She and your dog, Frenchie, survived because our angels were protecting them. I was well sheltered inside her body. And having her seat belt on made a great difference. The whole vehicle collapsed all around her, and was completely totaled. No one could believe that she didn't even get a cut or scratch. She was very bruised from the impact, however. When she didn't have her period, they thought the trauma to her body was the main reason. But luckily, I was the one that did that."

"Well, that's a miracle I'm so thankful for," said Larry. "We had five wonderful months of marriage. When she ran out of her birth control pills one weekend, we just thought that a couple of days without them wouldn't matter."

"And thank heavens you were wrong," said Becky enthusiastically. "It made quite a difference for my future! My guide and counselors sent an emergency message to me, through thought, of course: 'Get ready, get ready, we're sending you in. There is nothing to hold you back from entering the womb now. Get over to The Towers immediately.' I was prepared to go whenever they called, since I had finished my orientation to go back to Earth for my new growth lessons."

"I'm sure glad Linda ran out of the pills," said Larry with a sigh of relief.

"So they met me at The Towers," Becky continued. "They took me into a special departure room. The Towers is sort of like a large hospital on the Earth plane, but we don't need hospitals over here. It serves a need as a hospitality center and a place of rest. It's a 'stopping off' center for souls coming in and going out—like us, Dad."

"What a way to meet the child I always wanted!" Larry exclaimed.

Becky was very intent on telling the story of the beginning of her journey back to planet Earth, and she continued with the details of her departure.

"I lay down on a very comfortable table, and they covered me with warm blankets and put me into a nice, gentle sleep. I even had the sensation that I was shrinking down to a baby-sized soul as I was going into the sleep state. Then I think they hit some sort of energy-ejection button because suddenly I was in utero. It was dark and quite comfortable. I reserved my space by putting my energy deposit down on my new, warm apartment inside Mom!

"But there was no way that I was just going to stay there for the whole nine months. Some souls like the nine months of preparatory rest before going from an environment of pure love into an atmosphere of fear, negativity, and all the challenges of the Earth plane that help us to grow—that is, if we are able to survive them in one piece."

"Yes, I know," interjected Larry. "I was barely in one piece—and am just now brushing off the negative ions that must have penetrated my spirit body."

"You really look better, Dad, even as we're talking."

Becky continued: "On this side, there is no time, and it is a shock and confining to the spirit to go back into the 'time zone.' It's dark and boring in there—at least for me it is. I was told by my counselors that my soul could go back and forth for about five months of Earth time, if I desired. After that

I would be locked into the system controlled by the planet-Earth energies. When we are in our new apartments for good, the wonderful memories of our life here are blocked out. Our brains are then ready to process our Earth journeys. I wasn't in a hurry to get locked back into time, and took advantage of being free for a little while longer. And guess what I was doing when the accident happened, Dad?"

"What were you doing?" Larry asked affectionately.

"I was riding in the backseat, petting Frenchie, when the accident happened," she said.

"But I didn't answer your question about why they put you into a temporary sleep state when you first came over," Becky continued. "The reason is that it takes a lot of energy to leave the Earth plane. In your case a short period of rest was needed to recharge your astral body. Only the physical body can be injured, or diseased. The *real* body is indestructible. Now that you have gotten rid of your disposable body, you are 'Home Free,' as they say on planet Earth.

"So your counselors and your trained spirit therapists put you into a kind of cocoon state until you were rested and ready to start your new spirit adventures in this very beautiful dimension of pure Love. Since I was right there with you and Mom when the accident happened, I decided to come on back here to welcome you myself. I thought it would be appropriate that we meet each other before we start our new lives."

"That's quite wonderful of you, Becky. I wouldn't be able to meet you like this, otherwise. I'm sorry I abandoned you," Larry said somewhat dejectedly.

"I knew it was going to happen, Dad, because I had just had my orientation preparing me to go back into the physical world. I went through quite a detailed orientation to get me ready to go back to Earth. Here there is only pure Love and Light; and on Earth there is negativity and conflict, which nonetheless help in our spiritual growth, as I said before. It is time for me to go back for further spiritual growth. My Earth orientation council helped me to decide just what my Earth Contract will be."

"So I'm going through an orientation period coming in, and you are going through an orientation period going out," Larry replied.

"I've already gone through mine," said Becky. "We choose our primary life theme, which is our basic goal for our upcoming life. And then we select a secondary life theme, which is a conflict we set up for ourselves. Our secondary theme throws obstacles in the way of our primary goal so that we grow by overcoming them.

"Passivity is my primary life theme. I am a very sensitive person. Emotional discord will be a great challenge for me. My goal is to learn firmness to gain inner strength by dealing with controlling people. You are not controlling, Dad, nor is Mom. But I will come into contact with some very controlling people when I get back on Earth. I know exactly who they are, and I even shiver when I think about having to spend time with them. But I'm going to get a lot of help from God, from my guide and my orientation team, and perhaps from you, too, Dad.

"So my purpose is to learn to use my inner strength, to build a strong self-image, so as to be able to stand up for myself. Together, our orientation team plans the basic structure of our new lives in great detail. But there is room for lots of decisions as we grope our way through life."

"As your father, I'm already proud of you, Becky, for taking on such a challenging new life purpose," said Larry. "I do hope that I will somehow be able to help guide you and be able to follow your progress on Earth."

Becky's guide, who was with her during her orientation period and was standing just behind her, moved up to let Larry know that he would be free to visit with her at any time during her Earth journey. Because of his special connection as her father, and due to this period of time spent with her before she went back to Earth, he would have a special energy connection whereby he could look in on her at any time, and help give her support when she needed it. He turned to Larry and informed him that all humans have guides throughout their lifetimes on Earth, and that God is always good to us wherever we are.

Larry was sitting up now, and Becky said, "Dad, I'm going to hang around in my warm little apartment longer than I had planned because I want to stay close to Mom as she heals from the accident. You are in good hands, and she needs me more than you do. So I must go. I'll see you again when I return from Earth some years from now, which will seem only like a second in time."

Larry stood up and he and Becky had an incredible "energy merging" of spirit bodies.

Then Becky disappeared.

∞

Remember my Disconnect Principle? Sometimes we are instantly disconnected from people and things we dearly love. Sometimes we are reconnected with them—and sometimes not.

Now, forget it! This principle is relevant only to the Earth plane. Reconnecting with your loved ones in the afterlife *will* happen—and brings a whole new perspective to what we consider the "tragedies" of life on planet Earth. It adds a whole new chapter to the 9/ll story. . . .

PART II

New Horizons

4 Visit to a Lab in the Sky

It was a very cozy Sunday morning at my Heavenly Acres. It had started sleeting late the night before, and the ground was covered with a crusted snow. I felt very relaxed, and ready to see where Radiant Lady was taking me today.

But before I sat down at my computer, I did my usual morning chores of feeding all the little meowy mouths in my household, and emptying their litter boxes. I have lots of cats—and three dogs—most of which were brought to this heavenly spot in the woods because they were abandoned. Remember the Disconnect Principle that is only relevant on planet Earth? One of my biggest fears throughout life has been the fear of rejection, or abandonment—the greatest fear that most humans have. That is why I like to help animals that have been rejected or abandoned.

Many people ask me if I have names for all of the cats. Of course I do! They are all uniquely individual personalities. And I'm attuned to all of them. Mela, my cross-eyed Siamese, was so thin she could hardly walk when I found her in a bank parking lot. I have had her for many years now, and she is extra special because she is the only cat that told me her name. I thought when I took her home, "Now, what should I name her?" I heard very clearly in my head, "My name is Mela."

My cats are indoor-outdoor cats, so when the weather is nice I hardly see a cat in the house. They have many acres on which to roam, and are happy cats. Not all the cats I rescue stay at Heavenly Acres. I have gotten homes for many, many wonderful kittens. One of my main goals with cats is to help get them spayed and neutered. I have helped to get feral (wild) cat populations spayed and neutered.

"Sweet Pea," my latest little feral kitten, got out the pet door, and didn't know how to get back in. I looked and looked for her, and then opened the back door and called. She came running from under the porch, happy to come in the house and be reconnected with her brother and sister cats. She walked around the house, happily rubbing up against every one of them she could.

And speaking of having different personalities, there is Buster Chew-Chew. He is a little orange and white cat. His name used to be Buster, but he chews on my fingers and toes when he wants me to pet him. At first I thought it was cute. But it becomes a bit irritating when I get up in the night to go to the bathroom, and suddenly something starts chewing my toes! So as all you animal lovers know, they all have such different, and amazing, personalities.

Now that most of my cats had lain down for a morning nap, it was time for me to go back down into my relaxed-consciousness state to connect with Radiant Lady and my next journey.

∞

I sat thinking about lots of questions I would like to ask her. So many issues had come up since we had started these journeys together, and I had so many questions.

I suddenly heard her voice.

"Rosalind, good morning to you and your furry friends."

"Good morning, Radiant Lady," I replied. "Do you have furry friends where you are?"

"We certainly do. Every pet that you have ever had is here waiting for you when you arrive back at your original Home."

"Wow! I'm going to have a lot of pets waiting for me when I arrive there," I exclaimed. "I have had so many wonderful furry friends who 'disconnected' from me on this planet."

My black Labrador retriever, Mack, died such a tragic death and I felt so responsible. I had run outside to roll up my car windows when it began raining and he jumped on the floorboard of the backseat without my noticing it. I returned to my computer, and after about five hours I wondered where Mack was because he always stayed right at my feet.

I looked and looked for Mack, and then opened the car door to find him dead on the back floorboard. The sun had come out and overheated the car. The inside of the car was all scratched where he tried to get out. I was devastated, and felt so guilty and responsible for his death. Then someone urged me not to feel guilty because Mack at a deeper level chose that time to die.

"That is indeed so," replied Radiant Lady. "People choose when they are going to be born, and when they are going to die. And animals do the same. But the process of doing so is different for animals."

"So my brother Larry chose to die in the accident on that Thanksgiving Day many years ago?" I asked.

"Yes, he did. People give themselves several options for leaving planet Earth. Remember that Larry totaled his car in front of your apartment building in Newark, New Jersey, on New Year's Day of the same year he died?" she asked.

"I sure do. He totaled his car, but he wasn't even scratched. At that time, he hadn't yet married Linda. They got married on July 4 of that year," I said.

"He could have left then but he changed his mind because he had agreed before coming in that he would pave the way for his daughter, Becky, to come to Earth." Radiant Lady explained. "And he also had made a commitment to marry his true love, Linda, whom he had known before."

"Well, I'm glad Larry stayed around a while longer. I was so close to him. He had an energy about him that lit up the room whenever he walked in. He was such a joyful being, and always made me and others feel so good being around him. He has been with me a lot since he died. I have often been driving along and, realizing he is in the seat beside me, start talking to him."

"He also adores you and is part of the team helping to get this information out to the world," Radiant Lady said.

"So that means that I will get to visit Larry and find out what he has been doing on the other side for the last 32 years."

"You will be meeting him. But first you will meet another part of the team that is helping with the communication process," she said. "Now let's deal with the questions you were thinking about just before I signed on."

"Oh, yes," I said. "I was wondering what the real story is about why we humans choose to come back to this very dense energy field called Planet Earth, when life is so wonderful, loving, and stress-free where you are."

"That is hard for humans to understand. You come back to experience the special energy field that exists on Earth. It is an intense energy that helps in your spiritual growth."

"How is that?"

"There are seven known dimensions that humans gravitate to upon leaving the Earth. And within these dimensions are subdimensions. We use the word 'dimension' to represent a plane of existence. The Earth is the slowest vibrating plane of existence."

"Then we're in Hell?"

"No, the Earth is unique in that beings of all energy levels can coexist there," Radiant Lady replied. "There are beings from the lower dark levels of vibration that are sent back to grow. Many are sent back in by the angels that oversee them. Light energy beings from the higher realms come back to teach and serve, but also to grow closer to God."

"Are you saying that everyone on the Earth plane is here to grow closer to God?" I asked.

"It is the basic purpose of all beings in all dimensions to grow closer to God," said Radiant Lady. "God created us in His image. We were given the power to create with our thoughts. We got so carried away that we began to find ourselves farther from the Light. Darkness is merely the absence of Light. So, the farther we strayed, the more our light diminished."

"So we come back to Earth to have some tough experiences that help us lighten up. Is that what life is all about?" I asked.

"You've got it. Now let's go on to our next experience. Follow the instructions we gave you about relaxing. . . ."

∞

I sat in a relaxed state for a short period. Then suddenly I found myself moving through a denser energy field. I felt light. I felt like I was far away from my computer, even though my fingers were on the keyboard. Then I was in a room filled with light. It was a room that didn't appear to have walls, but felt like it did. The room's boundaries were made of a substance different from our walls, and the room felt very expansive.

Then I noticed several radiant energy beings seated about me. They were each dressed differently. One had on what looked like an embroidered golden robe. Beside him sat a handsome gentleman dressed in simple clothing similar to Earth clothes, but finer in substance.

And I saw Bob . . . Bob Monroe! He was wearing a loose shirt and comfortable pants, and sat before what seemed like a control panel. He looked so young and radiant. As I mentioned, I worked with Bob in the 1970s and 1980s back on Earth as an Explorer in his laboratory in Virginia. Bob was doing research on sound frequencies and the ways in which different frequencies affect our brains.

Some other beings were sitting across the room talking. There was furniture in the room, but nothing like the furniture in our homes. There were tablelike forms and comfortable-looking chairs.

Radiant Lady and I were suddenly in this room together with all these people. No one seemed startled that we instantly appeared in the midst of them.

Bob turned toward us, and said, "Welcome to my home, Rosie!"

"Hi, Bob. This is my friend, Radiant Lady, who is taking me on a tour of your dimension."

"I know," said Bob. "We're well acquainted. Hello, Radiance."

"Hello, Bob," she replied. "Thanks to the work you did with Rosalind in your Earth laboratory, we have finally gotten her here to your new lab."

"How exciting!" I exclaimed. "This is sort of like a Lab in the Sky."

"Call it what you want," replied Bob. "It is set up very much like the lab I had when we first started our work together at Whistlefield in Virginia."

As I walked around looking at his otherworldly lab, I said, "It looks a lot more technical than your control room was back on Earth."

"Certainly!" exclaimed Bob. "Since I can create anything instantly with my mind, I have created the master control room that I always pictured having. And it didn't cost me a cent. When I want to modify it, I can add and delete items instantly with my mind."

"That's awesome," I said with enthusiasm. "But I thought your Earth lab was awesome in the old days back at Whistlefield. We had some wonderfully interesting and amazing times doing brain research together. I was such a novice, simply working in your office as a typist. And you would say, usually late in the afternoon, 'Let me hook you up in one of our CHEC units, and see what happens.'"

"Yes," Bob said with a chuckle, "and you would often go sound asleep when I turned on the Hemi-Sync tapes."

"Let me see if I can remember what 'CHEC' unit stood for . . . Controlled Holistic Environmental Chamber!" I said gleefully.

"Good memory," Bob rejoined. "I had it set up so that there was no outside interference—no light and no outside sound. Then I would turn on the Hemi-Sync tapes and eventually you traveled to some very unusual places in the cosmos."

"Speaking of cosmos, Bob, what do you think of my book, *Cosmic Journeys*, which I wrote about our experiences together after you died?"

"Well, since I often dropped in to help you out while you were writing it," Bob replied, "of course, I love it!"

"I always felt that you were helping me write the book, and I'm glad to hear you verify that. And as far as working in the lab with you goes, I had a lot of help. I couldn't have done anything without my four Invisible Helpers, and my guide AhSo. And remember the time you put that psychologist from D.C. in my CHEC unit when I had to cancel our regular session at the last minute?"

We both laughed heartily as Bob said, "How could I forget! If anyone wanted to interview me about my sound system, they had to experience it for themselves."

"Yes, but I'm amazed that you got her hooked up in the lab because, as I remember, she was a real skeptic about what you were doing."

"Yes, she was—until your Invisible Helpers and AhSo rattled her belief system," said Bob.

"Actually, she was a great Explorer because after about ten minutes into the tape she saw someone in the room with her," I said with a chuckle.

"Well, not just someone," Bob replied. "She actually perceived four energy beings in the room, who were trying to lift her out of her body. I considered taking her slowly off the tapes—until I looked at the clock and realized that it was the precise time of your regular session."

"So apparently my Helpers thought she was me. We must all look similar when they view us as a spirit body and not a physical one," I said.

"Yes. And what I picked up from her replies to me over the microphone was that the Invisible Helpers were saying, 'That's her.' Until AhSo, the head honcho, said, 'No, that is *not* her'—and they all dropped her." We laughed at the incident as we had the day I had come back for my next session and Bob had related the story to me.

When Bob took the psychologist out of the CHEC unit, he told her all about my work as "Explorer ROMC," and how my Invisible Helpers and guide AhSo would always come to work with me, and take me out of body to various dimensions. Bob never heard from her again. She left not nearly as skeptical, but somewhat shook up at meeting five "spooks" that day.

I looked around me and then turned to Bob, asking, "So this is your home as well as your lab? I'm a little amazed that you have your own houses here. Lots of people seem to think that you float around on clouds over here, doing nothing throughout eternity."

"That's a boring concept!" Bob retorted. "In reality, it's completely the opposite. We can create and have anything we desire. If you want a house, you build a house, either with your mind or the old-fashioned way—with your hands! If you don't want a house, you can live anywhere in this wonderful atmosphere that you desire.

"And there is no weather here as you know it on Earth. It's neither cold nor hot. The temperature stays around 78 degrees," Bob said. "And if you like a change in weather, you can create a little rain or even a snowstorm around you. It's all created from mental energy."

"That is really wild and wonderful, Bob," I chuckled. "I have another question to ask you."

"I'm up for answering any question you ask. When we worked in the Whistlefield lab together, we were getting a lot of answers to many questions. What would you like to know?" Bob asked.

"Well, Bob, I'm really curious about your death. You traveled out of body so much during your lifetime that I wonder what it was like when you took your 'ultimate journey.'"

"Good question. I was very aware when I died, and was happy to get out of that tired and weary disposable body," Bob replied.

"If your physical body was tired and run down, did you have to rest when you arrived here, since it takes a lot of energy to cross dimensions?" I asked.

"I did have a period of rest and recuperation. And my beautiful wife, Nancy, was right there when I opened my eyes. I had so many friends that wanted to greet me that they had a big 'coming home' party for me! My parents, my ex-wives, and my friends were there.

"Even Laurie, my daughter—who is now president of the Monroe Institute, as you well know—dropped in for the celebration. Laurie comes by quite often, especially during her sleep state, and we do some important planning together," Bob continued. "Our institute has helped to expand the consciousness of thousands around the Earth. The programs and tapes we offer at our facility have made an important difference in many people's lives. That's why I continue to work with the institute's energies from this side. It's part of my commitment to help in raising the consciousness of planet Earth."

"I can understand that Laurie would come over to meet you because of your love connection. But you are joking about having ex-wives meet you, aren't you?" I asked with curiosity.

"Well, I've had my share of ex-wives. But to answer your question: yes and no."

"Yes and no?" I asked.

"Here, all that stuff that stands between us in relationships doesn't exist anymore. The love ties are what keep people together over here—basically just the way they do on the Earth. But the lower emotions of jealousy, pride, and ego—which I also had my share of—go out the window with the transition to this realm of pure Love."

"I have always wondered which spouse meets you if you have been married several times," I asked.

"It's actually the ones with the strongest love connection to you," Bob continued. "Here, all the negativity doesn't exist anymore because it was embedded in the cells of our disposable bodies, including our emotional bodies. With the physical body deleted, our soul/spirit bodies are cleared of the 'junk,' so to speak. The souls that hold on to that stuff remain in their astral, emotional bodies close to the Earth vibrations until they are ready to release it.

"Our 'astral' bodies are our physical bodies' emotional levels," Bob went on, "which we drop completely when we are one hundred percent into our new soul/spirit bodies. For one reason or another, there are a lot of souls who hold on to their astral bodies, with all the junk of negative Earth emotions. And there are a lot of helpers working with souls who have a fear of moving into new territory, souls so addicted to the garbage embedded in their emotional or astral bodies that they have trouble releasing it, mainly because they have never gotten acquainted with any of the aspects of their higher spiritual selves.

"Anyone who is attached to any addictive substance from the Earth plane has greater difficulty moving into their new spiritual bodies," Bob explained. "Many are locked into their flimsy astral junk bodies, in a no-time zone between Earth and the astral level, for centuries of Earth time. Their emotional body remnants become like security blankets, and they just won't let go and allow themselves to evolve to a higher level of vibration. It is so important to clear yourself of all Earth addictions before dying.

"That is one of the great challenges of being on the Earth plane: to be 'in the Earth, but not of the Earth'; not to be controlled by the slower vibratory energies created in our bodies while experiencing the Earth plane."

"Well, that sounds like a good reason to clear all addictions and negative emotions out of the body before you die," I remarked.

"Yes, it helps a lot to work on releasing your 'stuff' before you drop the body," Bob concurred. "While we are in the resting state after coming over here, we automatically have a life review through our astral body, which registers all of our life emotions. It is a good therapeutic technique that happens automatically to those who have addictions and a lot of emotional baggage. We view our stuff over and over until we get fed up with floating in our own Earth shit, so to speak. If we ask for help to be released from it, help comes immediately."

"That sounds good to me," I said. "Well, not the emotional 'shit,' but the release of it."

We laughed together again, happy to be reconnected.

"Well, there are those in the no-time grey zone who think they deserve a hellish existence. So they remain locked into their stuff for centuries of Earth time," Bob said pensively.

"Bob you look very different now," I interjected. "You look like you might have looked when you were 35 or so."

"I *am* young," Bob rejoined. "Our soul/spirit bodies are our *real* bodies, our prime-time bodies, and they're indestructible. So if you arrive here at old age, like I did, having dropped a wrinkled, old body, your radiant energy body steps forth and—ta-da!—here I am! I no longer eat the greasy hamburgers that I enjoyed so much while on planet Earth."

We laughed again because I remembered well how addicted Bob was to his greasy hamburgers.

"I'm impressed," I said. "I'm carrying around 70 years of Earth wrinkles, but I'm not ready to dump this body yet. I need to stay around until my last cat dies, which will be a good 20 more years or so."

"Well, you look good to me," Bob replied, "because I can see only your soul/spirit body."

"Thanks," I said. "I've been working enthusiastically at living from 'inside out.' Living through my soul/spirit bodies rather than my Earth body helps me to stay younger and to be continually radiant and joyful. My guiding energies gave me the affirmation, 'I am Light, manifested in Love, and expressed in Joy, Joy, Joy!'—which I repeat often. That means that I was originally pure Light . . . and I manifested into this Earth through Love, and express myself here in Joy."

"It's working," Bob replied. "I observe your joyful spirit lighting up the whole room when you are speaking to Guidelines groups at the institute."

"It's good to know that you drop in on us occasionally. Actually, as you well know, I speak in the house you used to live in—in fact, in your dining room. This house looks a little like your old home, but with more brilliant colors," I said.

"Actually, it is. This house was ready for me when I came over. Nancy created it with some help from others," Bob replied enthusiastically. "And we continually make changes. I have moved my laboratory into the house rather than have it in the log cabin outside my house as it is on the New Land at the institute."

"Bob, when you look back at the Monroe Institute, do you perceive it in a different way than you did with your physical eyes?"

"Yes," Bob replied, "I see it in a completely different way from this perspective. I see everything there at the institute in color and energy patterns."

"Can you describe them?"

"As a matter of fact, the colors surrounding the energies of the institute look quite beautiful. The patterns and energies have changed drastically since I came over to this side. Once I pulled my somewhat restrictive energies out, there was an expansion that hadn't taken place before. I had to hold down the energies to keep the growth from happening too rapidly. When growth takes place too rapidly, it can disintegrate as rapidly as it expanded. So it was important for me to hold on to the energies to accomplish what needed to be accomplished at the time."

"Bob, I want to congratulate you for doing such an excellent job in creating the whole Hemi-Sync scenario." I said. "For years, people came to your programs simply through word-of-mouth advertising, which says a great deal about the success of your programs."

"The plan was that after my male energy pulled out, the feminine energy of my daughter would take over and create a whole new balance of expansion. It certainly has grown rapidly since I was there. I am very pleased with the growth that is taking place."

"You should be," I exclaimed. "Laurie is doing a fantastic job. I think that all the years she was away doing her thing as a businesswoman, she was being prepared to take over the mission you started. So how do you see the energies now?"

"I can actually see the energies expand around the world." Bob said with excitement. "Those who come to the institute and then return to their own areas carry expanded energies back with them. These energies are encircling the Earth. Each individual who has had growth experiences at the institute has helped to accelerate the energies of the areas to which they return. We are encircling the globe like a spider spinning its web, and this web is light energy."

"That is very exciting. So where's Nancy? Does she live here?"

"She does but she moves around a lot because in this dimension you can move to wherever you want to be and back within seconds. So why not move around when it is so easy to do so? You just think yourself to where you want to be. Everything is instantaneous."

"So you don't get frequent-flyer miles over here?" I asked with a smile.

Bob laughed. "No, we do frequent flying, but no money is needed to exist. . . . Nancy always liked a lot of variety. People can follow any interests they desire when they come over. So Nancy has learned to move around in different dimensions at will. We have magnificent Halls of Learning here, and she spends a great amount of time in pursuit of knowledge. Over here, people can continue the pursuit of what they love the most. On Earth Nancy liked interior design."

"Yes, I remember how she so enjoyed helping to design all the homes she lived in," I said. "But I notice that you said that she spends a 'great amount of time.' I thought you didn't have time over here."

"We don't," Bob said.

"So with no time to function in, what does Nancy actually do?"

"She presently works on interior and exterior design, teaching newly arrived souls how to create and re-create their environment. If they want an environment similar to the one they had on Earth, she helps them re-create it through the thought process. If they want something entirely different, she helps them to create exactly what is in their minds. It's a grand and exciting process."

"So with Nancy gone all the time [chuckle], who cooks for you, Bob?"

Bob laughed as he said, "Ingesting food is not necessary for survival in this dimension. Our bodies are nurtured by the atmosphere. If people do miss eating food, however, they can create types of food substances through their thought process. And they can eat what they create, but it is merely absorbed into their new bodies. There is no elimination process as on Earth."

"That sounds like it would save a lot of time not having to cook, do dishes, and perform the toiletry routines of the Earth," I said.

"You're still locked into the time concept, aren't you?" Bob teased.

"To tell the truth, I really don't understand the no-time concept."

"Well, you should," Bob replied, "because you were in that space a lot when you were working as an Explorer at my lab. Focus 15 always took you into the no-time level."

"You're right, Bob. I forgot that. I can grasp a little more what 'no time' is. Another question: Do spirit people make love and produce babies like we do on the Earth plane?"

"No, we don't have reproductive systems in our spirit bodies. But people can express love by merging their soul/spirit bodies. And it's a much fuller experience than lovemaking on the Earth is," Bob said with a twinkle in his eyes.

"So people from the Earth die and come over here, dropping their bodies young and old. But when you progress to another dimension, do you 'die' again and go onto a higher plane?"

"No, there is no such thing as death after the death of the physical body. Well, in fact, there is no such thing as death at all. Soul/spirits whose energies rise in vibration just recycle into the next dimension. The soul/spirits of a higher vibratory nature coming in from the Earth plane will simply manifest on a higher dimension of light. Soul/spirits arrive at the level to which they have evolved at the end of their Earth journey."

"How interesting! So, Bob, what have you been doing since you arrived here?"

"I've been working with some scientists who are projecting new technologies to the Earth plane," Bob replied with animation.

"What do you mean by 'projecting' them to the Earth plane?"

"Exactly what I said. Everything that is made on the Earth plane originates from this plane. It is as if the Earth inventions are first created on this plane. This is the Realm of Manifestation. We can detect what is needed and project it in thought form to the Earth level. These thoughts are usually picked up at several places on the Earth at once."

"Does that mean that several people will 'invent' the same thing in several parts of the Earth at the same time?"

"Yes. It has happened on Earth for centuries. This plane functions as the 'mind' of the Earth. Mother Earth has her own body, but we are the mind, and she is the reproducer. Everything that exists on the Earth is merely a shadow of the real that exists in this plane and on higher planes. So I still do what I loved to do on the Earth plane."

"Speaking of 'planes,' Bob, you used to love to fly. I guess you don't do that anymore since you move by thought to wherever you desire to go."

"Well, as I said before, we can create anything we want. A group of us who love flying have gotten together to create the 'plane of our dreams.' You can't imagine how beautiful such planes are. Since we don't have air as you have, we don't need gas to propel our planes. We propel them with thought. So we have 'plane games' to see who can propel their 'thought planes' the farthest and the fastest. When we're finished with them, we can just dissolve them back into thought substance if we desire or we can keep them and play in them again and again. Some of my friends like to keep remodeling their planes."

"Fantastic! It sounds like all you do over here is have fun. That sounds like an exciting air show! I wish I could see it."

"Oh, you can see it. We'll have an air show in celebration of one of your many visits to our realm," Bob said.

"So I suppose people create boats over here as well."

"Oh, yes," Bob answered. "The water here is an amazing substance. Many people like to create their ideal water crafts. Some are as luxurious as the mind can conceive and many people live on their boat creations."

I had gotten so animated and excited to be talking with Bob after all these years that I had almost forgotten about Radiant Lady. I glanced over at her and realized she was also thoroughly enjoying the conversation.

"Do you have any more questions before we return back to the Earth level?" she asked.

"Yes, I have one more," I replied. "Bob, I notice that you have some cats lying around here just like you did back on Earth. I recognize a couple of them as the ones who lay on top of me while I slept in your gatehouse when you and Nancy lived there. And those dogs over there, are they the ones that ran away while you lived there? I remember how you and Nancy were so distressed about losing them."

"Yes, they are the pets that you met—and they were right here to meet Nancy and then me when we each came over," Bob said.

"Well, Bob, I think you win the prize for having the ultimate cat story. It's like a story right out of Walt Disney. Laurie told me that when you moved from north of New York City when she was young, you took your 22 cats with you to your new home in Richmond, Virginia. She said that two of the cats walked together all the way back to where you lived in New York. I can just see the two of them limping across the George Washington Bridge late at night thinking, 'It's just a few more miles—and I sure hope they don't send us back to that weird place where they took us!'"

"Yes, we were all amazed when the owner of the house we had lived in called a year later and said that two of our cats had arrived there in fairly good condition and wanted to know if they should keep them," Bob replied.

"I sure hope you told him to keep your two cats after all they must have gone through to get back to their original home." I said. "And if they could have told the story of their trip home, I'm sure it would have been a best-selling book."

"Of course, I told him to keep the cats since he offered to do so."

"Wise decision, Bob. Since cats are my passion and yours as well, have you learned anything new and exciting about them since coming over here?"

"I learned that cats throw off a different reflection than people do," Bob replied.

"What do you mean by that?"

"Well, cats are unique in that they exist in several dimensions at once. That is why cats are known to have nine lives. Cats are good 'shape-shifters,' and can appear and disappear in various dimensions easily and at will."

"That's an amazing concept, Bob. What do you mean by 'shape shifters'?"

"Cats in general have energy fields that help balance the human energy field. If they are treated well on the Earth plane, they pretty much stay in the Earth energy form. They are very independent and if they are abused, their spirits can pull out of their physical bodies even though they still appear to be in them, and come and live more fully in the energy field of this dimension. So they can go in and out of the Earth dimension at will. When they are sleeping the many hours on the Earth plane, their spirit bodies are on our plane having a good time. They even have the ability to disappear from the Earth plane."

"What do you mean by 'disappear'?"

"I mean just that. If they feel that they would rather be over 'here' than 'there,' they just shape-shift, and bring all their energies over here."

"Does that mean that they just take their bodies out of the Earth plane?"

"Precisely. And if a cat's previous owner is over here and their pet is on the Earth and ready to die, that owner can zap their beloved cat over into this dimension, body and all. It happens more often than you can imagine. When cats disappear, they usually are shape-shifting into their energy body on this side. In fact, some of our cats that are still alive on the New Land, who live with our son AJ, come up to be with us often. They appear to be sleeping there, but are up playing in this dimension."

"When I moved to Heavenly Acres, Bob, about four of my cats disappeared. It really devastated me, since I had to move from the mobile home park I was in for 20 years because I had too many cats. Would you know if any of them shape-shifted into your dimension?"

"Let me check that," Bob replied. "Hold on. I'm told that two of them came on over, your black cat, and your black and white one."

"That would be Julianna and Chunky," I replied. "I'm sorry they left because I miss them so much. I hope they are happy here."

"Don't ever worry about your pets. They'll be here to greet you when you make your transition. They always have the ability to bounce back. Most are basically happy wherever they are. Without animals, crawling creatures, and plants, the Earth would not stay alive."

"I don't know what I would do without my animals," I replied.

"And I know they appreciate you as well. I can see some radiant energies all around your home and property. You have a lot of angels watching over you and your furry friends."

"Bob, it has been amazing meeting and talking with you again. So you are an important part of a team that is helping to reorient humans on Earth to their true spiritual nature and the truth about the afterlife?"

"Yes, and we had planned this long before we were born," Bob rejoined. "So, I will be helping to oversee this whole project from my Lab in the Sky."

"Thank you, Bob," I repeated. "It's exciting to be working with you again!"

I looked over at Radiant Lady and could tell that it was time to go.

∞

Suddenly, I found myself back at my computer at Heavenly Acres.

What a trip! I needed to rest my eyes and body to prepare for work the next day in this time-oriented world. But I would be looking at stress in a different way and would be able to relax—and maybe even enjoy the stress of this dense plane.

"I'll go off to sleep, and my spirit will probably go right back out into the cosmos to have some more adventures," I thought. And actually, I would not be alone: everyone travels during their sleep—and yes, that includes you, the one reading this book. . . .

So when you put this book down for the night, just fly on out and join me. I would like to fly among the stars tonight. Join me for some astral fun together. Maybe we'll even run into Bob out there trying out one of his new plane creations. . . .

See ya!

5 What a Body!

It was a beautiful day in January, like a lovely fall day. I was sitting at my computer, with my window open beside me. My "big purr box," Gray Boy, was asleep in the window seat beside me with all four legs stretched out in front of him. And my very affectionate little tabby cat, Clover, was asleep on the desk by the window.

On the table behind me was my black and white cat Max, who looks much like a stunningly marked skunk! He has been with me for a long time, and knows how to manipulate me with his intense yellow eyes and a meow that says, "How about going to the kitchen and opening the refrigerator door and taking something out just for me?"

I dared not look at Max because I'd decided that nothing was going to interfere with my next Radiant Lady encounter. Once you put out the message that "I'm going to do this, and nothing is going to interfere," it seems that the message goes out through the atmosphere and someone you have not seen for a long time calls and wants to see you. That just happened. A dear friend that I hadn't seen for months left an "I'd-love-to-see-you-today" message on my answering machine just as I sat down to begin this chapter. But this was Radiant Lady's day.

Sooooo . . . I would sit there, relax, and wait expectantly for our next exciting encounter. And let me tell you that every time I got to this phase of the session my head would start getting fuzzy, and I would feel like I had to lie down and take a nap before proceeding. I think that many of us human beings come packaged with a built-in resister to anything unknown.

Since I had spent three hours cleaning my house before sitting down at the computer, I thought I would take a quick nap! I'm a night person, and it was around two in the afternoon. Two to four P.M. is the slower part of my day as far as energy is concerned. I can start working at six P.M. and go right to four A.M. without batting an eye. I get into the no-time zone during those hours.

But since I had to get up at 6:15 A.M. the next day and go to work, I needed to write then. "I'm just going to save what I've written, take a quick nap, and then get back into the 'afterlife zone,'" I told myself. This is embarrassing, but it is also part of being human and living in the rigid energies of the Earth zone. Good excuse! But also, all my cats sleep at this time of day, and it makes me want to go to sleep with them. . . .

∞

I'm so amazed at the nature of the human mind. I went to sleep at two and woke up 20 minutes later, as I usually do when I take a nap during the day. Our bodies are programmed so remarkably.

And now I must tell you an interesting story that relates to this book.

I took my nap in my guest bedroom. On the back of the bed is a little doll named Rosie that my sister, Polly, gave me for Christmas a couple of years ago. Speaking of being programmed, Rosie is programmed to sing "Ring Around the Rosie" when you hold both of her hands. She is wired so that if you make a circle of even ten people holding hands with her, the circuit is connected and she sings. When the circuit is broken, of course, she doesn't. That carries a message about our connection with each other and with universal energy. But that isn't the story I want to tell, which is as follows.

When I was teaching Death & Dying at a community college several years ago, a story about "Ring Around the Rosie" was in our textbook. During the period of the Black Plague in Europe, children began to sing this song, and it has been passed down by children generation to generation to this day. And it's about the deadly plague of smallpox.

"Ring around the rosie": the "rosie" was the red circle that formed around the deadly pox. "Pocket full of posies": everyone carried flowers in their pockets to override the stench from the dead bodies all around. "Ashes, ashes, all fall down" referred to the enormous number of people who died and were piled on huge funeral pyres to be turned to ashes.

How's that for a popular children's song, sung as they dance around in a circle, and all fall down to pretend being dead? Weird? Yes, we humans on planet Earth are rather weird when it comes to death. We're interested in nearly everything, but not about the truth about death, which is that there isn't any death.

So "Ring Around the Rosie" is put into the mouth even of a doll, showing how we are obsessed with death. I remember singing it and dancing in a circle with other children, so many times. When we fell down at the last line, we would giggle and giggle at how much fun it was to fall down and play dead. But maybe we giggled because we really knew the truth, that we were going to jump up fully alive.

So now I am writing a book about "death and beyond," and have a mini-death (sleep) before I begin each new section. Maybe sleep is a "play dead" game as well, as often happens when we first cross over to the other side.

∞

But after my nap I was rested and ready to begin!

A picture formed in my mind of standing in my bathroom the night before and looking into the new hand mirror I had just bought that day. I looked into one side of the mirror, and I could bear the image. But I turned it over to the high-magnification side and my face looked like a monster looking back at me: brown blotches on my cheeks, wrinkles all over my face, teeth jutting out of my mouth when I smiled. I quickly put the mirror down, and another thought came to me: "In five days you will be 70 so what else could you expect from a look into the mirror of life?"

I mused on this for a moment, and then said to myself, "Well, in the eyes of the world I may be ugly, but in my eyes I am stunningly beautiful"—at which point I picked up the mirror and gave myself a kiss!

That incident took me back to the time that I first realized that I didn't love me—and in fact, was very repulsed by myself. At that time I was

younger, had no wrinkles, and was fairly attractive. But I had read somewhere that we need to look ourselves squarely in the eyes in a mirror to see
what we really think about ourselves.

In the early 1980s, I was living in a mobile home, and my two closet
doors were mirrors. In all the times I got out of bed and looked at myself in
the mirror, I had never really looked at myself until the day I looked at
myself through the eyes of my inner feelings. I said out loud, "Yuck, yuck,
yuck!" and walked away in disgust.

But a few feet from the mirror, I stopped dead in my tracks, and was
absolutely astounded to realize that I didn't love myself. In fact, I realized that
I didn't even like myself. And that was the beginning of my turnaround in life.
I had suddenly found a new mission in life—to love Rosie unconditionally.

So I walked back to the mirror and said, "Hello, Rosie, I love you!" I still
didn't feel very comfortable. So I walked up to the mirror again, telling
myself, "I love you." Each time I did this, it got easier—until I looked forward to getting up in the morning, kissing my image in the mirror, and saying, "Rosie, you are absolutely stunning. You are *so* beautiful. God loves you
so much—and so do I."

That led me to feeling so good about myself, and so exuberant and joyful about life, that I finally came to realize that nothing outside myself can
control how I feel. I became fully aware that the control button for love and
joy was on the inside. So I found myself touching my love/joy button when
I awakened in the morning before even getting out of bed; continually
throughout the day; and before I went to bed at night.

Love, joy, and laughter help keep the endorphins in our brains working.
These are the chemicals that lead to a "high" without the ingestion of mind-
altering drugs. When the emotions of love and joy radiate throughout our
bodies, it's like a pinball game when the ball hits all the right points, and
finally sets off the "winner" lights that make the machine seem almost to
float off the floor. This is what the feel-good endorphins do to our bodies
and minds.

Well, guess what happened next. The world outside me began reflecting
back to me the same thing I was sending out. Not only was I now loving
myself, but I began to receive all kinds of loving responses from those
around me. I was putting out such a glow that even strangers felt compelled
to say, "Hello! How are you today?" To which I would reply, "I'm fabulous!"

∞

This scene began to fade, and I heard Radiant Lady's voice say, "Hello, Radiant Rosalind."

"Hello back to you, Radiant Lady!" I replied.

And then we were both giggling.

"I saw you kiss yourself in your new hand mirror last night," she said.

"I don't let that magnified image in the mirror discourage me anymore," I responded. "When I look in the mirror, I always look beyond the physical image into my soul and spirit. In fact, I feel that God is looking back at me and saying, 'You are beautiful, Rosalind, and I love you beyond any love that you can understand.'"

"God is definitely looking at you, Rosalind," she replied enthusiastically, "because God resides in every molecule of your physical body, your soul, and your spirit."

"Oh, thank you," I said. "It is wonderful that you verify what I have felt for so long. I know a little about my physical body from the experience of wearing it. But, I really know little about my soul and my spirit. In fact, I always thought that they were one and the same."

"No, your physical body, soul, and spirit could be used as an analogy for the Father, Son, and Holy Spirit within you," she said.

"Yes? That's saying a lot!"

"It is. But this is what I mean. We think of a father as overseeing the household. Your household is your body; and you are the 'Father' overseeing this very special home, which is merely loaned to you for the period of your stay on the Earth plane. It is very important that you, as the Father, treat your body in a sacred manner."

"That makes sense. Where does the Son come in?"

"The Son is the bearer of the good news about the makeup of the physical body—the real 'contents,' the unseen levels. Even though the Father is real, of course, your physical body is not ultimately real since it is merely a temporary vessel in which the soul and spirit reside during their stay on this plane. Since the body is with you when you are born but doesn't go with you when you die, it's not real, but only a temporarily helpful vessel. Again, it is sacred, however, and the soul and spirit try to keep it vibrantly alive during their temporary stay in it. The Son, or soul, being the bearer of good news, is the life source closest to the physical level and is your functioning body, your active body when the physical body dies."

"It's cool to hear it described this way," I replied. "And how does the Spirit fit into the picture?"

"The Holy Spirit, as I am using this analogy, is the spiritual energy that pervades the whole of life. It is the source of all that is. It is the energy food that nourishes all living matter."

"So is the soul then the energy form that houses the spirit?"

"Precisely so. We live in our soul bodies until such time as we evolve to the highest spiritual dimension—where the soul body is dissolved and our spiritual body of pure light resides in the very presence of the Godhead," Radiant Lady said with reverence and awe.

"So, Radiant Lady, I'm getting the impression that our 'soul' purpose for being on Earth is to be molded and tempered in such a manner that we evolve through level after level until we are back in the presence of God, where we first started."

"That is a very simple statement. But that is precisely the purpose for being on Earth: to learn, grow, live, and love through the real energy—the Spirit—and not be attached to and controlled by the physical."

"So when we wake up in the soul/spirit body on the other side, can you tell me what that body is like compared to our physical bodies?"

"Certainly, Radiant Rosalind," she said, smiling. "That is precisely the lesson to be learned during this visitation."

"I'm excited," I exclaimed. "But can we put this lesson on hold until I go feed my animals? I'm still on the Earth plane, and all Earth bodies, including mine, have to ingest food! So I'll eat, too, and get back to you as soon as I finish, I promise."

"I know you will. There is no time in my dimension, so I'll be ready when you are," she said, knowing that I was excited about completing this lesson.

∞

Two and a half hours later, I was finally back at my computer keyboard. While drying some clothes and realizing that they were not drying, I had to crawl behind the dryer and reconnect the metallic tubing that goes from the dryer to the outside of the house. Then when I was feeding my animals, two stray cats were trying to get into the house to get fed along with my regular tribe. Of course, I fed the two cats. But they were males, and I didn't want unfixed males in my house because of spraying.

So I found myself a bit frustrated as I sat back down to communicate with Radiant Lady. I was doing my best to get back into the relaxed state. In my mind, I asked, "Radiant Lady, are you there?"

"Of course I am, Rosalind."

"Whew!" I replied. "I thought that being so frustrated, I might not be able to make the connection with you."

"I have been watching you the whole time and keeping our connection, so it's easy to get back into communication."

"Good," I replied, relieved. "I tell you what, Radiant Lady, I sure hope it's an easier life on the other side than it is here. There is always some challenge, or something going just plain wrong. When you get one thing in life fixed, something else pops up."

"Well, actually, Rosalind, that is the beauty of being on the Earth plane. The greater the challenge you overcome, the faster you learn. You never really grow when things are running smoothly."

"Sometimes we humans would like just a little break from the challenges," I sighed.

"Well, dying is the break that renews you, and gets you ready to come back for further lessons," she said with warmth in her voice.

"Alright, then, why don't you tell me more about what it is like over there, so that I'll have something to look forward to—or know what I am in for—before I get there."

"Well, let's start with the body we have here," she replied. "Let's just call it the soul body, for simplicity's sake."

"So what is the soul body like compared to the physical body?"

"First, in the physical world bodies have brains through which the mind works."

"Yes, I'm aware of that, even though they say we use less than ten percent of our brains!" I retorted.

"But in the spirit world, our bodies *are* our brains."

"Say what?" I blurted out. "Your bodies *are* your brains?"

"Yes! You actually do have brain cells throughout your physical body there on Earth. These cells are the foundation of your emotions, and reside in the thin astral shell that is stuck like glue to your body and which will become unglued when you die. But as we mentioned before, many souls don't want to let this emotional shell go. Thus they relive their emotional memories over and over—until they get fed up with this and seek a change. But the cells in our soul/spirit bodies are the brain cells. Thus our bodies are constructed of brain cells through which our minds function."

"So how does that affect you differently?" I asked.

"For example, with our brain cells in our bodies, we simply think where we would like to go, and we're there instantly, since our bodies are very light and our minds are very powerful."

"That's absolutely awesome," I responded. "So when I die and find myself in the dimension that my energies vibrate to, then I can instantly fly around to check the place out?"

"Well, it is not as simple as that. When you are born into the Earth plane, you have legs to transport you around. But you do have to learn to crawl first, and you wobble when you first stand on your legs. Many residents here stumble and fall when they first arrive because they have to be taught how to move around in their new bodies. We call it the 'spirit walk.' You can walk from place to place if you desire. But when you want to go a great distance, you think very distinctly where you want to be and are there instantly. So that is why you have to learn to control your thought processes when you are back in your real body—your soul body."

"I love it, I love it, I love it!" I exclaimed gleefully. "So there will be someone there to help me think in a different way?"

"Absolutely. God is so good. Just magnify love on the Earth plane about a thousand—or maybe a million—times, and then you might know what Heaven is like. Everyone who comes here is met by masters, guides, and angels, who help them to adjust to their new world. The energy of the afterlife is Love, wherein no fear exists. Therefore loved ones are there to meet you, also. I'm particularly referring to the Summer Plane, or Mental Plane, to which most souls migrate," Radiant Lady said warmly.

"And what about gravity?" I asked. "Our gravity keeps us glued to the Earth. Do you have a different kind of gravity that allows you to propel your bodies so easily with your minds?"

"Yes, we do have gravity," Radiant Lady responded. "But it does not affect our soul bodies. Gravity has an effect on the environment in our dimension; but our soul bodies are exempt from this gravity."

"Are your soul bodies different from our physical bodies in any other way? Our life force is enabled by the good, rich blood running through our veins here on Earth. Do you have blood in your soul bodies?"

"Absolutely," she replied. "But we do not need food as you do to manufacture blood and energize your bodies. The air in the spirit world is much more powerful and invigorating than the air you breathe. You have to have food to energize and repair your bodies, but with the energy supplied by our atmosphere, we do not need food to survive. Breathing the clean, fresh, fragrant air here is the spiritual force that energizes our bodies."

"So what happens to your bodies when you get sick, or have accidents?"

"In the spirit world our bodies are in a state of absolute perfection, perfect health. We do not get sick or have accidents," Radiant Lady replied. "Here there is an eternal magnetic current that is forever charging us with force and power. We also receive sustenance from the Light of our realm. We have an abundance of color, an invigorating type of water, and flowers everywhere that are so beautiful that our spirits are uplifted just by being around them."

Almost in disbelief, I said, "On Earth we say, 'If it sounds too good to be true, it probably is!' Will Heaven end someday, just as life on Earth will die when our star, the sun, burns out? And when was Heaven created?"

"Heaven is, was, and always will be present because it is designed out of the molecules of God's essence. This dimension was here and populated with soul/spirit bodies long before the Earth was even conceived in the mind of God. And it will always exist because there is nothing to destroy it. The physical plane will eventually dissolve just like your physical bodies because it is not reality."

"I'm so overwhelmed to realize that we live forever. But returning to food, are you saying that you don't have to eat *anything* to get recharged?"

"Well, actually, there is a special fruit here that we can eat and get recharged. If juice from the fruit drips off, it just disappears, and goes back into fruit substance. There is no waste here. Nothing perishes. There is no decay, since physical matter doesn't exist in our dimension."

"So if there is no waste matter in the spirit world, then you don't have pollution of your air and water?"

"Absolutely no waste or pollution!"

"Then you don't have dumpsters for garbage—which a lot of dumpster addicts on Earth would miss! They love finding 'free stuff.' Of course, in your dimension everything is free. But certainly you must have germs, since they are living energies."

"We do not have germs, and therefore no diseases of any sort. Actually, pain is unheard of, and an impossibility, in our dimension."

"No pain? That's one of the main things that make life difficult in the Earth dimension. Most people say that they don't fear death as much as dying—meaning dying in pain. I know many people who can't live life fully because they are *so* afraid of dying. In fact, fear seems to be the most prevalent emotion in our dimension, and keeps us from living fully and truly enjoying the Earth experience. Does fear of any sort exist in the afterlife?"

"Well, not in our dimension. After leaving the Earth, most souls go to the Summer Realm, where only Love presides and there is no pain or fear. But on the lower realms closest to the Earth, where souls are still clinging to their astral emotional shells, there is pain and fear, which are part of the makeup of the astral shells. But we'll deal with that in another lesson."

"I'll tell you what," I said, "it sure sounds like Heaven to me! And what about digestive organs? If you don't have to eat, then you must not have stomachs, intestines, or elimination organs."

"Exactly."

"Actually, it seems like most of our life energies on the Earth plane are absorbed by the physical. Everything ultimately seems to rotate around the physical body. Our big businesses are drugs, makeup, food, clothing—on and on."

"That is the great challenge on the physical plane." Radiant Lady responded. "The physical dimension exists so that people can learn from it, as I have said over and over. The physical is there both to assist and serve you, and to assist you in overcoming it. The main issue in the physical plane is not to let the physical become a controlling factor in your lives. The physical challenge is there to strengthen the soul/spirit within. We do not have such physical challenges in our plane; and that is why people go back to Earth to have experiences that will help them to grow spiritually."

"So are you actually saying, Radiant Lady, that we should embrace our physical pain, fears, and so forth and use them as a means for greater spiritual growth?"

"Yes, that is what I am saying. You each go back to Earth with a special purpose for growth. You have a whole group of teachers, guides, and elders who help you decide what your growth challenges will be. Those who overcome the toughest challenges are usually the ones who reach a higher plane of spiritual growth."

"So there is no fear, worry, negativity, immaturity, competition, rebellion, or war in your dimension," I summed up. "I'm thinking that this explains the duality of the Earth plane. In most of our great novels and movies we portray bad guys versus good guys. And the good guys usually win out over the bad ones. So maybe at a subconscious level we are portraying the physical-body level as the 'bad,' and the soul-body level as the 'good.' We know at a deeper spiritual level that in actuality there is no fear, war, death, and so on, but only life, love, and joy in God's world. It appears to me that in the spirit world life is pleasure with no fighting for existence, and no discord."

"Yes, that is so."

"Then does that mean that animals that must kill for survival in this world live in the next world without the need to kill? Since they don't have to eat, they don't have to be eaten or kill for their survival?"

"That is correct," Radiant Lady said. "We have every kind of creature here, ranging from lions to tigers, cats, dogs, snakes, birds—even dinosaurs and unicorns."

"Really?"

"Yes, and all these life forms live in peace and harmony. They don't have to eat to survive; thus they don't have to kill—just as humans have no need to kill, since you can't die in our dimension. There is only life; there is only love; there is only joy."

"I have another question," I said. "What about age? When I die, will my wrinkled physical body have any effect on the age of my spirit body?"

"Well, actually, souls do come into our dimension carrying an energy reflection of their life on Earth. When babies, children, teenagers, middle-aged, and older people die, they normally come in looking like they did when they died. But with the ability to create and change everything with the mind, you are soon able to change your energy body back to the prime of your life—say, in your thirties.

"Now with children, it is different. Children are allowed to enjoy their childhood and grow into maturity naturally, unless they are very evolved souls who go back to Earth temporarily for one reason or another. When they come to a point of learning how to create and manipulate with their minds, they begin to build their environment, just as children do in the Earth plane.

"There is a lot of schooling that takes place in our dimension. Your brother Larry was a teacher when he came here. He had been working with young people in the Earth plane, so he chose to work with youth in this dimension."

(She said I would get to meet Larry before long, which I was looking forward to.)

"Radiant Lady, what about the clothes that you wear? I noticed when I was with Ray and Tash that people are dressed in all kinds of attire. Do you have clothes factories over there?"

"No, Rosalind," Radiant Lady gently admonished. "I think that even with ten percent of your physical brain, you can probably figure that one out!"

"Well, let's see," I said. "You probably have people over there who love to sew and do it as their form of service. Or perhaps people just create their own attire right out of their mental closets. Is that correct?"

"Both are correct. Spirit robes come with our new spirit bodies. When we are ready to wear our spirit robes, we just think them into existence. Each spirit robe varies, and expresses the nature of the resident wearing it. Many wear their spirit robes most of the time because they are so comfortable. And some souls wear sandals here, though many go barefoot."

"And do people have to pay in some way for the new clothes made for them by others? Do they barter and exchange services, or are they just given to them as gifts?"

"Often services are exchanged or gifts are given but we have no need for money in this dimension. Actually, people here love to serve others, just as you do on Earth. People all have unique talents, which carry over into this plane. So they perfect their talents even more over here. Since we don't have all the mundane activities related to life on Earth, souls are freed to follow their hearts' desires here. There are those who didn't have time to pursue their wishes on the Earth plane because of the physical obligations of earn-ing a living, raising a family, and so forth. So for those who are unable to develop their God-given talents on Earth, Heaven is something to look forward to greatly."

"Another question just came to mind," I said.

"What is your question?"

"Well, where does the ego come in? The ego gets a lot of bashing here on Earth as something that often works against the good of the human being."

"That's because the purpose of the ego is not clearly understood on the Earth plane. God would not give you something that is not useful."

"Well, that's what I suspected," I replied, "But what *is* the purpose of the ego?"

Radiant Lady explained: "The ego is a very important part of the energy of the physical body. Because the physical plane is so intense, the ego acts as a shield or protector for the human personality that is innate within the soul/spirit. It is like a reflector of fear, hatred, insecurity, and all the emotions that dissipate with the astral body when the soul body enters another realm. That is, it reflects these emotions back to the world as it checks 'thought IDs.' It often gets a bad rap because it becomes associated with the lower emotions. But the ego is not a negative emotion, but an energy that is stronger than any emotion, functioning like a parental protector of the human personality as well as the soul/spirit that resides within the personality."

"I'm not sure I completely understand what you are saying, Radiant Lady," I replied. "But whatever you say, I do accept."

"I certainly don't have the last word on everything," she responded. "But the human ego is not a part of your soul/spirit body because we have no need to have such protection in a world where there is no conflict and where only Love exists. The personality survives the death of the physical body, but the ego does not."

"Awesome. This is the best lesson I have ever received. You are so wonderful, Radiant Lady. Thank you for taking this time to teach me these truths of the universe."

"Well, since there is no time in our dimension, I don't consider myself to be taking time to teach. In our dimension it is a joy to serve. And it is a joy to serve you, Rosalind. Our purpose in getting this material out to the world is to give hope to those who are discouraged, and joy to those who are seeking a better life."

"Thank you, Radiant Lady. Well, I guess it's time for me to retire. I can't wait for my next lesson. I never know what you are going to teach me next. It gives an extra edge of excitement to my journeys! Good night."

"Good night, Rosalind. You are a wonderful student, and I look forward to our next adventure together."

6 When Our Earth Tour Ends

I sat wondering what determines exactly where we end up after we die.

"That is a good question," I heard in my mind.

"Radiant Lady?" I asked.

"Yes, it's me."

"I'm glad you're still with me, Radiant Lady."

"Of course, I am always with you. I think you are going through that human 'guilt' thing," she replied. "Just because you haven't communicated with me for a while, do you think I have given up on you?"

"Well, I guess I was thinking that," I said. "I drop back into my old guilt stuff now and then. It goes back to my self-image, and thinking I'm not deserving of your attention since I haven't held up my side of the bargain for a couple of weeks. I didn't sit down to communicate with you at all last week because so many people called, and we had long conversations just when I should have been talking with you.

"Then my electricity went off for ten hours on the coldest day of the year and, of course, I couldn't write then. I did go over to Barnes & Noble to write, but I had so much fun drinking my tea, watching people, and visualizing my book on the best-seller list that I didn't tune into you. But I did get the outline of the chapter headings done. I felt a great need to have an overview of what the book will cover. Did you help me with that?"

"Of course I did. We're not going to let you take off on your own with this. The outline was done—I just helped you to tune into it."

"Well, the outline came together so quickly, I knew you must have been helping me," I replied. "Thank you, as always, for your wonderful guidance."

"And thank you for being such a receptive part of our team," Radiant Lady said with a sincere tone in her response. "I'm really impressed with how together our team is. Remember that we have the ability from our dimension to project thoughts to you, and that's what we did. We have been projecting a lot of thoughts to you, Rosalind. In your dimension you might say that we are working on this '24/7.' And in our dimension we would say that the manuscript is already done, and we are projecting it to you in every possible way we can. In the no-time dimension, everything is done instantly."

"I guess it must be a real challenge for you to work with someone in the time dimension."

"Actually, no," Radiant Lady replied in a cool, calm manner. "In the no-time dimension, we don't have the pressures on us that you have. Judgment is something that doesn't exist here. On the Earth plane, you put judgment on everything. Someone could say that because I even said that, I am putting judgment on you, but I'm not."

"Oh, no, Radiant Lady, I don't feel that you have a judging bone in your body—oops, I don't know if you even have bones! It must be amazing to live in a no-time zone. Here on the Earth plane, time is always at our backs pushing us on and on. We wake up in the morning and are pushed through the day. We are pushed through the months. It seems like yesterday was the first day of the month—and now here it is the end of the month. It just never ends.

"Some*times* I would just like to get off the treadmill, and not have time blowing on the back of my neck—some*times* like a gentle wind, some*times* like a gale, and some*times* like a tornado! It seems like yesterday that I was four, and riding on the back of my friend Billy Boy's tricycle. And now it seems like a day later and I'm 70. Inside I don't feel older at all. I feel timeless. I don't feel like I have really changed a bit since my first Earth memories."

"Well, you haven't changed, Rosalind, because you have finally gotten in touch with your timeless nature, which is your Spirit Self. That Self never changes. And you have answered your own question that you asked when we started this conversation."

"You mean when I asked what determines where we end up after we die?"

"Yes. On the Earth plane, you are 'doing time,' and where you end up depends on the quality of the time spent. You are all doing time 'for life.'" Radiant Lady chuckled. "So guess what, Radiant Rosalind?"

"What?"

"Well, when your time is 'up,' you will get off your treadmill and get your breather!"

"That sounds encouraging. But what determines where in heaven's name I will be when my time is up and my tour is over?"

"*You* do."

"I do? But how do I do that?"

"You don't do it consciously. It's an automatic system, like your autonomic nervous system that controls your bodily functions. When you die, you have built into your physical, soul, and spirit bodies an automatic placement system that moves you to the realm that has your same vibratory rate."

"I'm fascinated by the way you discuss the bodies I am wearing. You talk about them like they are clothing that I dispose of when I am tired of wearing them," I said a little defensively. "I guess I've been wearing this particular body for so long, I'm beginning to feel a bit protective of it. You know, I'm so used to wearing it, I'm not sure I want to let it go.

"And I must admit that I picked a good one this time around because it has really been good to me. Now as I say that, I wonder who 'me' is if I am not my body, even though I do know that I am more than my physical body. But being human, doubts do come into my mind fairly often."

"Having doubts is normal for humans. But I want to emphasize that two of your bodies *are* like disposable clothing. The physical attire is stamped with a 'time' tag. The soul attire is stamped with a 'time/no-time' tag. Only the spiritual attire is stamped with a top-of-the-line 'no-time' tag."

I found it somewhat amusing to hear Radiant Lady's Fifth Avenue approach to our most precious possessions—our bodies. But she had really made me think. As I reflected on what she said, I could understand the "time" tag on my physical body, which I had been complaining about in my discussion with her. But when we got to the soul body, she said that there is a "time" *and* "no-time" tag on it. Now that one, I didn't understand. But I did understand the top-of-the-line spirit body: a spirit body would obviously be in a no-time zone.

"Rosalind, Rosalind, did I lose you?" I could almost hear her snapping her spirit fingers in front of me, as if to ask, "Are you there?"

"Oh, yes, I'm still with you, Radiant Lady," I replied. "I'm just trying to figure out what you mean by putting a 'time/no-time' tag on the soul body."

"Now we are up to our lesson for today. All the levels, realms, dimensions, or planes of existence you can end up in when you have done your 'time' all exist within you. There is nothing real that exists 'outside' you. Look at your fingers that are on the keys of the computer that you are typing on. They are not real!"

"What do you mean 'not real'? I can see them, feel them, hear them. . . ."

"They are not real because they are all disposable."

"Oh, yes, my fingers are part of my disposable body. And my keyboard and computer are also a part of the disposable world around me."

"Precisely. The only—absolutely *only*—thing that is real is Spirit, which is nondisposable. It is real because it can never be destroyed. Can you understand that?"

"I can, since you describe it so simply. That is, I can understand it mentally. But the pain that my physical body experiences *really* feels *real* when I am experiencing it!"

"Yes, but any pain that you had in the past is gone today. Shall we call it 'disposable pain'? So, here today, gone tomorrow. It is not real! When your tour on Earth ends, your awareness is going to open up on the level, realm, or dimension where your consciousness vibration is the strongest."

"You mean that if a person has something of a mean, angry, or, as we like to say here on Earth, evil, vibration, when they die they will end up at a hellish level of existence?"

"You've got it!" Radiant Lady said strongly. "And there are many of those levels in the nonphysical realm. But when the personality of a human is too attached to its lower, slower emotions—like greed, hatred, anger, fear, addiction, and so forth—these emotions remain attached to the soul body, which keeps the individual attached to the time zone. So the soul that has disposed of its physical body, but hangs on to slower vibratory astral-level emotions, wears the 'time/no-time' tags and experiences a 'locked-in' existence between Earth and Heaven, or Nirvana, as we call it in this dimension. The locked-in existence is what you understand as purgatory, or a place of mental anguish."

"When I was in my late teens, I went through such a state of mental anguish that all I wanted to do was dispose of my physical body," I said. "I thought that if I got rid of my physical body, all my inner pain would go away. I tried to commit suicide, but luckily I was dramatically rescued from doing so. From what you're telling me, if I had died when I tried to kill myself, I would have awakened at my strongest level of vibration, which at the time was fear, anger, and emotional pain. And I would have found myself in purgatory between Earth and Heaven in a time/no-time existence."

"You are a good student, Rosalind. You are catching on to these concepts very rapidly."

"Well, since I've been fortunate enough to be on the Earth plane for 70 years now, I've experienced some of what you are teaching me. Experience really is the best teacher—other than you, Radiant Lady. Now, as we talk, I'm starting to appreciate having 'time' breathe down my neck.

"And speaking of the pressures of time, when I was suicidal, it was *so* painful to wear the physical body that I sat down one day and counted how many days I would have to live if I lived to be 70. I was 18 then, so I subtracted 18 from 70 and came up with 52 years. When I multiplied that by 365 and came up with 18,980 days, I went into an emotional tailspin. I thought, 'There is no way that I can carry this pain around for that many more days and years'—and that's when I attempted to hang myself. But now that I have lived those 52 years and have processed so much of my emotional garbage, I feel thoroughly, thoroughly joyful most of the time, and am in no hurry to leave the Earth."

"It is your choice as to how long you are going to stay around here," Radiant Lady affirmed. "You decided that before you came on this Earth tour. But if you cut your tour short by disposing of your body before your time is up, you will either be sent right back to Earth to finish up with the contract you made with God or you will spend the time you were supposed to be on Earth in a much more challenging state than you would have had on Earth. There are exceptions to the rules about suicide, but they are so complicated that we won't go into that now.

"Rosalind, you would have been close to what you on Earth call Hell, because you would have been locked into that painful emotional state until the time that you were supposed to finish up your tour. It is ironic that you didn't think you could bear the emotional pain for so many more days on Earth, but if you had disposed of your body, you *would* have had to carry that pain around all this time in a locked-in time/no-time level between dimensions."

"Yes," I replied, "I have a good friend who just the other day told me about her father's suicide, and how he hung around her immediately after he died, sending her the desperate mental message that what he did was a real mistake. He kept trying to get into her body for a safer place to be, obviously trying to relieve himself from the purgatory-like existence he was wandering around in."

"Yes, most souls realize instantly after they murder their own bodies that they have made a terrible mistake."

"But these souls aren't condemned to this hellish existence for eternity, are they?"

"Well, Rosalind, knowing what you know about God, what would you think?"

"I would say that God does not condemn us to a hell-like existence for eternity, but we put ourselves there by choice—by our automatic energy system. So I guess the spiritual law behind where we end up when our Earth tour ends would be the 'like-attracts-like' principle. I believe that God functions solely on the principle of pure light, love, and joy."

"That is correct, Rosalind. At the physical level, the principles of 'opposites attract' and 'like-attracts-like' are in operation. The Earth level is the densest, slowest vibratory level. But when you move beyond the physical, it is always 'like-attracts-like.'"

"So, according to 'like-attracts-like,' people vibrating at the same level end up in the same space or dimension when their physical body is dropped," I said. "Therefore, the souls that are on a love vibration when they die end up in the mental dimension or summer realm, as you have called it."

"Yes, the summer realm is where the majority of souls from the Earth end up when they drop their physical garb. So when they have completely released their Earth 'stuff,' as you have been doing all these many years since your teens, they are in that loving, pure, light soul body that I spoke of earlier."

"Talking to you now, Radiant Lady, makes me really happy that I have made it through all my years of Earth challenges. The longer I live, the more I love life here. When I was young, I was really self-centered."

"You don't need to judge yourself, Rosalind. Everything you are experiencing while in your body is an important part of your soul growth."

"Thank you for reminding me of what life here on Earth is all about."

"It is my privilege, and my main reason for being in communication with you, Rosalind. Now do any other questions come to mind?"

"Yes, I do have one. When I was doing my exploration sessions with Robert Monroe, my guiding energies made it clear to me that there is really no such thing as out-of-body experiences. What is happening, as they explained it, is that people are merely shifting vibrations and going to different levels accordingly. So when I went to visit Ray and Tash, I was able to be there because I was able to shift into their vibratory level. Is that correct?"

"That is exactly correct, Rosalind. And it is why you are able to go to these different dimensions where I am taking you while sitting at your computer. You are gifted with the ability to shift your vibration so as to be in communication with those of like vibration."

"You know what, Radiant Lady? It's four A.M., and I'm finding myself shifting into the level of no-time sleep! So I am going to have to sign off for now and continue later today."

"I will be ready to continue when you are, Rosalind."

∞

Since punching my "time card" and checking out two days ago, I saw a short news item on the importance of sleep. A study was done with two groups of people: those who didn't get enough sleep, and those who received adequate sleep. The following day the two groups were given some problem-solving questions. Those who had adequate sleep solved them much more rapidly than the ones who didn't have enough sleep.

I was tired yesterday after a long day of work on this physical plane and I decided that instead of staying up and working the "night shift," I would get a good night of sleep and work the "day shift." I usually function better at night, but when I am tired, I don't.

So I came back to my computer wide-awake, alert, enthusiastic. Since I was sure that Radiant Lady doesn't have to sleep, I knew she'd be ready to continue as usual.

"Correct!" she said. "I detect a tone of jealousy in your voice over the fact that I don't have to sleep, and you do."

"Well, yes, I do feel that way sometimes. Well, I feel that way now," I said a little sleepishly—oops, I meant to type sheepishly!

"How you feel is okay," replied Radiant Lady, "But I do want to remind you that you have lived in the no-time dimension a lot 'longer' than you have lived in the time dimension."

"Thank you for reminding me of that, my no-time friend. Well, I'm ready to continue with my lesson for today. Every time I talk with you for even one minute, I learn something!"

"I'm basically giving you a crash course on the planes of existence. And I want to remind you that a plane is not a place, but a state of being. The first plane is the material plane, or the physical world, which you know a lot about. The second is the Etheric Force Plane. The third is the Astral, and the fourth, the Mental Plane. Very little is known about the fifth, sixth, and seventh planes because these constitute such a high degree of spiritual evolution.

"Now these seven planes are related to the energy centers—or what are called 'chakras'—in your body. The first is the root chakra at the base of your spine. The second is the reproductive center. The third is the solar plexus; the fourth is the heart; the fifth is the throat; and the sixth is the third eye, located at your forehead. The seventh energy center is on the crown of your head."

"Slow down," I exclaimed. "I want to process what you are saying as you go along. What you are basically telling me is that all these planes are 'states of being' and are related to energy centers within us, which manifest at varying degrees of vibration. So when we die, we are instantly in the same energy center, or plane, with which we vibrate. Therefore, if a million people from the slowest vibratory plane, the Earth, died today with their fourth energy center (the heart chakra) vibrating the strongest, they would wake up on the fourth plane, known as the Mental or Summer Plane. Is that correct?"

"Yes, Rosalind," Radiant Lady said, obviously pleased. "So what I am saying is that there is nothing 'solid' about anything, even the physical. Everything in this dimension, and the next, is pure vibrating energy. And since you are pure vibrating energy as well, you are attracted to that which you are most like when you drop your physical body."

"But you know what, Radiant Lady? That same thing happens while we are still in our physical bodies. We are attracted to those people who vibrate on the same level as we do. I've always been amazed to hear stories, say, of a woman from an alcoholic family who marries an alcoholic. And she divorces that husband, proclaiming she will never make that mistake again. So she carefully searches for a mate whom she is sure has no alcoholic tendencies, only to find out later that he is an alcoholic, too. And she chooses the same kind of man the third time!"

"That's correct" Radiant Lady continued. "That is the like-attracts-like law that is a functional part of the Earth plane. And if this woman ever changes her own energy within, and shifts to a faster level of vibratory energy, that is when she will pick a partner that will make her life more pleasing."

"But what about the law of 'opposites attract' that you said is also prevalent on the Earth plane? How does that work?"

"Because the Earth plane is a mixture of every kind of energy, there are times when one must be confronted by the opposite energy so as to learn a certain kind of lesson for growth. I won't go into detail at this point because this is the hardest thing for humans to process. There is often a discussion of 'why bad things happen to good people.' And then there are people who need to blame someone or something outside themselves—who get angry with God, say, for their child's murder. In the overall picture, the child possibly experiences little pain and goes directly to the plane of pure Light and Love, which is where the child's energy is vibrating.

"Now, the murderer ends up locked into his astral shell when he dies. He perceives himself to be in a dark, dense place—a low vibratory state. He continually lives his terrible deeds over and over until he is totally repelled by his experiences. Only then is he ready and willing to receive God's light into his dark world—which helps move him out of his dark state of existence.

"And often that child that he killed, being a highly evolved soul, is able to be a major factor in his transformation. These children of light often work with the angels in helping to raise the vibrations of those who become lost in the slower, darker levels of vibration. And the child may have chosen that kind of death before he came to the Earth plane for lessons at many levels. Often the parents of such a beautiful child soul have incredible energy transformations because of what they experienced with this highly evolved child."

"You know, Radiant Lady, I remember reading a story in the newspaper several years ago about a five-year-old child who was dying of leukemia. The story was written because the child had gotten in touch with a spiritually evolved guru, who came to visit him in the hospital. It was a glowing story because the child was on the same vibration as the spiritual teacher. They related on so many levels.

"The dying boy had no fear of death. He spoke of the fact that he had to come to Earth, and was leaving early, to teach his parents about the fact that there was no death—only life. He spoke of the love of God. He was such a radiant and joyful child. The parents were truly moved and grateful that this spiritually evolved little boy chose to light up their lives even for such a brief period of time. The child died shortly after the visit from his spiritual friend."

"Some very high spiritual beings come from the fifth, sixth, or seventh levels to bring more light into the world," said Radiant Lady. "They also reincarnate back to the Earth from a higher plane for greater growth themselves. All of the Earth's great spiritual masters, like Jesus, Buddha, and many others, come from the highest spiritual planes. Their presence on the Earth plane in and of itself lifts the vibrations of the overall energies of the Earth."

"It is such an awesome gift for God to send these messengers of Light and Love to our Earth plane," I said. "If we would just live in our light, love, and joy energy as much as possible while on the Earth plane, it seems that the vibration created would offer incredible benefits for everyone involved."

"Yes, Rosalind, that is correct. You have learned a lot since your dark days of despair years ago. Your vibrations have raised considerably, even though you have experienced much pain in the process or might I say *because* you have experienced much pain in the process. You have truly learned that living in love and joy is the answer to living a fulfilling life in the physical body."

"You're right, there. And I am certainly grateful for all the help I have received from the higher dimensions. If the Love of God that has come to me in the form of help from my guides and angels had not been there when

I needed it, I would still be wandering around lost in my darkest, slowest vibrating energy."

"So Rosalind, that brings us to our next lesson. Why don't you take a break and come right back, and we'll let time blow on your neck and move you right through time into the next dimension of no-time."

"That sounds good to me. And for you to tell me to take a break is something! Okay, I'll meet you again shortly between time and no-time. I just can't wait to find out what will happen next."

PART III

Help Always

7 Every Earth Traveler Has a Guide

I wasn't gone long. Back at my computer, I sat with my eyes closed, tuning into what my Spirit Team would like for me to do at this time. I began to feel I was being placed somewhere, or that an image from my Life Imprint, my Akashic records, was being sent to me.

I found myself sitting in a booth at a little restaurant. The memories started to flood in from an incident in my life.

I was going through some very hard times because I had just gotten a divorce and needed to seek employment. I had worked most of my adult life. But when David and I got married, we decided that since he had a good job in a local community college, it would be okay for me to stay home and not take on an outside job. It was really nice being a "kept woman," so to speak—that is, until I needed to get a job.

We lived in the country in a very nice farm home, with great pillars like a wonderful southern mansion. It was named Oak Hill Farm because it sat on a hill with a great oak tree in front. When we arrived in Virginia just after getting married, I found this house listed for $100 a month in the paper. Coming from the New York City area, I figured that the amount had to be a typo. But when I called about renting it, it was still available, and at the listed figure.

David and I lived in this wonderful house for several years, and the rent didn't go up. That was in the early 1970s and it would have been a good time to invest in a house; we didn't even consider that since the rent at Oak Hill Farm was so reasonable.

But one day my idyllic marriage came to an end, and it became necessary to find a job. I had very good credentials, but lived in a sparsely populated area equidistant between three cities in the Shenandoah Valley. I started by visiting the employment agency in Harrisonburg. They didn't have a job available for me even though they seemed impressed with my resume. Next I traveled south to Staunton. The employment agency there said they would keep my name on file until something came in that would fit my needs. Then I finished the triangle by driving east to Waynesboro, where the employment person said, "Oh, we had something about three weeks ago that would have suited you perfectly, but we don't have anything now."

I left the employment agency completely discouraged. I walked up the street to a little restaurant called the Mad Hatter. There weren't any customers because it was three in the afternoon. There were a couple of waiters standing across the room when I sat down in a booth. A waiter came over, and I ordered only a salad, since I wasn't flush with money, nor was I that hungry.

When the waiter walked back to the other side of the room and disappeared into the kitchen, I heaved a great sigh and sent out a very clear prayer request: "Please help me to know where I can go to get a job." Then I heard a male voice as clearly as if someone was sitting across from me say, "Go to where you've been before!"

I was so startled that I looked up and all around me, but saw no one—absolutely no one! Being surprised like this, and a bit uncomfortable having a voice come out of nowhere to answer my question, I thought, "If they are going to give me a message, I sure wish they would be more specific." I didn't know who I meant by "they." Angels? Guides? God? But as I sat there waiting for my salad to arrive, I kept asking myself, "Where have I been before that would be a good place to get a job?" I had lived in a lot of places, and I was hoping the voice wasn't referring to New York City! I loved living in Virginia.

I was still racking my brain when the waiter brought me my salad. "Go to where you've been before. . . ." What in the heck were they referring to? Then I suddenly received an image of Central Virginia Community College in Lynchburg. I thought, "Oh, CVCC. I taught a class there a couple of years ago. I wonder if Dr. Fralich is still there." He was the one who had hired me.

Lynchburg was a good hour and a half drive from Waynesboro. I quickly ate my salad, paid the bill, and rushed madly out the front door of the Mad Hatter! It was late in the afternoon when I arrived in Lynchburg. I pulled up in front of the college, went right into Dr. Fralich's office, and asked to see him. He welcomed me and invited me to take a seat in his office.

"Dr. Fralich, I need a job. Can I come back here to teach at CVCC?"

"Sure," he replied. "I can't give you a full-time job but can allow you to teach two courses at least. What would you like to teach?"

I quickly answered, "Parapsychology, and Death & Dying."

"Fine, you're just in time to get into the fall schedule."

I shook his hand, and walked out, saying silently, "Thank you! Thank you! Thank you for answering my prayer so instantly!"

This was the best tip I have ever received. And I don't think I would have thought of it on my own. I had taught a course in parapsychology for several terms at CVCC a couple of years before. But it was a long drive from Oak Hill Farm to Lynchburg, and since I didn't have to work I had given up the job. Now, here I was ready and able to go back.

That voice, which I now realize was my guide, completely changed the direction of my life.

∞

It has been almost 30 years since I moved to the Lynchburg area from the Shenandoah Valley—and I'm still here. I had never taught a Death & Dying class before, but I had done so much research on this subject after Larry died that I was able to put a course together without blinking an eye. I needed a master's degree to teach in the community college system, so I was grateful I hadn't allowed my father to talk me out of going on for higher education.

Actually, I would never have met David had I not gone to get my master's at Union Theological Seminary in New York City, where he was also a theology student. Upon graduation, I received a job offer to be an assistant minister in Pennsylvania. At the same time I was offered a position as a counselor at a YMCA in Manhattan. By my staying in New York City to work, David and I got better acquainted, and eventually tied the knot. We were married for ten and a half years.

Having reviewed this story in my mind, starting with the image of me sitting in the Mad Hatter, I imagined Radiant Lady was ready to comment—and give me some high-level advice. One of my cats, Sparky, climbed up and lay across my forearms. My fingers were working perfectly and I was able to type with a loving load over my wrists and arms!

∞

"That is indeed a loving load," I heard Radiant Lady say in my mind. "And I'm glad you were finally able to track her desperate meow and get her out of the closet earlier today. She was asking for help, just as you were asking for help those many years ago when you desperately needed a job and a new lifestyle. And, of course, you have continued asking for help through these many years on planet Earth."

"That's right, Radiant Lady. I'm glad I was able to track her plaintive meow and help her. But now I'm going to have to remove her since she just turned around and is sitting full body on top of my hands."

I put Sparky down, and she was not a happy cat, of course. I had disconnected the phone for the weekend. I had decided that I was absolutely not going to be disturbed, so I couldn't even allow my cats to disturb the flow of my typing.

"Radiant Lady, are you making some kind of point that we can be guides to each other here on the physical plane?"

"Yes, I am," she replied. "You are so connected to the energy of those around you on the Earth plane that you are a guide to others in many ways. Most people don't even realize how they can influence others' lives by just a simple smile."

"That's great to hear—and I do believe it. But tell me: how, and why, do we have guides from another dimension answering our every need, like, 'Where can I find a job?' Is there always someone out there listening to us, watching us, waiting to help?"

"Actually, there is. Remember what Tash said when he and Raymar took us on a tour of the Hall of Records? 'As you think, your thought is connected to the pure mind of God.' So when you ask for help, you *will* receive help. That is a universal principle. 'Ask and you *will* receive.'

"But when you ask, you have to be patient, and allow the answer to come in the form God or the Universe wants to send it. You cannot ask, and then decide exactly how the answer will manifest in your life. That is where faith comes in. You have to trust that at a higher level your needs are better understood than you can know yourself."

"It has taken me many years of Earth life to learn that," I said.

"You cannot imagine how much help is available to you. God's whole system is set up to help those on the Earth plane, those caught in the 'time warp' between dimensions. The souls in the higher dimensions, as we described earlier, are automatically nurtured by the atmosphere that surrounds them."

"I remember you saying that the air we breathe and the air they breathe is completely different."

"Yes, the molecules of the air they breathe are like the pure breath of God. The atmosphere is pure God energy because they are at a higher vibration and closer to the Godhead, since they are no longer in their physical bodies. Then at the higher levels—five, six, and seven—they have dropped their soul bodies and are living purely in their Spirit bodies with God."

"Goodness gracious! It's beyond my wildest imagination to conceive what it must be like to exist in a pure Spirit energy body."

"Very few have any understanding of what it is like to live in the sixth and seventh realms—and beyond. You are in such a slow, dense realm of existence that God has to provide many more sources to nurture your energy levels. But I do need to emphasize that God is as ever-present on Earth as in the Higher Realms. Your spirits are made up of pure God energy, but are sheathed by a soul and physical body. Therefore, the density of your vibration makes it more challenging to connect to your God-energy levels. There are, however, many on the Earth plane who do connect to the pure Spirit levels, through the help of their masters, Jesus, or Buddha and/or through dedicated prayer and meditation."

"So because of the slower vibrations of the Earth plane, and the mixture of vibratory energies, we really need to receive help and guidance from many levels beyond our dimension. Is that correct?"

"It is, indeed. Before you enter the Earth dimension you go through a very thorough orientation period with your group of elders, teachers, guides, and angels. It is decided then who your guide or guides will be when you enter your sacred new sanctuary, your physical form."

"That's so awesome," I said. "But it's still hard, I think, for humans to even imagine that the next realms are so incredibly organized. A lot of people think that you float around on clouds, or just sleep through eternity."

"They're in for a surprise when they die—or rather I should say 'become truly alive.' Your Earth realm appears completely disorganized, in a state of chaos, compared to the realms beyond."

"But why would that be?"

"God's creations are impeccable at all levels. In all realms, those dwelling there are created in the image of God, and thus have, in turn, the free will to create their surroundings through their mental energies, just as God created them. God is Light Form—Mind and Love Substance—and so is *your* spirit body, which will someday be reimmersed in the Godhead, where you will see God Face to Face and Spirit to Spirit. Those in the higher realms are living in God's *pure* Presence. Remember, if *you are* the image of God, God is, in turn, *the image of you.* You were created by your Father, God, so that you might have Life and have it *abundantly.* Every spirit is equal in the Light, Love, and Joy of God's Presence. Remember the affirmation: 'I am Light, manifested in Love and expressed in Joy, Joy, Joy . . .'

"So always remember that Love is not just an emotion but the Power and Energy that propels your soul and spirit, and your life on this planet as well as on *all* the higher dimensions.

"Now the levels beyond the Earth dimension are much more evolved than your dimension. On the Earth level, most of you have no concept of how you have created your own realities, your own circumstances of life. You are a creator; you create with your every thought and anything that you can imagine is yours to be or do or have. You are choosing your creations as you are choosing your thoughts. What is running in the programming of your mind eventually manifests in the outer world.

"If you want to change your outer world, you must first change your mental programming. Because of ignorance of how their lives work, most people on planet Earth try to change themselves by changing their external world. And that is like trying to change the picture on a TV screen by rubbing it with a cloth."

"I do understand that, Radiant Lady," I said. "But it sure took me many years to see clearly in my mind how I create my own world. I remember coming across a book in my college library that discussed creation. The statement 'All that is, comes from the unseen level' was the main theme of the book. There was a discussion of this concept. The tree is created by the Mind of God on an unseen level. The book I was reading came from the mind of a person, and the thought that created it was first on the unseen level. Then I started looking around and thinking about everything, figuring out how it either came from the Mind of God, or the mind of a human, on the unseen level. And then I realized how we were indeed created in the image of God."

"I am aware of the incident," Radiant Lady said in a humorous tone of voice. "You were walking through an aisle in the library looking for something and that book literally fell off the shelf at your feet."

"That's exactly what happened! And when I picked up the book and leafed through it, I checked it out from the library and never did find what I was originally looking for. I think the information in that book meant more to me than anything else I learned that year in college."

"That's an example of how guidance works. Many toes have been bruised by guides trying to get their trainees' attention," Radiant Lady remarked somewhat comically.

"So we're called trainees? That's interesting."

"That's my own term for humans. You are in training on how to live life more abundantly, more lovingly, more joyfully . . ."

"I like that concept. And if I'm in training here it makes me feel less guilty about making errors. I stopped to get gas yesterday and the young lady who waited on me was wearing a big red button with the word 'Trainee' on it. I felt the button was telling me that she might make errors because of not yet knowing everything, thus taking the station off the hook. Maybe I should get a big button saying 'Trainee' so I can take God off the hook for the fact that I don't know everything yet."

"That's why you have guides. God covers all the bases. If you need help, ask—and you'll definitely get an answer."

"You know, that's a very powerful statement and concept. When you really think of it, if we would drop our 'know-it-all' attitude and ask for help more often, we would become more functional as managers of our own businesses—our lives. I have been praying and asking for help continually for the past two years, and my life has literally been transformed."

"I'm very aware of that," Radiant Lady said joyfully. "You thought on September 5 of this year that your life was falling apart, didn't you?"

"I certainly did, especially when my part-time job of ten years disappeared in one day."

"You had asked for help financially, so everything had to fall apart so that it could come together at a higher level. It's like your tour guide experience to Scotland, which you spoke of in an earlier chapter. There is indeed order within all the chaos on Earth. Nothing in your world is random. Ask and you *will* receive. But you have to have faith to believe that you will get help, and then be willing to accept what comes to you."

"I sure learned that—and I learned it the hard way. A few days before my part-time job dissolved, someone called out of the blue and offered me a job that would triple my salary. Not seeing the big picture, I turned the opportunity down, saying 'Oh, I already have a good job I've had for ten years.' When I called back about the new opportunity, the job was taken. Thankfully, everything worked out for me to have the job. It was a miracle—and I love the job."

"That's a wonderful example of how God and guidance work in our lives when we ask for help. Just know that as you evolve into the Mental Realm, or Summer Realm, everything is meticulously organized, far beyond the organization of planet Earth. There is no experience of chaos there. The beings that exist in these realms know how to use their minds to manifest just what they want, and know exactly how to get things done. So a lot is going on at all levels of these higher realms.

"And remember, their bodies are their minds. In your world, getting things done is a two-step process because your minds are different. As we discussed before, on the Mental Realm you think where you want to go, and instantly you are there. But at the Earth level, you have to think of a goal and there is a two-step process in manifesting it instead of a one-thought process. Because you need a lot of help on your plane to survive this complex process, the guidance system is very much in place before you come into this seemingly chaotic dimension."

"So in my seventieth year of life on this planet, my main challenge, which I must have set up for myself before coming in, was suddenly transformed. All my life I have had an issue of not having enough money, not feeling prosperous. Since I finally realized that I am absolutely and amazingly prosperous, and that the nature of God's world is unlimited supply, everything is opening up to me. I feel different inside, and miracles are continually happening. Just at the time my new job dropped into my lap, I received a contract on this new book. I realize now that there is unlimited money out there, but I just have to allow it to come into my checking account."

"Your wonderful guide has been working overtime to help you to understand this message on prosperity," Radiant Lady said.

"Oh, do you know my guide?"

"Of course I do," Radiant Lady exclaimed. "We are both a part of the team that helped to sculpt your Earth life before you came in."

"Oh, that's good," I said, still not quite understanding what this planning committee was all about.

"Well, it's more than good. As a matter of fact, it's quite wonderful, if I must say so myself."

"You're right," I replied. "In fact, it's amazing. Most of my life I have been fumbling around, not knowing what the heck life is all about, and what the heck I am doing! I have been searching, searching, searching all my life. I have traveled the world looking for the answers that I finally discovered were right within me—you know, like the little book *Acres of Diamonds*, in which an entrepreneur looked all over the world for diamonds only to discover them right in his own backyard."

"Well, that is the attitude that many humans have," Radiant Lady responded, "and the main purpose of this book is to help people get an overview of themselves and their many dimensions within. That is the basic purpose of your first book, *Cosmic Journeys*—to help people realize the nature of the many realms within themselves."

"So is it possible for me to meet my guide or guides?"

"Of course it is. That is part of our plan. We're glad you asked."

"So I'm ready to take another trip?"

"Certainly, and you should take a break before that happens, since it might be a while in Earth time before you will be able to attend to the needs of your body."

"Yes, like getting a bite to eat, which I need. I don't want my stomach to be growling when I meet my guide."

"So take your Earth break, and we'll be waiting."

∞

"I'm back. . . ."

"That's good," Radiant Lady replied. "We've been waiting for you for 24 hours!"

"Oh, gosh, I've done it again. I ate something and sat back down. It was midnight, and I suddenly realized that eating that leftover Chinese food had made me sleepy, so I went on to bed," I said sheepishly.

"I'm just kidding you, Rosalind. There is no time here. When you get to this side, you will never have to apologize for 'being late.'"

"Oh, what a relief! I never like to be late for an appointment. But with all the activity going on in your dimension, how do you know 'when' to meet friends or attend meetings or anything else that involves more than one resident of your realm?"

"That's quite easy. It works in the same way that we meet with you. It is all done by thought. Someone thinks, 'Meet with me' or 'with us' and zip, I am there instantaneously. If there is more than one person I'm to meet, they receive the same message. We never have to talk in this dimension if we don't desire to do so. Most of the time we communicate through thought. There are times when we prefer to simulate Earth talking, especially when we meet a newcomer to this dimension. We teach them that their thoughts are like an open book, and instruct them in a new way of thinking, just as we show them a new way of walking."

"It's sure good there are lots of folks over there ready to help others who need help, such as newcomers. We can send thoughts to each other here on the Earth plane, and that type of communication quite often happens spontaneously. The love connection of mothers helps them pick up on something happening to their child. I taught a course on extrasensory perception for a number of years. I always told my students that everyone has ESP, and that it just needs to be developed. What is ESP in regard to the thoughts you send in your dimension?"

"What you call ESP is the mind function of your Soul/Spirit body. Yes, everyone has ESP because everyone has a Soul/Spirit body. That's why your ESP can be developed. By concentrating on it and speeding up your vibration, it can be developed quite successfully."

"When I used to teach parapsychology, I dealt with the subject of extrasensory perception and did ESP exercises with the students. These fell under the category of mental telepathy, and I would break that down into clairvoyance (clear seeing), clairaudience (clear hearing), and clairsentience (clear sensing). Then we would view telepathy as either precognition (knowing the future) or retrocognition (knowing the past). So from what you are telling me, in doing all these tests, I was really teaching the students how to function from their Soul/Spirit bodies rather than from their physical minds?"

"That is correct, Rosalind. You have been working with Soul/Spirit bodies for many years without realizing it."

"You've triggered one more question in my mind," I said.

"And what is that?"

"You spoke of 'speeding up our vibrations.' I wish you would give me a definition of vibrations. You've frequently spoken about vibrations in regard to the realms and dimensions of the afterlife. What do you mean by vibrations?"

"Everything on the Earth plane is broken down into molecules. Molecules are the makeup of energy. And all energy is in motion at varying speeds all around you at all times. Some molecules vibrate at slower speeds, and those vibrating at very slow speeds are what you presently perceive as the material world. Molecules vibrating at hyperfast speeds are the invisible energy of your thoughts. So the only difference between you and the keyboard you are typing on is the configuration and speed of your molecules."

"So our thoughts, which are at the unseen level, vibrate at a much faster level than our bodies?"

"That is correct."

"Well, then what about the levels our guides and angels are on? They, too, must be vibrating at a rate of speed that goes beyond our physical perception."

"You are correct, Rosalind. We know of seven different planes of existence, but levels five, six, and seven are at such a high rate of vibration that we know very little of what happens there—unless one of the residents comes down into our dimension to teach us. And, of course, when these highly evolved Light Beings arrive, the word spreads by thought."

"Sounds a lot better than cell phones on our Earth plane," I said jokingly.

"You see, the residents of the higher realms can descend into the lower vibratory realms, but the lower cannot ascend into the higher. So to take you to meet your spirit guide, we are going to help to raise your vibration so that you can ascend into the realm where he exists. You are personally invited to the home of your guide, by the way."

"Awesome," I replied. "But I have one more question while I am thinking about it."

"Certainly."

"Well, I'm a card-carrying member of 'Planet Earth.' And ours is just one planet of nine that revolve around the sun. As we speak, we have a land rover on our neighboring planet of Mars. And there are millions, and perhaps even billions, of galaxies in space. Our astronomers never cease discovering the presence of more and more galaxies. And all of them must be physical matter, since we can see them through our Hubble telescope. So do all of these physical energies that we perceive in space have a unique spiritual component or special higher planes associated with them, just as we do? Or are we all part of the same planes of existence?"

"You are asking very good questions, Rosalind. Everything physical—visible to the human eye—has its unseen levels. Your dimensions of existence radiate out from the Earth as their center. And every other planet that exists in the billions of galaxies is created in the same manner as planet Earth, and all have their planes of existence at varying vibratory rates."

"God is becoming more and more awesome as we speak!"

"Well, God has always been awesome, and is not becoming more so, because the Godhead, or God energy, is the only reality that exists. When your star, your sun, explodes, then all of the planets surrounding it, including your beautiful planet Earth, will no longer exist. And thus the physical realm is not the real realm."

"So there are quadrillions of spirit worlds out there that surround all the quadrillions of planets that exist," I responded somewhat flippantly, as it was hard for my mind to process the concept. "So do some of the spirit beings from the spiritual levels of a planet several millions of light years from Earth ever come to our Summerland to visit?"

"Oh, all the time," responded Radiant Lady. "Our Summerland, or Mental Level, is one of the more lovely spirit lands, and travelers from many spirit worlds from other galaxies love to come and visit. And since we are a Love realm, with no fear or dissension, all are welcome. Also, there is a great spiritual hierarchy, or rulers' council, that gathers from all of these various realms."

"Oh, that makes me feel like a grain of sand on God's great beach of life."

"Just remember one important thing, Rosalind. The pattern of all that exists in God's universe exists in every cell in your physical body. And every cell is important to the continuation of life. Every cell in your body is important in keeping you alive. Therefore, every planet is important in keeping the galaxies alive. You are very, very loved and important in the eyes of God. In just the same way, you should love, respect, and revere all life-forms around you because Spirit is the All That Is—and that includes you."

"Thank you so much, Radiant Lady," I said. "You radiate so much love just through your voice. You make me feel so loved, welcomed, and appreciated. So now I am going to get to see you in person again—or rather in spirit—along with my guide."

"Yes, and now I want you to close your eyes and relax. We will be raising your vibration in order to bring you into a higher vibratory realm."

"I will do that. This very quiet, snowy day certainly helps me to relax . . . but I'm so excited that I will probably have trouble relaxing!

∞

"Hello, Radiant Lady," I began. "I hope you are here. Actually, I'm sure you're here."

"I am."

"Well, then, I'm also quite sure you are aware of what happened when I closed my eyes this afternoon with the certainty that there was nothing around that would or could interrupt my session. But the inevitable happened!"

"You might as well tell the story now that you've brought it up."

"Well, I was thinking as I sat here, with my eyes closed going into a relaxed state, that there was nothing I could think of that would interfere with my session with you and my guide. But suddenly I felt that someone was watching me—like the night many years ago that you were watching me as I was going to sleep.

"You know how my computer is right beside a window here in front of my house. Well, I opened my eyes and turned—and looked at a face staring in the window at me. I screamed because it startled me. Luckily, I didn't do that with you when you were watching me at my parents' house and I first saw you!"

"Yes," she said, "like you did when you were a young girl and got out of bed one night because you couldn't sleep, and as a joke, stood with your arms raised at a window making shadows beside your sisters' bed. When they woke up, saw you, and started screaming, they scared your father so much that he almost had a heart attack as he ran up the stairs to rescue them."

"Yes, and I *was* really in trouble then. My only escape was to crawl under my bed as far back as I could so that Dad couldn't get his hands on me. By the time he forced me out from under the bed, he had calmed down and I didn't get a spanking. But it was a close call, and I really did deserve one. But getting back to what happened this afternoon, there looking right in the window at me was my 14-year-old neighbor, Cristin (a variation of Kristin). I call her my 'grandneighbor,' since I don't have children. And she has a younger brother, Cody, who is my movie buddy. It's because of this family that I was guided to my present house. Cristin's mother and stepfather were my guides.

"Cheryn (a variation of Sharon), Cristin's mother, had answered a personals ad that Mark put in the paper. They ended up marrying, and lived by me in the mobile home park. Next, they built a home in my Heavenly Acres neighborhood, out in the country. So when I had to leave the park because of having too many cats, I came out here to find out if I could purchase an acre from Mark and Cheryn to put my mobile home on. They weren't allowed to sell any part of their acreage, but as I drove back to the main road there sat a house with a 'For Sale' sign at the end of what is now my driveway. I hadn't even noticed the house when I drove in. And the price was right. It was the first house built in this housing development and is on the best piece of land. It was an FHA house; the government was selling it because the original owners couldn't keep up with the payments. The price had just dropped from $56,000 because it hadn't sold in eight months. So I bought the four-year-old home on nine acres of land for $49,500. Elsewhere (like in California) the house and acreage would have gone for much, much more. And because I had just written *Cosmic Journeys* and had received an advance, I was able to get a mortgage on the house.

"So I often thank Mark for putting that ad in the paper to find Cheryn. Isn't it amazing how guidance can happen? And I feel that my cats were also my guides at the time. Because if it weren't for them, I wouldn't be here now. They were the reason I was kicked out of the mobile home park."

"It certainly is amazing how things happen," Radiant Lady said. "But there are never any accidents. Everything in life on planet Earth is 'on purpose.'"

"Well, I guess Cristin was staring me right in the face when it was time for me to meet my guide as an illustration of how we are each other's guides all the time. She was watching me as I sat at my computer with my eyes closed, thinking that I had gone to sleep at my computer. She was really puzzled and even amused as she stood outside my window with her nose pressed against it. So I had to stop and take time to talk with her since I hadn't seen her for a while. I believe that 'the secret to life is life itself,' so it is very important that we love, respect, appreciate, and take time to communicate with each other. Life is *so* temporary. Now I realize that Cristin's presence was a part of our session.

"I am again ready to continue. I'm eager to see what will happen. Let me ask for a favor: no surprises, please!"

"Relax, and we will again help to raise your vibration," said Radiant Lady. "And, yes, Cristin was an illustration that all on planet Earth and beyond are each other's guides. We are all One with no separation between us."

"Okay, and thank you, Cristin, for the guidance I get from you often," I said.

∞

"I will describe what I am seeing, hearing, and feeling," I began.

"That's good," said Radiant Lady.

"Well, I feel my body vibrating and starting to get warm. I am feeling very light-headed. Now I feel like I am moving through space. I am moving through an energy tunnel. I know that I am not really moving, but just changing vibrations.

"A view is beginning to open up in front of me. There is a sparkling green field. I see a very beautiful landscape, with trees that seem to be vibrating. The horizon is quite expansive. Now I am coming down near a dwelling that is surrounded by an amazing garden. Not only are the colors of the flowers otherworldly, but the smell is intoxicating.

"I am now on a walkway that goes into the garden. The house is a very unique structure. The walls have a golden glow about them, and the house is nothing like the structure of our dwellings on Earth. Rather than walking, I feel I am floating just above the vibrating surface of this glorious garden that surrounds the house.

"As I move into the garden, I see two people sitting on a very beautiful bench among the flowers. I am coming closer to the beings, who stand up and turn to me. One is my Radiant Lady, in a stunning, flowing white gown with golden embroidery. The other, standing beside her, is a very handsome gentleman also in an embroidered robe. He has very piercing eyes and a wonderful golden glow to his skin. He has a somewhat Asian look, with a striking goatee. He bows to me as I come closer."

"Rosalind, welcome to our dimension," said Radiant Lady, reaching out her arms toward me, which gives me an energy surge—it would be a hug on planet Earth. "I want you to meet your dearly beloved guide, AhSo."

I stepped closer to him and our eyes met as we touched hands. An electrifying energy impulse went right through my body—not just from our hands touching, but also from our eye contact. It was such an incredibly familiar energy flow that I found myself speechless.

"What do I say to a great master such as the one I am now meeting in person for the first time? Or should I say meeting in spirit for the first time."

"Rosalind, it has been a privilege to serve as your guide throughout your years on planet Earth. And I am no more of a great master than you are. In the eyes of God, we are *all* great masters," his thoughts projected into my mind.

"I should have realized that you would be able to read my mind."

"That is not unusual in this dimension. To read your mind in your dimension, I must be given permission by you to do so. And you gave me full permission to work with you in any way necessary to achieve the goals that we set forth for you before you entered the Earth womb," AhSo mentally projected to me.

"I really want to apologize to you, AhSo. I was not taught to believe in guides when I was growing up. So when you came to me during my exploration sessions at the Monroe Institute, I really didn't believe you were real. I thought it was my imagination—that is, until the time all the material came together in my *Cosmic Journeys* manuscript. When I read over the things that you taught, I knew it was not my imagination because I wasn't capable of discussing such amazing concepts that I knew nothing about."

"I accept your apology, but it is not necessary. Coming to know and accept my presence in your life was an important part of your growth process. So you now have overcome the first barrier that you put in front of you after entering your life in the physical body."

"I know your name isn't AhSo, because you chose not to give a name when Bob Monroe and I were working with you. So Bob gave you the name AhSo because of your Asian accent, which was strong when you first started speaking through my energies. Also, Bob would often say, 'Ah, so that is what it is about,' when you would give him some important information."

"A sense of humor in this dimension is as important as it is on planet Earth," AhSo said. "Many in our realm got a real chuckle out of Mr. Monroe's need to give me an 'energy identification,' which ties my energy to the Earth plane. But actually, I looked at it as an 'affection identification' on Mr. Monroe's part because he seemed to so appreciate me and thoroughly enjoyed our many conversations.

"I also became very fond of him in our wonderful sessions. It was such a privilege to meet him when he arrived on our side, and we often get together socially. I respect and appreciate his very inquisitive mind. He continues to seek and probe the minds of many in this dimension, desiring as he does a continual flow of universal knowledge."

"Does he come to visit you, AhSo, or do you go to his home?"

"Both. I have been to his home many times, and he has similarly been to mine. As you know from what Radiance has told you, it is very easy to get around here in this golden dimension. It's a good place to retire," he said, which made us all chuckle. "Mr. Monroe and I have been working on the *Soul Journeys* project, together with Radiance and several others. It has taken us a while in Earth time to get where we are now, but we are all pleased with the progress."

"I would say you have pulled off a miracle to get me settled down and in the right energy space for the transcription of this book."

"We knew you would get around to it eventually because you had made the contract with us before entering the Earth dimension," AhSo said.

"So Bob Monroe and I must have made some kind of contract before coming in as well. Is that correct?"

"It is."

"I have some questions I would like to ask you person to person, or spirit to spirit, however it works!"

"That is why you are here. What would you like to know?"

"I read over the chapter entitled 'The Nature of Guidance' in *Cosmic Journeys* before coming to visit you. Almost everything in that chapter was information you had given on guidance. You mentioned that you had been on Earth many centuries ago, but have not been back since. So why haven't you been back to Earth?"

"First, I want to say that to be a guide in your dimension, one has to have the experience of living there at least once before taking on the challenge of being a guiding energy to an Earth soul. I wanted to learn what it would be like to be a guide, so I was willing to enter the Earth experience. And it was a good experience.

"You and I have worked many times together because we are on the same ray or vibration. Our purpose has been to assist people in the Earth plane to be aware of their own spiritual pathways. And on this dimension we have assisted many souls as they began their spirit journeys here. Our basic purpose has been to help people realize that there is no death—only life."

"It's so wonderful to hear that we have worked together before, AhSo. My life seems so mundane that it's hard for me to imagine that I have done all the things you say I have done.

"Another question I have is in regard to the four Invisible Helpers that worked with Bob and me at the institute. You mentioned that they are from a completely different energy system than ours. I took that to mean that they were from another galaxy, or something like that. Is that correct?"

"Yes. There is a very elevated system of wonderful spiritual beings who work as, let us say, missionary guides through the many higher levels of the galaxies. Our friend Radiant Lady has told you that every planet has its own spiritual dimensions.

"The four wonderful light beings that we worked with at the institute have never been in a physical body on planet Earth. But they were willing to serve the Earth in this different capacity. As they served, by helping to guide you into many dimensions and experiences, they were also evolving in their own spiritual growth. And I also want to say that you often travel with them throughout the galaxies during your sleeping state."

"Perhaps when I wake up feeling so energized, I have been traveling with them during the wee hours of the morning," I said with great enthusiasm. "You know, in my religious training, I was always taught to believe in angels, but spirit guides were never mentioned. Could you tell me the difference between a spirit guide and angel?"

"I would be happy to comment on that. Everyone on Earth has a spirit guide, with some exceptions, which we will discuss later. We, as spirit guides, watch over and advise you whether you are consciously aware of our help or not.

"Now, angels were created by God to be our messengers and protectors. Angels will appear on Earth to accomplish this service as messengers or protectors, but they never incarnate on Earth. They live exclusively in the higher dimensions. They are neither male nor female, even though they might have a male or female name. Angels are collective energies of Light. Some live among us but don't mingle with us. Angels are a completely separate species. They always appear as illuminated beings, and are very, very special messengers of God. They exude extremely powerful light and love. When you call upon the angels, they are always there to help.

"You can never become an angel because they are a specially created species, but you could become a spirit guide, as I have been many times for you and for others. Just as you earn advancement spiritually, so do angels earn advancement through their good works and the miracles they perform in the name of God.

"You have heard that 'every time a bell rings, an angel gets its wings.' All spiritual beings are continually advancing—you, me, Radiant Lady, the angels. What life is all about is evolving back to our pure essence of Spirit, as Radiance told you . . . to the All That Is—back to our original life in the pure God Energy."

"Oh, thank you, AhSo," I said, as I began to feel my energies waning. "I'm just human, and my vibrations are slowing down."

"Yes, Rosalind," said my tour guide, Radiant Lady. "It is time to return back to your level. And it has been a privilege to have you with us for this brief encounter."

"Yes, it has been a privilege, and a blessing, to serve as your spirit guide, Rosalind—to watch over and advise you when you have needed help," said AhSo.

"Thanks to both of you," I said. "It's such a privilege to be in your presence, and to work with you. I will do everything I can to help carry my load in getting this information out to the planet. And let me add that on the Earth plane, I could not do this without the help of my wonderful agent in New York City by the name of Barbara Bowen and the exceptional staff at my outstanding publishing company, Hampton Roads, and my proofreader and ex-husband, David, who are all behind this project 100 percent. So thanks to the team on your side and the team on my side for helping to complete this project that has been in the 'heavenly hopper' for what might be considered eons of time, and one eon is a thousand million years, according to the astronomy and geology unit of time."

$\mathcal{P}$

I was aware of being back at my computer and pumped up with energy, now that I was sure that when I went into the sleep state I would be taking a trip into the spirit worlds of the unlimited cosmos with my four Invisible Helpers, my cosmic missionary Friends.

Come on out and join us. There is plenty of room out there for all of you who are reading this book—all one hundred million of you—and since there is no time in the spirit dimensions, we are all together *now!*

And we'll certainly recognize each other when we meet because we are on the same mission of spiritual growth!

8 Angels: Our Caretakers

It had been a wonderful day for me. I love rainy days because they make me feel so cozy inside my home—and also cozy inside myself. I feel so connected to all aspects of myself—body, soul, and spirit. But this day was more than a rainy day; it was an icy day. The ice completely covered the roads and everything was closed. As I sat down at my computer, I heard a truck chugging up the road at the end of my driveway, so someone was out. But I was enjoying being inside.

And I was ready to welcome a special guest into my home—or, should I say, into my heart. I sat quietly to see if I had a visual assignment to start off the session with my dearly beloved Radiant Lady, to whom I have gotten very attached.

∞

I allowed my fingers to hit the computer keys gently as I awaited any visual "TV shows" in my mind's eye. Yes—I saw blue sky and then my eyes panned down to treetops. I found myself out for a walk at my own beautiful Heavenly Acres. I was moving through my backyard with my walking stick in hand, calling for any kitties and dogs who would like to walk with me. Some ran after me with the same sense of excitement that I always have when we start our walk through the sacred wooded spaces of my nine acres.

I feel strange saying "my nine acres" because I look at this divine place as a loan from God. It is such a privilege not only to be here on this magnificent planet, but to be enjoying my limited time at this temporarily allotted place. And to have all my wonderful cats and dogs also on loan from God: what a joy! Everything that we have is such a marvelous blessing and reason for deep appreciation.

On this blue-skied, sunny day with ten or twelve cats and two of my four dogs following me into the woods, I felt especially grateful. Nine acres seem expansive, especially when they include lovely hills, some quite steep. I like to choose different paths, but I always move in a circle around this outdoor sanctuary. On this day, we wound through some brush to a slight incline, crossed over a path, and there before us was a very special spot with two large, elegant stones protruding from the ground, seemingly happy to serve as benches on our Heavenly Acres outdoor sanctuary.

I took my place on my own stone, and three of the cats gathered around me. Two dogs sat right at my feet. Four cats cozied up in a line on the narrow stone in front of me. Then I heard a meow from behind, toward the house. One of the younger cats was saying, "Wait for me, I can't walk as fast as the rest of you."

Trees circle the stone outcropping, reaching toward the sky and giving tribute to the greatness of God in their own unique way. I feel that the trees are akin to God in their reliability—always being there for me when I seek them out. These trees were here when I came a few years ago, and I expect them to be here when I exit the planet.

We all sat for about 15 minutes, absorbing the magic of the moment. One tree has a broken limb that leans down to rest on the Earth. Three of my furry friends were doing their "cat walk" on this favored limb. I talked to the trees, thanking them for growing on my Heavenly Acres and being faithful companions to me and my animal friends.

As I sat there drinking in the moment, I thought about other sacred places that might be the next resting spot on our walk. Another 15 minutes of hiking would lead us to a pasture on land owned by the cattle farmer who had to sell off a large number of acres to pay for his wife's lengthy stay in the hospital. My property connects to the pasture that feeds his cattle. I'm sorry for the stressful event that forced him to sell some of his land, but I have to admit I am grateful for what the sale of his property has done for me: It has given me a home and land that has brought me and my animals great joy.

We always cross a creek that runs through my property and walk up a steep incline to the pasture. When we arrive, the cats and dogs make a run for another favored spot. I am forever amazed to see these incredible creatures break out in a run as if to say, "Who will be first to sit at the seat of the Tree Master?"

This awesome tree rises high above all the other trees in the woods. Its branched arms are always outstretched toward us, as if to call us to sit under its shade and tune in to its hundreds of years of Earth wisdom, which silently gives strength to our spirits. It stands like a King Oak with the smaller trees around it showing reverence for its grandeur. By the time I reach the tree, the cats and dogs are seated at their special places with their legs outstretched toward the tree as if to show their appreciation for its presence as Master of the Woods.

Eventually, we rise from the first leg of our hike and curl down the trail to the creek. We play there for a while, with several of the cats jumping from stone to stone, trying hard not to fall in. We then follow the stream for a ways, and when it turns to the left, we turn right and go up the hill to the pasture.

On this particular day, I felt something very different in the air. The animals didn't run toward the great oak tree. Then I felt sick in the pit of my stomach as we neared our once-sacred sanctuary. I saw only sky where our Master Tree had once stood. We walked closer, and the animals begin to sniff the earth. The ancient tree had been cut down, and the limbs sawed off.

I was so grief-stricken at the death of this stalwart friend who had stood for centuries as evidence of God's grace and glory, that I threw myself across its barren trunk and cried and cried and cried. Two cats climbed on my back as if to console me, or perhaps to mourn with me. We all felt empty because our old friend had been killed. And we never go back to that spot, it being too painful to experience our sacred sanctuary so ravaged.

On a later walk I followed the sound of a chain saw and found two men cutting down a tree. I learned from them that they cut down our great oak at the request of my farmer neighbor, who felt that the oak trees were dropping acorns that he believed were poisoning his cattle. I walked away, still in sadness at the loss of our great beacon, which had stood for so many long years and then suddenly was gone . . . Here again is the Disconnect

Principle, only relevant on this dense Earth energy level of pain, fear, frustration, and anger. I wonder if the tree will be awaiting me when I arrive Home in the next dimension? I invite it to be right on my true Heavenly Acres in the dimension where only Love is relevant and even trees cannot be destroyed.

Another thing that captures our attention on our walks in the woods is the presence of the snakes whose home it also is. In my first summer at Heavenly Acres, I had approximately ten snakes as visitors in my house, thanks to my cats, who wanted to proudly display their finds or possibly bring me some food in return for my feeding them so well.

When I would walk into my kitchen and see about five cats in a circle staring at something in the middle, I would approach very cautiously to see what was capturing their attention. Twice when I did so, I saw a baby copperhead curled up in the middle with ten or 12 big eyeballs staring down. The young snake was petrified, and I shooed away the cats and got a dustpan with a little brush to sweep it gently into the dustpan's plastic container. Then I put the brush down on the copperhead, so that it wouldn't fall out, and I carried it all the way down to the cattle crossing, out of the vicinity of my property and safely away from my cats. Many, many people have told me that the baby copperheads are much more poisonous than the adults. So I was always careful to shelter them under the brush so that they wouldn't be tempted to strike at me. They evidently hadn't had an opportunity to strike at the cats that carried them into the kitchen.

One evening I came home at dusk and walked into the bathroom to use the commode, without turning on a light. I felt something squishy under my shoes, and when I got up to turn on the light, there was a live blacksnake curled up on my rug in front of the toilet. Of course, I carefully carried it out as well.

When I talked with Esthmus, my farmer neighbor, and asked him about the history of snakes in our area, he told me many stories about the rattlesnakes and copperheads who share our magnificent land. And he, in turn, had a passion to kill any snake that came into his sight.

I learned that snakes don't feel comfortable around cats, so the snakes must have moved farther away from my house to deliver their babies. There were no snakes in my house after that first summer. From then on, we mostly took our hikes in the winter months when the snakes were in hibernation. I have always been petrified of snakes, so this was a wonderful lesson to help me live up to my belief that "the secret to life is life itself" and respect all living forms, even those I was afraid of.

Actually, I was most afraid that my cats would bring some copperheads or rattlesnakes in and drop them on my head or my bed while I was asleep. But I realized that I should stop visualizing that fear so as not to create the event. Of course, this was my fear of dying. I did find about five snake skeletons in my shoes in the closet when winter came around. They must have been dropped right inside the back door in the mud room and scurried through the furnace room into my master bedroom closet to find shelter. I respected the snakes, however, and the snakes respected me so no one got hurt, with the exception of the snakes whose burial containers became my shoes. They weren't the shoes I wore in the summertime. Luckily, I always wore open sandals!

The pictures of these events slowly faded from my mind . . .

∞

"Rosalind," came the voice of Radiant Lady, "we want to commend you for your sensitive awareness of and passionate respect for all forms of life."

"Oh, Radiant Lady," I responded, "I think I must be too sensitive to the loss of life around me. To cry for ten minutes at the death of a tree seems a little much. But I felt despair, and I actually felt the confusion in the minds of my little animals. We really do miss our very special sacred sanctuary."

"Awareness helps to keep your soul and spirit attuned. If humans on the Earth plane would become more aware of the presence and needs of all levels of life forms, they would also become more attuned to the Invisible Helpers that are continually in their presence."

"You mean to become more aware of our spirit guides and guardian angels?"

"Yes, so many humans just call upon them or become aware of their presence in times of crises. But they are always present, and . . ."

There was a scratching on my office door and I got up to open it. When I returned to the computer, I said, "I'm sorry to have interrupted you, Radiant Lady, but it's hard for me to be discussing sensitivity and awareness and ignore the request of one of my cats to open the door! As you no doubt know, I asked my beautiful little orange cat Blue Boy, with his blue collar, what he wanted. And, of course, his answer was obviously love and affection, which is all everyone—animals and people alike—really want. I lay down with him, and he walked around my head and meowed in my ears and licked my cheeks. When I told him that I love him a lot, he replied by touching my cheek with his cold paw. He just came in from outside and simply wanted to tell me he loved me. After our little love session, I put him out of my office so we can continue our conversation."

"You don't have to apologize for doing what I'm saying is important— being sensitive and aware. We in our dimension are so grateful that you are fully aware of our presence."

"Well, my dear Spirit friends, I haven't always been this way, as you well know," I said. "But how do spirit guides and guardian angels get the attention of the ones they are assigned to who aren't sensitive to their presence?"

"Your 'gut feeling' and intuition are two important ways that your helpers can get your attention. Also, when you get that 'knowing' feeling, you should always heed it. It is very hard for spiritual helpers to work with humans that live so much through their heads and ignore their heart levels."

"So tell me more about angels, Radiant Lady. Do we all have a guardian angel who is with us all the time?"

"Yes. You are born with a guardian angel who is assigned to you before you are born, and is with you throughout life."

"But isn't it sort of a boring job for the angels to be with us all the time and not have a life of their own?"

"Your life is their life; and they *do* have a life of their own. It's difficult for you to understand the fluidity of spirit when you are in the physical body. Spirit is in a no-time existence, and multitasking is one of the angels' prime talents. They can perform a thousand tasks at once if necessary because in no-time everything is possible. Life on the Earth plane is linear, but in the spirit world it is all-encompassing. The angels exist in the spirit world but are in tune with your spirit at the same time. Any time you call or pray for help and guidance, they are instantly aware, and are with you to protect and guide you."

"So what is the difference between angels and spirit guides?"

"Your spirit guides have lived on the Earth for at least one incarnation, as AhSo told you, so they understand life in your dimension better. Angels are a completely different species and have never lived on the Earth."

"So how are they able to help us if they have never walked in our shoes?"

"They were specifically created by God to be caretakers at all levels of creation. They are pure Love, and know no other emotions. They are collective energies of light. They are from such a high vibrational level that they do not talk, but communicate only by telepathy. They can be anywhere at any time. They can appear on Earth temporarily if need be. They can shapeshift into human form to perform miracles on the Earth plane. They are all-powerful because they are molded out of the Spirit of God, which is pure Love.

"I want to take you back into your Akashic record to a Life Imprint when your angels saved your life."

"Oh, I have more than one angel?"

"You certainly do," Radiant Lady rejoined. "You have your own specific guardian angel and you also have legions of angels at your service to call upon for help."

"That is good to hear. I have a good friend in Florida who was able to stop smoking because whenever the desire to smoke came to him, he immediately prayed to the angels to take away his desire. Each time he prayed for this help, the desire was taken away from him until he was able to stop smoking completely and has remained smoke-free for years."

"That is the best approach to any addiction that you can have. Smoking is the toughest addiction to overcome. So if you have a smoking, drinking, or drug addiction that you want to have taken from your energy system, call upon the legions of angels available to you at all times.

"It is not important for humans to decide *how* the angels do what they do, but merely to have *faith* that all things are possible for them to do. Your human minds cannot even begin to comprehend the ways in which the universe functions. Miracles are the natural activity of angels. Therefore, miracles are the natural experience of humans as well. Many human beings think of miracles as something out of the ordinary. But miracles are God's natural state. If you truly look at life, everything is a miracle. That awesome oak tree that you loved so much is one of God's great miracles, and at the same time is an integral part of the natural universe," Radiant Lady said with great passion.

"You started to take me back to a scenario when the angels saved my life—I'm ready now if you are."

"Of course, Rosalind. You know that in the no-time level, I am always ready. So go now into your mental travel mode. We will send the images to you, and you can pick them up and tell your story. . . ."

∞

Strangely enough, every time I got to this place I felt a little resistant or nervous inside. I guessed it was that fear of the unknown, or just plain fear of . . . well, I didn't know what. I just needed to keep fear out of my life and vocabulary, and concentrate on staying in the Love-energy mode. So I told myself, "I won't resist; I will relax and go with the flow. . . ."

I found myself breathing deeply and remembering a time several years before when I had been having a great deal of trouble breathing. It seemed to come upon me all at once. I remembered lying in the back bedroom of my home, when I lived in the mobile home park. I had always slept on my back, but I was having so much trouble breathing that I tried lying on my stomach and putting the pillow under my chest to help me breathe better. But I began to feel more and more like I was smothering.

I came to the conclusion that I was either getting asthma, like my mother used to have, or was allergic to my cats. I used to be allergic to cats. But when they started adopting me, I just ignored my allergy, deciding that love would override it, which it eventually did.

I concluded that my breathing problem indicated a need for more exercise, to get back to working with my rebounder, which through bouncing stimulates deeper breathing.

I happened then to see in an advertisement for a health conference in Baltimore that a rebounder specialist would be giving a workshop.

So I went to Baltimore with two good friends, wheezing all the way. As we walked the three blocks from the car to the hotel where the conference was being held, I kept falling way behind my friends because I was so short of breath. And that was not like me. I usually bound around with lots of energy.

The rebounder workshop was on the last day of the conference. I was so excited when the time came for me to attend the workshop. I walked into a very crowded room, and found a seat right up front. We waited, and waited, and waited, but the speaker didn't arrive. After a while, people started walking out. I turned around and began talking to a lady sitting behind me. We introduced ourselves, and I told her I was really looking forward to this workshop to help me to breathe better. I described my symptoms to her and she got a strange look on her face.

"I have worked for a cardiologist here in Baltimore for 20 years," the lady said, "and from what you are telling me, I think you have congestive heart failure. I advise you to get to a cardiologist as soon as you arrive home."

"Congestive heart failure—I don't even know what that is," I responded. "I thought that I was getting asthma or having an allergy to my cats. Are you serious? Do you really think I should see a doctor when I get home? I'm afraid that a doctor is going to tell me that I'm allergic to my cats—and I just couldn't live without my furry friends."

"I think that you should go to the emergency room as soon as you get home," the lady replied firmly.

The speaker never showed up. But I see now that I was meant to go to Baltimore and attend the rebounder session so that I could talk to this woman sitting behind me, instead of listening to a speaker recommend rebounding, which might have killed me.

When I arrived home, I stopped by to see my best friend and told her what the lady had said. It was Sunday evening and she wanted to take me to the emergency room immediately. I was wheezing terribly, but I told her I wanted to wait until Monday morning.

The next day I found myself in the emergency room. Finally, a doctor came in to see me and I told him my symptoms. Before I knew it, the room was swarming with nurses who started doing all sorts of things. I don't recall ever being very sick, let alone being in the hospital, so this was a brand new experience for me. They gave me shots and then started a process of taking fluid from my body.

Then the cardiologist on duty appeared from behind a curtain. With a grim look on his face, he said, "Mrs. McKnight, I have to tell you that you have congestive heart failure, and that we will have to keep you in the hospital for at least the next five days.

I looked at the doctor and laughed, exclaiming, "You mean I only have congestive heart failure and I'm not allergic to my cats?"

He stared at me with a puzzled look.

"I can't believe it," I continued. "I'm so happy that I'm not allergic to my cats."

Then I suddenly realized that my cats were home with no one to take care of them. "But I have to go home to take care of my cats," I blurted out.

"Well, you will have to call someone to take care of them because we do not want you to leave this hospital, Mrs. McKnight. You don't seem to realize that you are in bad shape. Congestive heart failure is an extremely serious matter; the only solution for it is a heart transplant. And we don't do heart transplants for people older than 50." With that, he walked out of the room.

I lay on the table, giggling under my breath, as the nurses worked to get the fluid out of my body, and prepared me to go to the intensive care unit.

Then I thought to myself, "What did the doctor say? A heart transplant was the only solution to my situation, but I couldn't get one because I'm older than 50? That's a hoot!" I was so happy because I wasn't allergic to my cats, and I finally knew what was wrong with me. Knowing what is wrong with you is the beginning of the healing process! The unknown leaves one in a lot of fear that isn't helpful in the healing process.

I decided that being in a hospital was a new adventure for me, and that I was just going to relax and enjoy every minute of it, especially since I was too old to get a heart transplant.

My hospital stay was an amazing experience. I received phone calls from so many people. Then my room started filling up with flowers. I was very grateful to be alive and not allergic to my cats, and to have so many friends who cared.

All kinds of tests were done, including an echo scan, from which they learned that my heart was pumping at a rate of only 15 to 20 percent instead of the 65 percent rate that is normal. I learned later that many patients die when their heart efficiency is that low.

They put me on four different medications and sent me home on Friday—possibly to die. But I had decided early on that when I die, I want to make my transition in a happy state, without fear, but I wasn't ready to make my transition yet.

It was so wonderful being home and lying in bed with my cats all around me! My neighbor who took care of my cats while I was in the hospital stopped in occasionally to see how I was doing. Then a lady I had met a couple of weeks before telephoned. She asked how I was doing, and I told her that I had to go back to work the next week because I had no savings. She replied, "Oh, no, you must not go back to work yet. Meet me at the Coffee Cup Restaurant tomorrow at noon."

When I met her the next day, she handed me an envelope, and then drove away. I looked in the envelope and found ten hundred-dollar bills—one thousand dollars. I realized that I had just been visited by another angel. The first angel had gotten me to the conference to meet the nurse who worked for a cardiologist. And now a second angel. Wow!

As I rested in bed, I realized that over the many years my heart had served me, I had never thanked it. So I named it Strongheart, and started thanking him and talking to him on a regular basis. Strange to call my heart "him," but that seemed natural to me.

I had been home for about a week when I was asked to come to the hospital the next day for a stress test. It was during that night that I must have had a special visitation from the healing angels. When I woke the next morning, I felt *so* good, better than I had in a long time.

When I got on the treadmill at the hospital, they had to tell me to stop because I was actually running. They sent the report to my doctor, and he called me a couple of days later to have the echo scan done again. Halfway through the test, the lady asked me when my birthday was. She thought she had the wrong chart! Learning that she didn't, she then brought in someone else to check the test because my heart was pumping at a normal, healthy rate of 65 percent. The doctor saw me right after that and said he had never had this happen before. He seemed elated and sent me the following letter:

Dear Ms. McKnight:

Hallelujah! I am very pleased to report that your echocardiogram demonstrated that your pumping function has returned to normal. The chamber size is normal and there is no evidence of residual weakness. Although somewhat unexpected, we should be very excited about this finding as it tends to be a rarity. This also explains why you have been feeling so well.

When I visited the doctor the next time, he took me off my medications, saying that I didn't need them anymore.

Then the next miracle happened. I had no health insurance, and no money to pay my hospital bill. The hospital business office asked me to send a copy of my income tax return. When they saw what I earned, I never received a bill from them. The angels were at work again!

Suddenly these images of my experience stopped, and I knew Radiant Lady was ready to speak again.

"Radiant Lady," I asked, "can you give me a rundown on what actually happened?"

"Well, on the Earth level you might call it a miracle, but in our dimension it is God's laws functioning in a normal manner. Yes, you had several angels working with you through the whole experience; they were having as much fun at the hospital as you were. They also enjoyed the ride as you were whirled through the halls to one of your treatments!"

"So a lot of prayers were being offered for me. I assume that they helped a lot."

"Of course. The angels were bombarded with requests for your healing. And with your perpetual state of happiness throughout your whole exciting ordeal, the extra supply of endorphins in your brain made it easier for them to orchestrate the shift in your bodily functions."

"You know, Radiant Lady, as I write this story, which I have never done before, I am awestruck to see so clearly how the sequence of events points to the intervention of angels. Thank you so much for walking me through this experience. My faith in God, and the angels, and you—and everyone—is renewed. Thank you, thank you, thank you!"

"Thank you for thanking me. I was there with you. We have been together since before you were born. But I want to keep you in a little suspense, and wait until the end of our conversations to reveal just *who* I am to you."

"Well, I appreciate the mystery! If you will excuse my Earth lingo, I do want to say that you are really a 'classy lady,' and I feel privileged to have you as a friend and, I can even say, as a business partner in helping me produce this manuscript."

"As you well know, Rosalind, we on this side have waited a long time for this to happen. Your guardian angel, spirit guides, and healing angels have done a lot of 'patching up' throughout your life.

"You are always telling people that you have four angels riding on your car, which you do, indeed. You can tell story after story about how, when something happens to your car, an angel is right there to help you. That is an example of how the angels work through humans—like your neighbor who showed up twice when you needed assistance with your car."

"I like the way you say that I have been 'patched up,' which I have been. I used to tell friends that at times I have felt like I'm held together with safety pins, or maybe I should have said taped together. But knowing that God has such an amazing crew waiting in the 'wings' to protect us, heal us, advise us, watch over us—or do whatever is necessary to get us through this Earth experience—is simply awesome. There is so much going on behind the scenes of life. If we were able to see and understand the whole picture of what's taking place in our lives at all times and all levels, it would probably 'blow us away.' But instead of being blown away, I think I need to get to bed!

"I guess you noticed that my cat Max scratched on the door so persistently that I had to answer. I pulled up a chair beside me, and told him that he had to sit there and be good. And he did, other than poking his cold nose on my arm to let me know he cares.

"So goodnight to you, Radiant Lady, and all my angelic beings and guiding energies. I feel so exalted that I have a feeling I will be flying out for a visit with you tonight."

"You are welcome at any time to visit with us during your dream state, which you do often. Continued blessings to you, Rosalind. It is always a privilege to work with you, spirit to spirit," said Radiant Lady, as her voice faded away.

9 Getting Stuck—and Unstuck

As always, I was excited to learn what would happen next. It was time again to receive my imprinted memories from Radiant Lady, so I sat quietly at my computer and allowed the pictures or the words to be sent to me from the next dimension.

∞

The image of my driveway showed up clearly in my mind. I could see a strange dog walking slowly toward me. He was limping. I walked out on my porch to meet the dog. I had only been in my new home for 18 days. I stood in front of my steps, waiting for this dog to come up to me. I stooped down and put my hand out to him. When he got closer, I realized he had a terrible stench. He was moving his head around and whining, as if to ask me for help.

I said to him, "Listen, dog, I don't know who you are, but you smell so bad that I can't talk to you until you get a bath. You stay right there; I'll draw a bath, and come back and get you." I went into the house, plugged the drain, added some bubble bath, and filled the tub with warm water.

I went back outside to get the dog and he was lying in front of my porch steps, obviously knowing what I had said to him. He was a medium-sized dog, but was so thin and scraggly that I was easily able to pick him up, carry him in the house, and put him in the tub.

As I started splashing the water on his body, I was amazed to find that he was thoroughly enjoying the bath and the attention. I took about half an hour washing him and talking to him. The more I washed, the happier he became.

When his offensive odor was gone and I began to see the real color of his fur, I said, "Hey, doggie, you're a real neat dog. You have such a calm personality." He was so content that he had stopped whining. After I got him dried off and brushed, he pranced around my house, smelling things, as dogs do, as if trying to decide if he wanted to stay or not. It didn't take him long to decide that he wanted to stay, in spite of the cats who had already taken up residence with me.

I didn't have any dog food to give him, so I gave him some dried cat food mixed with a can of the wet cat food. He was starved and gobbled it up. Then he lay down at my feet and went sound asleep.

The next test of whether I would keep him was his relationship to my cats. I really had mixed emotions about mixing him with my cats. But the cats didn't seem to be an issue for him, and he was such a calm dog that he was not an issue for the cats. It was as if he had always belonged with us.

The next question was a name. Well, he came on May 12, which was my friend Patty's birthday. And I had a very special friend in the next dimension, named Patrick. Patrick had become well known at the Monroe Institute during the time I was doing research with Bob Monroe. So Patrick became the dog's name. Eventually, some people called him Patty, short for Patrick. But I always preferred to call him by his full name.

The longer he stayed, the closer we got. I soon learned that he loved to ride in my car, so everywhere I went, he went with me.

He was such a friendly, charming dog that if I ever visited friends without him, people would say, "Where's Patrick? I wish you would have brought him along."

In October of that first year, I even took him to a Halloween party with me. I dressed him up as a witch. He wore a cool black hat and an orange cape. He made such a hit at the party that three people said that if I ever wanted to get rid of him, to let them know first. In fact, the hostess of the party invited him back for the next year's party. We went again the next year, and he was dressed as an angel. So Patrick became very much a part of life at Heavenly Acres.

He soon picked up a friend named Jesse. Jesse was a neighbor dog, and was always on a leash chained to his doghouse. Finally the neighbors began letting Jesse off his chain to come over to play with Patrick. Then Jesse's owners had to move, and asked me if they could leave Jesse with me since the place where they were moving was close to a major highway. Jesse was elated to live at Heavenly Acres, where he didn't have to be on a leash because in our county, way out in the country, there was no leash law.

A year later, two little stray dogs arrived when I was giving a birthday party for a friend named Ann. Her husband was Jim, so I called the dogs Annie and Jimmy. I knew they were hunting dogs and that they had been badly abused because it took several months for them even to come close to the house. I fed them at the end of my driveway. They would sneak up to eat and go somewhere down the road to sleep in the woods. Annie and Jimmy loved each other greatly and always stuck together. Jimmy would lick and lick Annie. After several months, they began to take up with Patrick and Jesse. Then all four dogs slept on mattresses under my house.

They still do, with the exception of Patrick, who was hit by a car and killed after being with me for three years. Patrick died doing what he loved to do. He loved to chase cars; one night he ran up through the field and right under the front wheel of a car. He died so suddenly that I'm sure he didn't feel any pain. But as I write this, Jimmy, Annie, and Jesse are still with me. Jimmy and Annie were scrawny little dogs when I got them, but they are fattened up now, and are happy campers here at Heavenly Acres.

The images of my dogs faded, and I was sure my wonderful teacher from the other side was ready to talk with me.

∞

"I certainly am, Rosalind," Radiant Lady said. "And I want to tell you that Patrick is a really happy camper here in our dimension. In fact, I have two Patricks right here beside me: Patrick the man, and Patrick the dog. So perhaps we will call Patrick the dog 'Patty' to distinguish between them. Patty just glows, like the little angel that he is. We don't even have him in an angel outfit! He's just a natural angel and everyone over here loves him just as much as they loved him in your dimension."

"Oh, Radiant Lady, I'm so thrilled that both Patricks are there with you.

I do have trouble calling my dog 'Patty,' but I will try. I really miss Patty, and I have a tinge of jealousy because he is with you and not me."

"I understand that. But it will only be a matter of time, and Patty will be one of the first ones to greet you when you come over."

"That sounds great. But I hope the 'matter of time' is far in the future. I'm really enjoying life on planet Earth, and now I want to stay as long as my body will hold together."

"You will leave when it is time to leave, as you agreed in your Earth Contract before going on your Earth vacation."

"So what brings you and Patty together?" I asked.

"You do," she replied.

"Oh, so I get to speak to Patrick, and perhaps even Patty?"

"Better yet, Rosalind, you get to come over and visit with both of them at once," Radiant Lady said with excitement in her voice.

"Yes, yes! That sounds exciting to me. I can't think of two spirit beings that I would rather visit with than my two beloved Patricks. So what is on the agenda when I get there?"

"I'm glad you asked because I think it would be good for me to do some orientation work before we shift your vibrations to this level. Many people who are reading this material right now have no idea who Patrick, your dear Scottish sailor, is. So I'm going to let you do some orientation for the readers, and then I will do some orientation for you before you come over. A good way to do this is for you to talk to me about the 'Patrick Event,' and I will ask some questions to keep the orientation interesting for the readers."

"Well, it's time for a commercial then," I replied. "Chapter 21 in *Cosmic Journeys* tells the full story of the Patrick Event. It is one of the famous happenings that took place during the Monroe Institute Explorer Sessions of the 1970s and 1980s. It was such a powerful event that an audio recording of what took place is played at every 'Gateway Voyage' program at the institute."

"You spoke about the Explorer Sessions earlier, but what is the Gateway Voyage program?"

"The Monroe Institute offers weeklong training programs in consciousness expansion, using 'Hemi-Sync' tapes, which Bob Monroe developed in his laboratory many years ago. In fact, these Hemi-Sync sound frequencies were something Bob was experimenting with while we were doing our exploration sessions. Everyone who goes to the institute to take these weeklong programs takes the Gateway Voyage program first."

"What are some of the available programs?"

"Well, their titles include Guidelines, Heartline, Lifeline, MC², Exploration 27, Timeline, Starlines, Remote Viewing Practicum, and Exploration Essence. To learn about individual programs, readers can turn to the back of this book for the Web address and phone number of the institute."

"The titles sound interesting to me," Radiant Lady said. "Where do the program participants come from?"

"People from all over the world come to attend these programs. It is the most amazing experience. I tell people that it's like taking a trip to Heaven for a week—and it is! People keep coming back to take program after program."

"And why is that?"

"It's a life-changing process because you go into yourself and discover aspects of your own inner dimensions. That is what this book is all about: helping people to understand the many dimensions of which they are made up. When we talk about dimensions, they are not 'out there' somewhere but are within us. The training participants relax in 'CHEC units' to experience the Hemi-Sync tapes just like I did when I was doing my research with Bob Monroe. I speak at the Guidelines programs throughout the year. So if you attend Guidelines after you take Gateway Voyage, bring your book or books and I would love to sign them!"

"Well, Rosalind, that is a good commercial for your books, and for the Monroe Institute," said Radiant Lady. "But now I would like you to share information about the Patrick Event. The reason I want you to do this is because we will be learning about the lower dimensions during our session today."

"Yes. When Bob and I met Patrick during one of our lab sessions, he was 'stuck' in one of the lower dimensions. He was in the time/no-time dimension between Heaven and Earth, which we discussed earlier. He had no idea that he had died. He was on a ship that blew up in the 1800s. He spoke about being in the 'kitchen' when the ship blew up. Someone from Scotland who heard the tape and heard Patrick say 'kitchen' instead of 'galley' said that they called them kitchens during that time period. So Patrick, thinking that he had survived the accident, was floating out in the water, holding on to a log, waiting for help to come. Patrick thought that he had only been in the water overnight but he had been holding on to his log for 120 years of Earth time."

"So when you refer to him as being 'stuck,' you're referring to the fact that he was not just stuck in the water, but stuck between the Earth time and the afterlife no-time dimensions, as we discussed earlier."

"Precisely," I answered.

"So how did he get 'unstuck'?"

"Well, we just took a crowbar and pried him out from between dimensions. Just kidding!" I said, as I heard Radiant Lady chuckle. "Bob Monroe did an incredible job of helping to rescue Patrick."

"What do you mean, 'rescue'?"

"Since Patrick was not aware that he was dead, the angels and guides from the other side could not get his attention because he was still in the Earth vibratory level. Therefore, it took a person on the Earth plane to get his attention, convince him that he had died physically, and direct him toward the 'Light' of the other side."

"And Bob was able to do that?"

"Yes, Bob was able to get Patrick 'unstuck,' with the help of AhSo, who gave him a good orientation before the rescue began. Even though Bob had never heard of 'rescue work' or souls being stuck between dimensions, he handled the session like a real pro. So after Bob convinced Patrick that he had died in the explosion on the boat, he urged him to look up for a Light and see if he noticed anyone he knew from the other side."

"And what did he see?"

"Well, this is when it really became dramatic because he saw his mother and father, and started crying uncontrollably.

"Now the setting is that I am in the CHEC unit, and Patrick is speaking through me. Bob is talking to Patrick, and when Patrick sees his mother and father on the other side, Patrick and Bob become very emotional. Then Bob says to Patrick: 'Go with them. . . . There are many friends waiting for you. Go on and away.' And Patrick responded, 'Thank you! Thank you!' and disappeared into the next dimension."

"That is very touching," replied Radiant Lady. "In fact, Patrick is sitting here beside me, and has tears streaming down his cheeks. He is very appreciative toward Bob and you for helping him to get 'unstuck' from between dimensions and rejoin his loved ones in a new world of fuller life and growth."

"Well, he has become quite well known in certain circles here on the planet. Since Bob is now over there, I hope they have met."

"They certainly have. In fact, Patrick was among those who met Bob when he came over. That is one thing that Patrick has been doing since being here in our dimension—helping to bring people over smoothly from the Earth dimension. Bob made the transition without difficulty, but Patrick knew he was coming over, so was there to meet him as a way of saying 'Thank you!' for what Bob had done to help him."

"That must have been very moving," I said.

"It certainly was," replied Radiant Lady.

"And I do want to put in another commercial," I continued. "If people reading this book want to know the details of Patrick's crossing, they are contained in *Cosmic Journeys*. And those taking the Gateway Voyage program hear the actual tape of Bob helping Patrick get unstuck."

"Thank you for reviewing the Patrick Event," said Radiant Lady. "Now I want to give an orientation to the lower dimensions, and you can ask me questions as I proceed."

"I'll be happy to do that," I replied.

"We're going to raise your vibrations to bring you into this dimension. And then we're going to take a journey into the Lower Realms of Darkness.

"Now, I want to make it clear that Patrick was never stuck in the realms of darkness. He was merely caught in the 'grey zone' between dimensions before he was rescued. He is a very delightful, highly evolved soul, and has been of great service to many, many others since coming over. In fact, he is going to lead the tour into the dark realms.

"When Patrick first came over, he started working with the souls caught in the grey zone between dimensions. And he has done so well with this work that he has begun working with the angels in the dark dimensions. It takes very committed and qualified souls to do this work."

"I am so proud of Patrick," I said. "I want to take the tour, but I could never do that kind of work on a regular basis, though I admire people who can. Here on planet Earth I've learned that I don't like to work with people's problems, but prefer to work on a creative level, like writing this book, for instance. There are so many ways that we can share with others. As I understand the other side, people can continue doing things they loved to do here on Earth."

"That is correct," replied Radiant Lady. "Now I want to discuss with you why and how people end up in the dark dimensions."

"It sounds like what we think of as Hell. And I know that many people here on Earth are taught that God condemns people to Hell. I believe that God is pure Light and Love, and condemns no one. So how do people end up in the dark dimensions?"

"Remember your Poison Ivy Principle, when you purposely rubbed poison ivy on your young friend when you were a child?" Radiant Lady asked.

"How could I forget? I certainly hope I won't end up in the dark dimensions because of that!"

"Of course you won't. But according to the Law of Karma, everything a person does creates a result somewhere. In your case, you were the cause that created the effect of poison ivy on your own body. By your own actions, you judged yourself.

"If at an early age you had gotten hooked on doing bad things to people and didn't care about the results, by your own actions you would have been consigning yourself to the dark dimensions. Ugliness of mind and deed produces nothing but ugliness. The spirit world is a world of strict justice, which we mete out to ourselves. That is the free will that God gave us when we were created."

"So I was right in thinking that God in no way judges or condemns us to some eternal hell, but by our own thoughts and deeds we judge ourselves," I stated.

"It's as simple as that. So in understanding this law from the standpoint of the higher Light realms, the beauty of the spirit world is the outward and visible expression of the spiritual progress of its inhabitants."

"So for the people in the dark dimensions, how can they get out of that level of existence?"

"By desiring to move toward the Light, even just one fraction of an inch. Darkness is merely the absence of light. So if beings in a lower dimension have an 'ah-ha' moment, forgive themselves for what they have done to themselves, and desire help in changing, their light will actually glow in the darkness. The angels, and helpers like Patrick, will be right there to pull them over into the Light realms.

"Light helpers will stay with these repentant souls, and nurture them in every way they can. The help that is there for everyone on the Earth plane is also always there for those stuck in the grey zones and in the lower dark dimensions. God *never* abandons us. We abandon God when we choose darkness over Light."

"This is very helpful. I'm really glad I didn't repeat my poison ivy type of activities over the years. I'm a fast learner. I got the message immediately when I broke out with poison ivy—'I did this to myself, and I'm sure not going to repeat such actions!'"

"We're glad you did get the message immediately. And now we're ready to bring you and Patrick and Patty together for a visit."

"I'm ready to go, and I know what to do," I said. "But before I go into my altered state and shift consciousness to enter your dimension, I would like to mention what the Hemi-Sync sound system is since it ties in here. Hemi-Sync is the process that Bob Monroe developed in his laboratory—not his Lab in the Sky, but at his Whistlefield laboratory in Afton, Virginia—many years ago. It's the process that is used at the weeklong training sessions mentioned earlier. Hemi-Sync safely alters your brain-wave patterns, helping both sides of your brain to function in unison. Then an electrical signal is created, becoming like a whole new program in your brain, which allows you to explore the realms of your own consciousness.

"So, Radiant Lady, that's what this book is all about: encouraging individuals to get in touch with all the various dimensions of their own energy systems. Once your brain learns this pattern through Hemi-Sync, then you are able to transition this new program in your brain on your own. I've used this Hemi-Sync process for so long—through 11 years of research in Bob's lab—that I can quickly tap into this brain-wave pattern and begin the exploration of my own inner realms."

∞

"Well, now I'm ready!"

"So, as you continue to relax, Rosalind, we are using some techniques to help raise your vibration so you can move into this dimension more easily."

"My physical body feels very heavy," I reported. "But at another level I feel so light . . . so light . . . And now I see a tunnel, and at the end there is a magnificent light glowing, almost like a twinkling star that pulls me toward it. I feel I am moving rapidly. It's a wonderful feeling of freedom from the more intense vibrations of the physical body. I'm moving rapidly, and suddenly I'm floating, and now beginning to settle, like a feather descending to the ground.

"The atmosphere around me is so intense. The colors are brilliant. The vibrations are very different from on the Earth plane. I look around, and now realize that I have landed on a boat. No, it's more than a boat—it's a ship, a beautiful ship. I see some lovely glowing light forms at the bow of the ship. I will use my mind to move myself toward the light forms. I'm getting closer. And there you are, Radiant Lady, with your sparkling energy radiating all around you. 'Hello!'"

"Welcome to our dimension, Rosalind," said Radiant Lady, with a wonderful smile on her face. "Your trip was rapid. This is the best and cheapest way to travel, isn't it?"

"I agree, since flying has now become a bit challenging on planet Earth in the same way that so many things are challenging in our very wonderful dimension. Wow, Radiant Lady, what a unique outfit you have on today. It looks like a sailor's outfit with all the feminine touches. Such radiant blue with silver embroidery! And you have a beautiful sailor suit skirt instead of pants. I've never seen anything like it. The design is so unique and stunning."

"I created it just for this occasion, Rosalind. I pictured in my mind just what I wanted, and manifested it directly on my body."

"Oh, yes, you described earlier how residents of your dimension can create whatever they need right from their minds, including new outfits." I looked down to see what type of outfit I had on. "Oh, wow! I'm wearing an enhanced version of the pink and maroon outfit I'm wearing at my computer. And my clothes are vibrating and radiating. Say, can you create an outfit for me like the one you're wearing?"

"Here, everything is made to order. What would you like to put on your newly arrived soul/spirit body?" Radiant Lady asks.

"I would love something like you have on. The top can be just the same, but I would love brilliant blue pants, since I wear pants most of the time." I realized excitedly that we were reading each other's minds. Just as I finished that thought, I looked down and was wearing this stunning spirit garb.

"How do you like your sailor cap?"

"You certainly do know me and how I love caps. I wear my black and maroon ones all the time when the weather permits." I reached up and took my cap off, and then put it back on my head. "This is really cool! Thanks. I wish I could take this back to Earth with me. People would ask me where I got my incredibly beautiful outfit, and I would say, 'From Instant Solutions for Heavenly Garb.'" We both laughed. "And it is a wonderful feeling to experience the laughter vibration throughout your entire energy body."

"Now for the next surprise, Rosalind. I want you to close your spirit eyes, and when I say 'open,' I want you to look around. Okay . . . open!"

I opened my eyes to see before me in a sailor outfit one of the most handsome young men I have ever seen. Our eyes met and I said, "You are Patrick!"—at which point we stepped toward each other's energy fields and I experienced a kind of electric impulse. It was some kind of warm-fuzzy feeling, like a love connection.

"Hello, my dear Rosalind," said Patrick. "The last time we merged energies was in that no-time zone between dimensions. It was a little 'damper' experience than this, since we were in some mental water!" he said, with a twinkle in his eyes.

I could tell that Patrick has a great sense of humor. "It's a privilege to meet someone as famous as you are back on Earth," I said. "Is this your ship?"

"It certainly is. Since we can create any living environment that the mind can conceive, I definitely wanted to live on a ship, since that is what I lived on most of my time on the Earth."

"It's an awesome ship," I said. "And you designed and created this all on your own?"

"I did—once I learned the art of manifesting what I desire directly from my mind. But it took some practice to come up with this one. I was a little timid when I first started creating what I wanted. I was always used to living on someone else's ship while on Earth. So at first, I created just a little boat, feeling, I guess, like I didn't deserve anything too large and elaborate. But it was my first boat, and I loved that little craft.

"Eventually, as I became more confident and started receiving more and more guests, I decided to create the *Patrick Express*. I have had lots of visitors who are taking programs at Mr. Monroe's Institute. They listen to the

Patrick Tape while enrolled in the Gateway Voyage course, and when they retire to their CHEC units after listening to the tape, they are still thinking about me and zip right up into my boat. So I had to enlarge my boat into a ship."

I turned and scanned the horizon, stunned by the beauty of the scene. His ship seemed to be docked in a nice seaport. The water looked so different from our Earth water. It seemed "thicker" and more resilient. And it had an incredible sparkle. The colors were many times brighter in this dimension than on Earth. I felt like I was in the middle of a Walt Disney movie! The horizon stretched on and on, with many different shades and hues of green—green water, green grass, green trees. I noticed there were no roads.

"No, there are no roads, Rosalind, because we don't have to use vehicles like you do on Earth. You notice that there are no electrical poles or lines either," said Patrick.

"Well, I guess you didn't have any when you were on Earth. But we sure have plenty now. It's awesome to look at a landscape that isn't marred by poles, wires, roads, smog, and so on. So how do you get to your boat, Patrick? Can you walk on water if you want?" I asked jokingly.

"Absolutely. We can walk over the water, we can float in the water, or I can just manifest myself right onto the boat."

"Well, now if you fall into the water, can you drown?"

Patrick and Radiant Lady both laughed. Radiant Lady said, "Remember the lesson I gave about the nature of spirit bodies over here. We are indestructible."

"Oh, of course," I said. "I forgot. I'm so used to everything being breakable on planet Earth. I'm glad to have this little preview so that it will be easier when I move here. But Patrick, where's my dog Patty?"

Patrick replied in a humorous tone. "Who says he's your dog?"

"Well, I remember that you specifically sent Patty to me, didn't you?"

"I certainly did. But he was my dog, and I sent him to Earth for some special lessons. He works very closely with me, and I wanted him to get some Earth experience since he helps me meet the souls/spirits of people and animals who are crossing over."

"I'll tell you what, Patrick, it was an incredible experience to have him with me for three years. He came quickly, and left just as quickly. I knew that there was a reason that he died instantly under the front tire of a car. Then

I also knew that he needed to be buried at sea. Since I didn't have that option nearby, only a large river, I took him down to the riverbank, gently rolled him in the water, and watched as he floated out of sight. I kept a lock of his fur, which I occasionally take out of the book I store it in. I just hold it and say, 'Hey, buddy, I miss you, but we'll be together again after being disconnected from each other here on planet Earth—be sure to meet me when I get there. . . .'"

"It was very appropriate to drop him into the water," said Patrick. "He appreciated that and his spirit body swam back to you to say goodbye one last time as you stood there on the riverbank talking to him as he floated down the river. I was there to greet him when he passed over, of course, and we both came back for his memorial service. Since we both have had Patty as a pet, we can each use the term 'our' dog instead of 'my' dog. So look over the side of my ship and tell me what you see."

I walked over to the railing and looked—and there was Patty swimming toward us.

"Patty is in the water a lot," said Patrick. "That's another reason I have chosen to live on a ship."

Just as Patrick finished his last word, there before me was the spirit version of "our" wonderful dog Patty. And he had on a darling little sailor outfit, and a hat just like mine. I howled with laughter, as he was howling with joy to see me.

I bent over as he rolled over my feet like he always used to do. I said, "Patty, are you ready for another Halloween party with your marvelous sailor outfit as your costume?"

Then I was amazed to hear his thoughts come right back to me: "I'm ready, and I would go back to Earth with you if I could. But I have more important work to do than going to parties. Oh well, I'm just trying to impress on you that there was a good reason for me to leave. I must admit that we actually do have our share of parties over here. I do miss my buddy, Jesse, but I have some wonderful new spirit animal friends here. Do give Jesse a special rub for me, and tell him I miss him. I miss Jimmy and Annie, too, but not as much as Jesse. We all had some exciting experiences together."

"Yes, you did, Patty. But I never did quite forgive you for killing two or even three cats that came onto our property."

"I'm really sorry about that. But you must remember that on Earth we have the killing, survival instinct that we don't have over here. Actually, those three cats were right here when I came over, and they are part of my clan of friends."

"Well, that makes me feel better, and I forgive you, my friend. I really was holding that against you even in death."

"I appreciate your forgiveness," Patty responded, as he licked me affectionately.

"Now Patty—I have trouble calling you Patty, because I like the name Patrick—I do want people who are reading this book to realize that we are communicating telepathically. But your thoughts are received so clearly in my mind that I use the phrase 'Patty said' instead of 'Patty thought.'"

Patty sent the thought right back to me. "That's fine. And I do want to let you and everyone reading your book know that when they meet their pets here on this side, they will communicate with them telepathically as well. Actually, animals are highly revered here in the spirit world, and all on Earth should know that we do have souls and spirits. Many humans on the Earth plane are very self-centered, and think they are the only ones to survive physical death.

"Just as the angels are created by God as a unique species, so are your animal pets. We are sent to the Earth with the same qualities of the angels— Love only. We are created by God to teach humans Unconditional Love. We love our masters no matter what they do to us."

"Oh, Patty, that is wonderful to know and I want to say that you and all my other furry friends have given me a special purpose for living. If not for all my animal friends, I'm sure I would have left the planet some time ago."

"We knew that, and that's why all my brother and sister cats and dogs kept adopting you."

"Thank you for saying that, Patty. I love you so much. Just the short time you were with me gave me a whole new perspective on the meaning of love," I said admiringly.

"I'll tell you one thing," Patty continued, "there are a lot of humans stuck in deep pits of the dark dimensions, but there are very few animals there. There are a few committed animals that took on the energies of their masters so completely that they stayed with them when they came over to this side. Most of those animals had been badly abused by their masters. But even in death, they are still committed to them.

"Many animals are on a higher vibration than humans. God created us directly out of pure Love energy, which is how He created the angels, as I said. So animal pets are always there to help humans evolve spiritually, just as angels are there to help when needed. The only difference is that the angels do not reside on the Earth plane to perform their sacred services of human protection. But we animals are committed to living on the Earth to have direct contact with humans who need Unconditional Love—which is most of them!

"And we animals continue to be God's special servants here on this side. One of my special assignments is to work with the animals that are locked in between the time/no-time zone with their masters. In many cases, if we can reach the animals and convince them to move toward the Light, it creates a spark in the 'locked-in' consciousness of the human soul."

"Oh, Patty, I love you so much and really miss you. I have told many people that I had a 'knowing' that you left the Earth so suddenly because you were needed on the other side," I said with tears in my eyes.

At this point, Radiant Lady said that she would like for me to jump overboard to get revitalized in the "spirit water" before we descended into the depths of the Dark Realm.

I got excited, went right to the railing, and jumped overboard. The water was amazingly resilient and I found myself bouncing, as I pictured it would be like to bounce on a cloud. Patty jumped in right after me, losing his sailor cap as he jumped.

"Oh, Patty," I said, "You have lost your cap, just as you kept losing your halo and your witch's cap at the Halloween parties on Earth."

"Yes, I have had trouble keeping my hats on in both dimensions," came the instant thought from Patty.

We splashed and floated around in the stunning water that was indeed so energizing. I looked up toward the deck of the ship, and Radiant Lady and Patrick were enjoying watching the fun that Patty and I were having. Then I received the thought that it was time to descend. . . .

The next thing I knew, we were standing in a field, the color of which was dimmer than the radiant green we had just left. I looked down at my clothing and noticed that I had on a dark brown cloak, as did Radiant Lady and Patrick. Patty wore his regular furry cloak, which seemed toned down from its original luster.

There was a hush as Patrick began to send thoughts to us about what would be happening next.

"You will notice," Patrick said, "that as we descend into the slower vibratory levels, the atmosphere will change completely from what it is here in the Light Realm. And the vibrations of the Dark Realm are much slower and denser than anything you know upon the Earth, Rosalind. Darkness is merely the absence of light. As we move deeper into the Dark Realm, we will be met by two angels who help oversee the spiritual work that takes place there.

"As we enter the level of complete darkness, we will still be able to see because we are on a higher spiritual vibration. The angels, too, can always see. But the residents of the Dark Realm cannot see us. If for some reason the angels want to be seen, they can be, just as they can make themselves visible in the Earth dimension if need be. Angels have all the powers necessary to shape-shift, or appear in whatever form is needed to perform the miracles of God's work."

Everything was quiet as we moved into a grey zone. There was no color. Everything around us appeared dead. There was no sound of the wonderful birds we had observed flying over Patrick's ship earlier. There was nothing growing. We moved farther, and it seemed even darker. It was like walking on a lunar surface—barren and deserted. I observed no form of life.

We wound down a pathway into what appeared to be a crater, and suddenly my sense of smell was fully activated. I experienced a stench that made me feel like I wanted to vomit. We were winding down the pathway around deep, dark pools of what seemed like water, but were more like Earth's cesspools.

Suddenly, I was shocked to notice movement in the pools: Human arms and legs reached up out of the water and then dropped back in. I realized that they must belong to people who had died. And since they were already dead, being immersed in this unbelievably foul liquid could not kill them.

My next sense that was awakened was hearing. As we rounded a corner, there were a large number of deformed bodies beating on each other. Each one would scream and howl as if being murdered. Here again, they were already dead, so they must have been replaying incidents (experiencing the Life Imprint) of Earth happenings.

Then gunshots rang through the air. I noticed a grotesque form that

---

was repeatedly stabbing something under the water. And a head would bob up from the water, and go back down as if trying to hide.

As we moved farther down into the darkness, I was aware that standing all around us at a higher level were numerous angels, patiently looking for any ray of hope, a ray of light coming from any of the grotesque figures that inhabited this Dark Realm.

I received the thought from Patrick that all of these grotesque beings were replaying over and over the horrible deeds they had performed while on Earth. Many of these monstrous forms had been in those cesspools for centuries of Earth time, unable to admit that they had done anything wrong.

But some had gotten tired of, and even bored with, replaying the same horrible scenario, and therefore would cry out in their demented minds for something or someone to save them from their horrible fate. At that point, a glimmer of light would flicker in the darkness, and the angels and spirit helpers, like Patrick, would converge upon them to offer assistance in raising them out of their mental muck and mire.

And if one of these depraved beings had an animal on Earth that they once loved, Patty and other animal spirits would go in with the team to offer their own kind of assistance.

I later learned that there have been rescues performed solely by animal assistants helping move the depraved being into a higher vibratory level. In many cases, Patty had been the only reason that the seemingly lost soul was motivated to make some type of change. The angels would help Patty to shape-shift into the form of the past pet of the depraved soul. Or if that pet was still accompanying its master in the pool, Patty would get the attention of the spirit of the pet, which would trigger a spark of light that helped them both ascend into the higher vibrations.

Once this transition had taken place, the angel and animal assistants were able to transport the lost soul mentally to a hospitality center somewhat like our hospitals. It is a place of rest where the souls sleep and also watch life records move before their eyes. But here, the angels can re-create new scenarios for the souls. They are able to show scenes of incidents in the lives of these newly regenerated souls where they succeeded and were on target with personal goals they had set for themselves before they were born.

In their resting state, such souls are attended by different levels of helping beings to aid in any way possible. Often, these very loving, kind, nurse-like figures are right there when one of the transitioning souls wakes up, looks around, and begins to ask questions.

Suddenly, we were back on Patrick's ship, Radiant Lady, Patrick, and Patty bringing me along with them.

Radiant Lady said, "And now you know, Rosalind, what Patrick has been doing since you helped rescue him."

"Yes, and it's amazing—and takes great commitment," I said.

"It is something I love doing," said Patrick. "And Patty very much loves his part in helping to bring souls in the dark realms closer to God."

"Well, Patrick, this is very intense work. I hope you have other activities you participate in," I said.

"You'd better believe it," said Patrick. "I have lots of activities, including flying with Mr. Monroe in one of his many planes. In fact, he has helped me to create my own planes as well. We have become very close, and even party together when we finish with some intense projects. Patty and I also enjoy Mr. Monroe's pets, both cats and dogs."

"Well, Rosalind," said Radiant Lady, "Your energy level is beginning to wane, and we must allow you to shift back to the Earth vibration. Again, it has been a privilege being with you, and I hope you enjoyed the special treat of being with Patrick and Patty.

"The journey into the Dark Realm is challenging, but it is a lesson that must be understood by humans on the Earth plane. God did not condemn these needy souls to Hell. Rather, they, through their own thoughts and actions while on the Earth plane, consigned themselves to exactly the vibration in the other world that corresponds to their inner vibration while on the Earth plane."

"Thank you, Radiant Lady; you have gotten your point across," I said. "It's difficult for me to think that those reading this book will not understand what you are teaching. God is pure Love and Light, and continues to love all beings no matter how low they have fallen into the pit of despair and darkness. . . . I notice that those fallen ones' bodies seem to take on the likeness of their minds."

"That is so, Rosalind," replied Radiant Lady. "This is actually true on the Earth plane as well. Humans become exactly what they think. Those with dark thought energies have a dark aura around them. Those who express light, love, and joy exude the Light of God. That is what life upon the Earth plane is all about—living in the Light, Love, and Joy of one's spiritual energy so as to evolve directly back into the presence of the Pure God Essence. We can never tire of expressing the importance of God's love. And now I say good night."

"Yes, good night, Radiant Lady. And good night to you, Patrick, my friend, and Patty, our precious and saintly dog. In dressing you up like an angel for the Halloween party, Patty, I didn't realize how close I came to portraying your true spirit."

I heard Patty's "thank you" bark fading in the distance as I became aware of being back in my office at Heavenly Acres.

∽

So, goodnight, friends who are reading this book. Just remember that you are Light, manifested in Love, and expressed in Joy.

That is an affirmation you can say over and over: "I am Light, manifested in Love, and expressed in Joy, Joy, Joy." You came directly from the Light of God's pure energy, were manifested in the Earth plane by the Love of God, and express yourself upon the Earth plane in Joy!

Thank you! . . .

PART IV

Local Tours

10 The Children's Dimension

One of my favorite images was coming to me: the silo I see every time I pull onto the road leading up to my house. It's very picturesque, and always makes me feel good when I see it. The big white farmhouse with the barns and silo beside it sits on a rolling pasture. Long before I found my house in the country, I had an image of driving up a narrow country road, with daisies lining the sides, and a farmhouse and silo in the background. When I thought of moving from the mobile home park, I always had that image in my mind's eye. So every time I see the silo, barns, and farmhouse, which is almost daily, I thank God for bringing me to Heavenly Acres.

In my mind, I was stopping my car at the turn onto my road to get my mail. I walked leisurely across the road to the mailboxes. When I looked inside my box, there was a large brown envelope from my oldest brother, Willis. I seldom hear from Willis, so I assumed this was something important. I got into the car and opened the envelope right away. Much to my amazement, inside was a black-and-white photo of Larry with my mother standing beside him.

It was a somewhat eerie faded photo. My brother and mother have been in the spirit world for many years. It was strange to me that Willis would send a photo of them after so many years. He included a wonderful little note that said he had run across this old photograph of Larry and Mom, and wanted me and my brothers and sisters to have copies of it.

That was just after I had started writing this book. I put the picture in a wooden frame and have kept it on my computer desk in front of me.

Something like this always amazes me. Larry has been in spirit for 32 years, and Mom for 27. And just when I was being taken on a tour of the afterlife, here came a picture of them—like a greeting saying, "Hi, there! We're looking forward to your visit!"

A month before, another interesting thing happened relating to Larry. I went to my local dumpster down the road, and there walking on top of the trash was a beautiful little kitten looking for something to eat. I turned and looked behind me, and over in a field was his mother's head sticking up from behind a grassy knoll, watching him, seemingly sending nonverbal guidance on how to find food when she was no longer supplying it.

I took my trash out of the car, walked over, and threw it into the trash bin. Seeing me, the kitten jumped off the dumpster and ran over to me. He was basically a white cat, like his mother in the field. But he looked like he had walked under a can of black paint that had dripped on him. He had little dots of black on his face, a black blotch on his back, and his tail was black. Underneath, he was all white.

I thought, "Oh, no, I shouldn't get another cat," as I reached down to pet this little purr box, whose volume magnified with each touch. I figured that when I left, he would rejoin his mother and they would go on to the farmhouse on the hill behind the dumpster.

After two more visits to the dumpster, each time with the kitten gleefully running to greet me, I decided that he had chosen me. His mother was nowhere to be seen.

I always let a cat name itself, so after a few days I thought about his main qualities and what name would suit him best. He was so friendly and my other cats liked him. So I asked myself, "Who is really friendly, liked by everyone, and makes the room light up when he walks in?" And the name "Larry" jumped right out at me.

So the cat's name is Larry. Larry follows me around the house, wants to be where I am at all times, and sleeps right by my head at night. It's as if we have known each other forever. So perhaps this kitten is a gift directly from Heaven—and from Larry. . . .

These scenes faded from my mind and I realized that Radiant Lady was ready for our next tour.

"Hello, from Heaven," I heard in my head.

"Hello, Radiant Lady," I replied. "I have missed talking with you. Everything in my Earth life went into overdrive and made it difficult for me to continue my tours with you during the past two weeks."

"Understood. You needed to get your picture taken and sent to your publisher. And, of course, we knew that you needed to tend to other matters in your Earth experience as well," she said.

"I think you must have had something to do with my finding the right photographer to take my portrait."

"I did my best to guide you in the right direction."

"Well, I was headed to the Wal-Mart photo studio. But when I got onto the expressway, the thought came to me that I should go to the Sears photography department instead."

"Yes, I had to use some special energy to direct you in the opposite direction. You see, we on this side can work through your intuition as well as your mind energies."

"Well, you sure knew what you were doing," I replied. "When I got to Sears, the young lady in the photo department said that it would take 20 days to get the negatives back. It was the eleventh of the month, and I needed to have them to my publisher by the fifteenth. But the Sears saleslady said a woman who had previously worked at Sears had started her own photography studio. She gave me her name, I called her immediately, had the photo taken right away, and it arrived at Hampton Roads Publishing on time. Thank you, Radiant Lady, for your guidance."

"Guidance is what life is all about," she replied. "We are meant to help each other in every way we can. Everyone's energies are connected in every dimension. We are all one, shaped out of the energies of God, and connected to each other through the Love of God."

"Yes. It has taken me a whole lifetime on this challenging planet to get this message loud and clear."

"Speaking of being connected through the Love of God, there is someone connected to you by a strong love tie who is eager for us to visit him," Radiant Lady said with higher mental intensity.

"Larry, Larry, Larry! Oh, how I have missed him!" I explained. "And I've missed him more as the years have passed, realizing fully the relationship we've been denied here on the Earth plane. I was more connected to Larry than to anyone in my life, and then he was taken away. You know, that Disconnect Principle."

"Yes, but remember, as you yourself said, the Disconnect Principle is only relevant on Earth, which is the unreal world. In the real world of God, nothing is destructible. But on the Earth plane, which is only a shadow of the real, everything is destructible—just as, when the sun sets, the shadow disappears."

"Thanks for reminding me," I replied. "It's just that when someone we love suddenly disappears we're left with only grief and memories of what we thought would continue."

"Grief is an important energy for those on the Earth plane," Radiant Lady said sympathetically. "It could be thought of as a rubber band of love that is connected to those loved ones who have stepped out of sight. It is very painful because there is a strong pull on your energies. You always have the strong wish that the rubber band could pull the loved one right back to you."

"But it doesn't happen, and the longer the band is stretched, the more the grief diminishes."

"Which is, of course, good," Radiant Lady replied, "because if the grief continues too long, it holds the loved one down in the Earth's energies. When the whole world grieves for the loss of one loved by many, that soul is held down in the Earth plane for a longer period of time than most souls who have passed over."

"So that means that if we understand the beauty of death, we should be happy for our loved ones beyond, and grieve only for ourselves and our loss. Then we should go on with our lives here, knowing that the band of love is forever connecting us to the lives of those in the next dimension."

"That is a good way of looking at it," replied Radiant Lady. "But it's easier said than done because grief is a natural substance in your Earth bodies that helps you process the energy of loss. Truly loving beings will grieve intensely for a brief period of time, and then release their loved ones to go about their new life in the spirit world."

"Well, Larry and Mom have been in the spirit world for many years of Earth time, so they might be completely different beings by this time."

"No, you will always be you. Everything else might change in your energy body, but your basic personality will remain the same. And you will always recognize your loved ones in the spirit dimension even though outwardly your appearance might be very different."

"So what if a baby dies a few months after it is born?" I asked. "Would the parents and child recognize each other when the parents make their transition?"

"Yes, the love bond keeps the connection firm. The spirit within us knows all, just as God knows all. We are made in the image of God, which is God's gift to us. It is difficult for our physical minds to comprehend the magnitude of spirit. Our spirits are always there within our physical bodies, but they have a different agenda. Often you become aware of a Silent Observer that is there with you, quietly observing everything. That is your spirit within."

"Thank you," I responded, grateful for this information. "So what do I do now in order to make the journey of love into the afterlife?"

"Relax, and I will help to shift your energies. You have been here before to meet Larry and your father. I will send the Akashic images to you so that you can connect again with their energies and be here instantly."

Immediately, I found myself in the magnificent green field. My heart was pumping. I felt lighter and extremely joyful. I looked to my right, and there indeed was my Radiant Lady beside me, reaching her hand out for me to grasp. I reached over, touched her beautiful hand stretched toward me, and felt an instant energy explosion.

The next thing I realized was that we were walking together down a sparkling pathway toward a beautiful cottage nestled within trees and flower gardens. Radiant Lady stopped, bent over to gather some of the soil from a flower garden, and let it slip through her fingers. It sparkled—and even gave off a melodious sound. The sky was very blue. The atmosphere was rich with the living energy, compared to Earth's air.

As we got closer to the cottage and gardens, I noticed three figures sitting on benches. One, wearing a beautiful flowing robe, rose and came toward us. As the person got closer, our eyes met, and I recognized the energy of my beloved Larry.

Something in his hand caught my eye and I saw that it was a rubber chicken dressed up like Santa Claus that he was carrying upside down! We both started laughing. Then we stepped into each other's energy fields, equivalent to a hug in the spirit dimension. It was like stepping into a large sunbeam or spotlight that greatly energized both of our spirit bodies.

"Larry, you still have the rubber chicken Santa that you carried around to everyone's house one Christmas," I exclaimed laughing. "You haven't lost your sense of humor! You always lit up every room you ever walked into. You exuded so much joy. I often think of you, and hope that I can be the same. And now you're emitting an even greater light than when you were on Earth."

"I re-created the Santa chicken as a special welcome to you," Larry said, smiling. At that point he dropped the chicken. Its Santa's beard and hat disappeared, and I realized that it wasn't rubber at all, but a real chicken. It cackled as if saying something to Larry, who thanked it as it bounced joyfully under a rosebush. "We retain our strongest personality traits over here, and I guess my sense of humor was my strongest," said Larry, with the same magnetic sparkle in his eyes.

Larry was in the prime of his life when he died, and as I looked into his eyes, I felt a pool of spirituality so deep that I was moved from laughter to tears that ran down my cheeks. I felt so much joy in his presence. . . .

"Larry, I was so moved when Radiant Lady took me through the Akashic records of your arrival into the spirit world. I'm sure you are aware of your daughter Becky's latest adventure back on Earth," I remarked.

"I certainly am. And I have her dog, Spirit, right here with me."

"Great," I said. "Becky will be so happy to know that you are taking care of Spirit, who was killed just after she left recently to study in Australia."

"It was very hard on her to hear the news of Spirit's transition," Larry said. "So Spirit and I have been spending time with her while she is so far from home. I feel that she has sensed our presence because she is adjusting much better now to her new surroundings."

Radiant Lady, Larry, and I, along with Spirit, who was followed by the joyful chicken, moved into the garden toward the other two figures. We could now clearly see the home that sat among the trees. It had a familiar feel, and was designed somewhat like our wonderful old farmhouse homestead on Eichelberger Avenue. The two figures walked closer—and there standing before me were my mom and dad. I felt tears of joy welling up in my eyes. The three of us merged into a powerful group spirit hug. My dad had his usual overalls on and my mother was wearing one of her soft cotton dresses. Her long hair was flowing down her back. So many times when I was growing up, I had stood behind her while she sat in her lounge chair and combed her hair.

"Rosalind, dear," Mom said. "We decided to wear clothes like we wore when we were raising you."

"They're cool outfits," I said. "And, Dad, I love your bib overalls."

I looked to one side of the garden and there was a beautiful barn. Then I looked in another direction and there was another barn.

"Dad, you finally got the farm you always wanted."

"I certainly did. After I got adjusted to my new life here, and realized that I could have anything I wanted, I decided to build our own house and barns."

"And, Dad, I am impressed that it didn't take you long to get adjusted in your new spirit-body form. You were adamant in your belief that there was no afterlife. Was it a shock when you woke up on the other side realizing that you were still alive? And what convinced you that it was real?"

"I was shocked at first but my shock turned to joy when my mom and dad and all my brothers and sisters were there to meet me. I'm glad my belief system didn't keep me out of Heaven!"

"And I am, too," Mom said. "Your dad was right there to meet me when I arrived. We used to argue about the issue of life after death when we were on Earth, but I was so happy to see him in the Love Dimension that it didn't even occur to me to say, 'Ha, ha, I was right and you were wrong.' That is Earth-type thinking anyway."

"Mom, I can remember vividly the flowers that you grew in our front yard when I was growing up. Did you plant all these beautiful flowers?"

"The ones over by the barn are spirit flowers that grow on their own here in this dimension, like wildflowers on Earth," she said. "But the ones all around the house are the ones I planted. I have learned so much more about flowers and plants since being here. And I've been taking courses in writing, and have written several books!"

"Mom, I am so proud of you. You're finally writing the books you always wanted to write, but were too busy raising us kids. What books have you written?" I asked.

"I've written one book about the art of raising Earth flowers as compared to raising Earth children," she said with great animation. "There are a lot of similarities. I loved raising both children and flowers!"

"Yes, Mom, I remember that after you raised us eight children, you wished that you would have had more," I said, laughing. "Gosh, Mom and

Dad, I'm so thrilled that you have finally realized your heart's Earth dreams."

I looked over and saw many chickens in a chicken coop. And there were three pigs lying in the sparkling soil that Radiant Lady had pointed out to me as we approached my parents' spirit dwelling. It brought back memories of my childhood, when we had a huge garden through which we walked to get to the chicken coop to gather eggs, and to the pig pens beside it. We had a mini-farm, not a large farm like Dad now has. And then a little dog came up to me and started wagging its tail.

"Speck! This is our little dog Speck," I said gleefully.

"I'm sure glad you recognize me," came the thought from Speck.

"Speck, are you talking to me?"

"No, we don't talk. We just communicate with thoughts. We animals have always communicated with thought and can understand humans. But being less evolved than we are, humans often can't understand us. God creates us directly out of Love vibrations as a special species just like the angels. We always give unconditional love to help raise the vibrations of humans upon the Earth.

"And God also did something very special for us dogs by giving us his name spelled backward! Just turn God around and you have 'dog.' However, many humans don't even believe that we have souls. We love them anyway."

"Speck, you are wonderful, and it's awesome to see you again."

"Rosalind, I have elevated your energies so that you could visit in this dimension," my tour guide said. "So we need to move on before your energies begin to wane."

"I have a question to ask Larry first, Radiant Lady," I replied.

"Go ahead and ask it."

"Brother Larry, have you seen my new little kitten that I call Larry?"

"Of course, I have, I sent him to you," Larry responded. "And look over there—that's Larry following you."

"It looks just like him," I exclaimed. "Larry, how did you get here?"

"Just like you did," he replied with thought. "I come up here often when I sleep. This is where I am from and I love to hang out here with all my friends."

"That's amazing, Larry. So when you are asleep I know you are probably here on this Heavenly Farm with Mom, Dad, Larry, Speck, the chickens, and pigs. So you move from Heavenly Acres to this Heavenly Farm. You are something else."

"Oh, yes, I know. I am a very special cat and sent to you with love from your brother Larry. I'm glad you took me home with you and didn't leave me at the dumpster."

"Well, I am too, Larry. Stay as long as you want. I must move on with Radiance and my brother."

"I want to take you to the Children's Dimension, where I taught when I first arrived here in the spirit world," Larry said. "I was ready to begin teaching young people when I exited the Earth so suddenly. Because of that unfulfilled dream, and because of having my own child on the way, I had a passion for working with younger spirits here."

"Stand between me and Larry," instructed Radiant Lady, "and we will transport you with us to the Children's Dimension."

It was no sooner said than done! The colors here seemed even more magnificent than on my parents' spirit farm. We walked into a little village that seemed like something out of *The Wizard of Oz*. There were many small, colorful cottages that wound through the village. The pathway seemed like the "yellow brick road." We passed children playing in beautifully structured playgrounds. And we saw others sitting in groups reading books, with teachers instructing them.

"I'm taking you to where I taught before," said Larry, as he picked up his pace and moved out in front of us. As we rounded a corner, the view took my breath away. There was a path winding up to a large castle that seemed to be made out of diamonds. It appeared to cover acres of land, with the most magnificent landscaping one could imagine.

As we moved into the castle, it was abuzz with activity. There were long corridors with many different kinds of rooms. I realized that as large as the building was, everything was scaled down to children's size. We passed rooms where children were being instructed in music. We heard the most glorious music and laughter as we moved through the halls. This was a Hall of Learning for children of all ages. One room was an art room. And beautiful pictures lined the walls of the halls.

Then we arrived at a room with a "Library" sign over the door. Larry motioned for us to follow him in. We were greeted by a most radiant light being. We stopped behind Larry as he motioned for us to move up.

"Rosalind," said Larry, "I want you to meet my teacher and guide, Astara."

She held out her hand, and sparks flew as we touched. I was greatly recharged by the touch of her hand.

"It's a pleasure to meet you, Astara," I said. "I'm pleased that if Larry couldn't be on the Earth with us, he has been with someone as beautiful and powerful as you seem to be."

"Astara has taught me so much about the true meaning of Love," said Larry. "She has dedicated herself to working with children for many centuries of Earth time, and I was fortunate to be under her care shortly after I arrived in the spirit world. She would be happy to answer any questions you might have about the Children's Dimension."

"What happens when children die and have no family over here to meet them?"

"There are always sensitive souls who love children, and who are here to meet them, along with their guardian angels. And there are always some relatives here even if they are great-great-grandparents. There is so much love and warmth when the child arrives that it experiences a much more secure reception than when it entered the Earth plane."

"I can imagine the difference. I once saw a baby born in a hospital, and it must have been a horrible experience for the child to be squeezed like a sausage through a painfully small enclosure, and immediately spanked upon its entrance into the Earth plane."

"That never happens here!" said Astara. "Very young babies come into a nursery environment and are immediately embraced by the helpers and angels. These very special beings are trained to work mainly with babies and children. There is soft music, soft lighting, and a very 'warm, fuzzy' environment surrounding them as they arrive in our nurseries."

"What about older children?" I asked.

"They are greeted in the same manner, first by the angels of Love and helpers, and then by their relatives. Since this is a realm where only love exists and there is no fear, the children experience nothing but affirmation when they arrive and throughout their time spent in this dimension," explained Astara. "Some are raised in caring homes, like foster homes on the Earth. Some are raised in larger children's homes, and some in small cottages with loving adults taking care of them."

I said, "I understand that when adults arrive in the spirit world their spirit bodies often take on the appearance they had in the prime of their Earth life, their twenties or thirties. So what happens with children?"

"Children grow up naturally in this dimension, and the energies of the dimension itself know when to move them on through growth levels. But they do grow up here more rapidly than on the Earth plane," Astara explained.

"We passed many delightful cottages and group homes as we came through the village to this Hall of Learning. The homes are so colorful and look like something right out of storybooks," I said.

"Actually, the storybooks get their inspiration from the Children's Dimension, and not the other way around. Everything originates here in the spirit world," Astara said. "Larry was such an inspiration to the children he worked with. He gave them so much love and attention; even his daughter, Becky, would visit during her sleep state to absorb his loving, caring energies."

"They say on Earth that losing a child is one of the most devastating things that can happen to someone," I said. "But if parents really can understand what loving care their children receive when they arrive in the spirit world, it should ease their pain somewhat. Do parents ever come to be with their children during their sleep state, when their souls are freed from their physical bodies to go where they desire?"

"Absolutely," replied Astara. "Parents often come to be with their babies and young children, especially right after the children arrive in the world of spirit. It helps them to adjust to the loss of their children, and helps the children to adjust more fully to their new life in spirit."

"That is awesome. So what happens if a child dies from being abused, or murdered, or from an accident? Do you have Halls of Rest for young spirits, just as you do for adults like Larry when he came over after dying suddenly in an accident?"

"Actually, we have many angels overseeing Halls of Rest for children whose physical bodies have undergone some sort of shock before entering the world of spirit. Many children who die from what the world would consider a 'horrible death' are often very evolved spiritual beings who chose to reincarnate into such a condition so as to evolve much more rapidly," explained Astara. "Or these highly evolved souls often appear on the Earth plane in bodies that have major challenges so that they can, in turn, aid their parents in their parents' spiritual evolution."

"It is so consoling to learn that when these young souls come into the spirit world, they are embraced by nothing but absolute Unconditional Love," I said.

Radiant Lady looked at me and sent the thought that it was time to descend back into the Earth energies. I began to feel those heavier energies just as I received her message.

"Thank you Larry, Astara, and Radiant Lady," I said. "I feel overwhelmed with the love in this Children's Realm. I'll sleep well when I arrive in my intense dimension so laced with fear and challenges. But the more I visit these realms of pure Love, the more I bathe myself in this Love and Light when faced with Earth challenges. Goodbye for now."

∞

I was back in my office, aware that several hours had passed since I had started the session. It seemed like it was only a minute.

I was also aware of the scratching on my office door, which was Max. I opened the door and let him into my sacred sanctuary, and he looked at me with those big eyes and talked to me about food, of course.

Max knew that it was about time for me to go to bed. He always meows me into the kitchen at this point, where he jumps up on the table and encourages me to open the refrigerator door as quickly as possible. And then there always comes my most beautiful cat, Peanut. They sit side by side, looking at me with large eyes. Max's coat looks like a skunk's, and Peanut looks like a lion. What a team they make!

And there is Lucky Prince, a large cat with large paws. He knows how to open the refrigerator door. The day before, I had bought some wonderful chicken and when I went in to get a piece to eat during a break, the refrigerator door was open and the container for the chicken was on the floor, with the chicken nowhere to be found. There were three cats with other stuff pulled out of the refrigerator, licking their chops. I really don't like them to eat chicken bones—as well as the wonderful chicken breasts. I would have to tape the door shut. Oh, well, at least they don't ask me for the keys to the car! My dog Jesse did jump into the driver's seat once while I was taking groceries into the house. Somehow he hit the gearshift with his paw and ran the car a few feet into a picnic table in front of the house. But that was his first and last time driving. . . .

Come on out and join me tonight and bring your animal spirit with you. My cat Larry is going to take me out tonight and show me some new territory. And since all my cats sleep a lot, I'll probably find some more waiting for me out in the Animal Dimension. I have a whole chapter on this dimension in my other book, *Cosmic Journeys*. It's an exciting chapter. You might just buy the book and read that chapter or just come on out and visit that dimension during your sleep state.

Whatever you do . . . Enjoy!

11 Meeting Some Local Builders

The images were coming. . . . I was in an airplane with one of my European tour groups. The pilot announced that we were getting ready to land in Iceland, and instructed us to fasten our seat belts. I looked out my window to see very barren land. If I hadn't known better, I would have thought that we were coming in for a landing on the moon. I had never in my life seen a landscape like this. I was sitting beside Ike, whose knuckles were white as he clutched the armrest of his seat.

"Are you okay, Ike?" I asked.

"No, I don't feel at all good about landing in Iceland," he replied. "I don't like the looks of the landscape. It's dark and barren. And look at the houses on the side of that hill; they all look alike, and colorless."

"Actually, I disagree about the houses. They all seem to be quaint and colorful to me."

"I have a bad feeling in the pit of my stomach. I think I must have lived here before, and must have had a bad experience," Ike said. "I've never before felt this kind of resistance about arriving somewhere."

"Well, Ike, there isn't much you can do about it," I advised. "The wheels of the plane are just about to touch down, and we're going to be staying here overnight. So you'll have to grin and bear it."

"At least we have a wonderful group who will be spending the night here with me. I'm sure I'll get through this. I'll just go to my room and go to bed, and be the first one on the plane in the morning ready to get the heck out of here," Ike said, with a tone I had never heard in his voice.

Ike had always been so upbeat and positive about everything. This was a part of Ike I had never experienced.

The plane landed and we were transported by bus into the capital city of Reykjavik. The country being about the size of Virginia might help our tour group of Virginians feel at home, I thought. We were on our way to Europe, where we were going to have a retreat in a castle in a small village in Germany. But for the first week everyone was going to go wherever they wanted to on EuroRail passes. So the tour members would pair off in groups of two and three and head off to France, Switzerland, Austria, Holland, or wherever they wanted. Everyone had the address of the castle in Germany and the time to arrive for our second week together.

We had dinner in our hotel restaurant in Reykjavik. When we finished, I noticed that Ike immediately headed up to his room. We had to leave the airport by eight A.M. the next morning.

When I got to the bus in the morning, Ike had already taken his seat just behind the driver. We all piled into the bus and were soon on our way back to the airport to continue our flight.

We were ready to get off the bus at the airport when I heard a loud, "Oh, no!" from Ike.

I walked up the bus aisle to him and asked, "What's the matter, Ike?"

"I left my passport in my room," he said in dismay.

"I'm so sorry, Ike. You'll probably have to spend another night here and join us tomorrow because we cannot miss this flight."

I looked at Ike and he was as white as a sheet.

"I can't do that," he said. "I can't spend another night here."

"Okay, Ike, I'll see what I can do." I replied.

I walked up the aisle to the bus driver and told him the situation, and he immediately got on his phone to talk to someone at the airport. He turned around and asked what Ike's hotel room number was, and Ike told him. He said that another bus was ready to leave the hotel and the driver could pick up the passport and bring it to the airport.

When the passport arrived, Ike was tremendously relieved. After checking in and getting on the plane, I noticed that he had a large safety pin on his coat pocket with his passport securely pinned in. His wife, Nancy, concerned that he would lose his passport, had made sure at the start of the trip that it would not be easily lost. She hadn't anticipated that Ike would take it out of his pocket and put it on the desk in his hotel room.

And so another passport glitch—I was glad it wasn't my story this time.

The trip was marvelous for everyone. Ike went with a group on a tour of Germany and was elated about his experiences. He had found other places where he was sure he had lived before; these had left him with good feelings rather than bad.

Ike was so freaked out about his dislike for Iceland, however, that he found someone to regress him hypnotically when he got back home, to find out what his problem was with Iceland. And he was regressed back to a lifetime in Iceland that was very distasteful to him. It was a great learning experience for him about a very upsetting lifetime.

The images faded. . . .

∞

I felt Radiant Lady with me. I always feel a shift in my energies when she is in my presence. I had interesting experiences after two of my sessions in which she elevated my energies for entering into a higher dimension. And twice, when I came out of the journeying sessions, I thought I smelled smoke. I went from my office to the living room and kitchen to make sure that nothing had caught on fire. I wondered if, in elevating my energies, some of my Earth dross burned up.

"Actually, it did," said Radiant Lady. "We have someone in Mr. Monroe's Lab in the Sky who sends a ray of highly intensive energy down on you. You experience the change in energy in terms of an odor, which is interpreted by your senses as smoke. What this ray does is transform some of your Earth thoughts of doubt and resistance so that you are free to receive communication from a higher level of intensity."

"That sounds good to me," I responded. "I was just happy not to find anything burning in the kitchen. I did have a fire once. A friend was helping me hold one of my animals while I was giving it some medicine. She moved her body up against one of the stove knobs and turned it on by accident. We then went to my office and closed the door to give some more animals medicine. When we opened the door and looked toward the kitchen, the curtain was aflame. We were able to put it out, but there was damage to the stove top. So that's why the smoke odor made me nervous."

"There is a lot going on that your physical mind can't perceive when we are having these communications."

"I believe you," I replied. "I used to think that such statements as you just made were a lot of hullabaloo. But I have had so many experiences working in Bob Monroe's lab that can't be explained, that I know something is functioning at a higher vibrational level. For instance, at least twice after intense sessions in the lab, car batteries outside the lab building were dead when we came out to leave. We had to call someone to get us started so that we could go home!"

"You were drawing on the energy of the batteries to keep you charged during your intense sessions," said Radiant Lady.

"Yes, and when we made the Patrick Tape, the energy was so intense that it blew out the electrical systems in three of the CHEC units near where we were having the session with Patrick. So I realize that something happens in my energy system to create this."

"Well, since you have slept almost all day, you should be recharged now."

"You know, we finished at four this morning and I slept until one in the afternoon. But I got sleepy again when it was time to start my session, and slept again from four to eight P.M. It was such a deep sleep that I wondered if I left my body to do some work in your dimension before starting our next session. Did I?"

"Yes, you did. We were trying something new. We decided that if you went into a very deep sleep before a session, your spirit body could come to our dimension to be recharged. Therefore, when you started the session, you would be highly energized—and not smell smoke when we're finished!"

"I did wake up feeling very recharged and ready to start this session. Thanks for the boost."

"Okay, we're ready to go on this side, if you are."

"I'm ready. What is on the spiritual agenda tonight?"

"I'm taking you to meet two friends you were fond of when they were on the Earth."

"Who would that be?" I asked.

"Your friends Ike and BC."

"Oh, my traveling buddies. I took them on tours here on planet Earth. So are they taking me on tours of the afterlife?"

"You are right on."

"I can't wait to see them," I said. "They were two very special people. They were involved with construction here on Earth and were very successful builders. BC and Ike both built housing complexes. BC also owned a restaurant and apartment complexes. But they both were also very committed to the spiritual level. And they were into helping people, and were two generous souls."

"That's why we want them to give you their view of the afterlife as they see it. They were always so interested in spiritual issues, and therefore when they came over, they were extremely curious about what is happening in our dimension! I remember when you had sessions with them on Earth where they would ask your guide many questions. They were much like your sessions with Mr. Monroe when he would talk with AhSo."

"Oh, yes," I said. "Those sessions really bonded us in our passion to learn more about the world beyond. And so here we are—they, in the 'beyond,' and I, here. So now they can give me an update on what their lives are like there."

"They are ready for your visit. So go into your level, and I will get Tash and Ray to rev up your Akashic energy system so that your spirit will be able to visit with us."

∞

When I closed my eyes, I saw an absolutely grand view of purple mountains in the background, and a beautiful blue sky. I felt my energies shifting. Strangely, my body was itching all over, which began to distract me. It must have had to do with the change in my body vibrations. I told myself to ignore the itching, and keep moving into my inner dimensions, which I know is where all dimensions are.

I felt a very strong ray of light shining down on me and found myself sitting in an open-air amphitheater. It was very quiet. There were a large number of seats, in a circular seating arrangement, though with no one in them yet. I was sitting in the first row, with the edge of the light beam hitting me. There was a chair on a platform in front of me. And then there was a faint sound of music coming from the ray of light. The light was changing color, and as it changed the music intensified.

People began to appear in the seats around me and I felt a growing mood of energy and joy. Then two beings took shape in the seats on either side of me. I turned to my left and recognized Ike. Oh, wow! Then I turned to my right, and there was BC. Wow, again! I got a message from them telepathically that we would listen now, and communicate after this special event was over.

There was a hush, and I realized the amphitheater was much larger than I had sensed earlier and every seat was filled. The light on the center of the circular stage was brighter. A being of light appeared. There was a reverent and powerful silence as the being's form became clear.

Then I could see all the features of the powerful presence in the center of the stage. He was tall and stately, and wore a white robe with gold and blue embroidery on it. Tremendous love and joy emanated from this being. He stood to speak. He raised his hands to the heavens, and the light intensified as he sent thoughts of praise and thanksgiving to the great God who rules over the universe.

I knew that everyone present was sending up the same thoughts of praise and thanksgiving, and I felt myself light and uplifted. The joy and love were filling my every cell. The colors of the light beam changed from glorious gold-white to a calming blue.

The figure did not speak, but I perceived his thoughts as he sent them out to all who were gathered.

"I bring greetings from the higher dimensions of pure Light and Love. The Father, the Giver, the Ruler of the universe, pours down every level of Love upon you. We are all a part of His Kingdom of Light, and you must always remember that you are each very special.

"Always ask for whatever you desire to aid you in your spiritual growth, and it will be given to you. And your praise and thanksgiving are always deeply appreciated. Every one of you is so connected in Spirit. That which you share with others is instantly given back to you tenfold.

"As you serve and share your Light with others, it will intensify in God's Kingdom, from whence you came originally. Our sole purpose for rising into the higher levels of Light is to return to the Pure essence of God's Light. God is the All That Is, and His High Light pervades in every dimension.

"I bring blessings to each and every one who hears this message. Your own energy levels will be enlarged because of your presence here. Remember that your happiness and joy are an expression of God's Love for you.

"Thank you. Now I shall leave but will return."

Suddenly, he was gone. The light in the center again began to change color and with each new color came a new and beautiful sound. Then many of the people in the chairs just began to disappear, while others got up from their seats and walked out through the aisles.

BC and Ike both stood up and motioned for me to stand. I did so and we merged our spirit bodies, which brought a great energy charge. I looked around and Radiant Lady was standing right behind me. She sent the message that we were going to leave the amphitheater. Then the three of them surrounded me and transported me.

It was beautiful outside! The amphitheater was at the center of what looked like a town or city. The building was made of a marblelike material, with large pillars, and was open around the sides and at the top. All around it were incredibly beautiful flowers and trees. I could see other buildings radiating outward, though none were over two stories high. There were no streets, but rather beautiful pathways between and around the buildings.

"Hi, Rosie!" said Ike. "Let's sit here in this garden and talk before we go anywhere else."

"Hello, Ike. It's amazing to be here. I'm glad you haven't reincarnated back to Iceland," I said, with a smile.

Ike had always had a wonderful laugh, and a great roar of laughter came from him.

"Hey, Rosie," BC chimed in, "We're happy to have you on our turf now! The last time I saw you was at my funeral."

"Yes, yes, BC. That was one of the most amazing funerals I have ever attended. So you were there? So you know what an incredible job David McKnight did of honoring your life on Earth. Everyone agreed after leaving the church that day that they would love for David to outlive them so that he could do their service."

Everyone laughed.

"But David came close to joining us," Ike said. "We would have loved to have him over here, but he still has work to do on the Earth plane. Everyone loves him so much that it is going to be hard for him to get away."

"I know, Ike," I said, "David is one of a kind. But I can imagine that when he gets here in the spirit world, he is going to be busy zipping in and out to see everyone he knows, and he knows a lot of people. He has fun now being around people, but when he can move his body just by thought, watch out when he gets here."

Everyone laughed again.

"So what did you think of the special Light session you just attended?" Ike asked.

"I felt very privileged to be invited to attend. Who was that great spirit who spoke?"

"He is the ruler over this realm," said BC. "But he lives in a higher dimension than this one. When we have requests about anything, we take them to him. He has been around for eons of time, and his mind has registered everything about everyone who is under his rule. He is a powerfully loving being of Light."

"So how do your lives differ now from when you were on planet Earth? Are you guys still building? It's obvious that you are still friends or you wouldn't be here together."

"Relax, Rosie," said Ike. "We have plenty of time to answer your questions, one at a time. First let me say that life here is so different from life on Earth that I hardly know where to begin."

"Well, begin with what we have on Earth that you don't have here."

"They always said on Earth that there are two things you can't escape: taxes and death," BC jumped in to say. "But here we don't pay taxes and we don't die. So we don't have an IRS, nor do we have funeral homes!"

"And there is no crime or war here," said Ike. "So we don't have police or soldiers."

"We don't have to eat, so we don't have supermarkets or restaurants," added BC.

"We don't have cell phones either," Ike went on. "We send thoughts telepathically. I'm glad you taught us how to do that in your ESP classes, Rosie."

"Well, I am, too," I replied. "So, you probably don't have TVs, radios, computers, cars, trucks, and superhighways!"

"You're right, Rosie," said Ike. "And we don't miss all that stuff that so absorbed our lives. It was a material world, and we were mostly involved in material matters. There was so much concentration on the physical body and not much attention given to spiritual matters."

"So, as building contractors before, can you still use those skills here?"

"We certainly can," they chimed in together.

"We're still contractors," said Ike. "But we don't need all the paraphernalia that contractors have to use in the material world. We still develop the designs for people, but then we create their homes or buildings with thought. This is the Mental Realm, so most of what happens here comes directly from mind—our minds and the Mind of the Source."

"By the 'Source,' you mean God," I replied. "Does that mean that you are closer to God here than you were on planet Earth?"

"No, it doesn't," said BC. "You are always as close to God as you allow yourself to be. We are calling more fully upon the power of God because we are taught how to do that. We have many helpers coming from more refined dimensions closer to the pure energies of God. Therefore, we don't get caught up in all sorts of belief systems about the wrath of God, the fear of God, the punishment of God, which don't exist. We are only involved in the Love of God."

"That's right," Ike continued. "This is the Love Dimension. There is no negativity here. There is also no sickness. Fear, anger, doubt, and all those negative emotions are nonexistent here. Those who leave the Earth with all those negative emotions get stuck in the lower vibratory dimensions closer to the Earth. They will remain there until they see and understand how they have put themselves there by their own thoughts and actions. Then when they ask for help in changing, it will be granted. A self-centered and greedy person would never enter here because their energies don't match the energies of this realm."

"So, Ike and BC, other than working as mental contractors, what do you do for recreation here? Do you have sports here, like football, basketball, golf, and so forth?"

"Actually, there are no contact sports," Ike replied. "Individual sports events like golfing (where you move the ball with your mind), fishing (where you can't harm the fish, so you release it), and croquet, sailing, and flying are great pastimes for many. And the reason we don't have contact sports is that our bodies are different—and we don't have to work out or jog to keep in shape. Our bodies are perfect and never deteriorate. We never get tired and we never sleep."

"Now the things that governments cut first in their budgets on planet Earth are the events that are most popular here—the arts," said BC.

"Yes," added Ike. "We have music concerts of all kinds. We have great halls of learning where all types of courses are offered. Nancy has been taking courses in weaving beautiful rugs, and she loves it."

"Oh, yes—say 'hi' to Nancy for me."

"You just sent the thought to her yourself!" said Ike. "Didn't you hear the 'hi' back from her?"

"As a matter of fact, I did," I said. "I seem to forget that this is a thought world. Well, of course, it's also a thought world on planet Earth, and most people don't realize we attract everything to ourselves by the way we think. If we think poverty thoughts, we get poverty results; and if we think prosperity thoughts, we get prosperity results. But on Earth the strong emotions added to these thoughts help to manifest them faster."

"That's correct," said BC. "So now instead of talking so much, what would you like to do, or where would you like to go?"

"I would love to see you build something. Now, I take it that since you don't have to earn money, you do your building as a service to people who need help in building their homes and so forth?"

"That's correct," said Ike. "And it really is a privilege to be able to do this as a service to people. It does take some training to learn the art of building with the mind. We had to take classes under some master builders and architects."

"Well, it's so good that you can continue on here in something you really like to do," I replied. "It's interesting that doctors, nurses, funeral directors, and law enforcement officials always have jobs on planet Earth because of illness, death, and crime. So when those people come over here, are they going to have to learn new skills?"

"We have met many in that category who are very relieved that they are out of that negative energy level and can concentrate on developing hobbies and skills that enhance their lives and the lives of others," said BC. "Their lives were ones of service to others, which helped to get them here. However, when they arrive in this realm, they can develop new interests and talents that will help them serve in different ways."

"It sounds like service is a key part of life in your dimension."

"That's true," BC affirmed. "And it is true on planet Earth as well. But many have not gotten the message that we are all one, and everything we do affects all others—and ourselves, as well. If we harm others, that comes back to us. If we help others, that comes back, too. Everything is based on a universal principle: As you sow, so shall you reap."

"Yes, that's the same as my Poison Ivy Principle. I tried to play a joke on a childhood friend by rubbing poison ivy on her, and I was the one that got it. That was 'instant karma,'" I said.

"I'm getting ready to add an addition to my home," BC said. "And I would like to invite you to attend the event."

"Thank you. It would be a privilege."

"Now, Ike and Radiant Lady know how to project themselves there. So you can stand between them and they can project you with their energies."

"I'm ready," I said, as Ike and Radiant Lady each put an arm on my shoulders.

There was a flash of light and suddenly we were in a most gorgeous setting. There in front of me was a house with many windows nestled in among some beautiful trees and flower gardens. Beside it was a lake, with deep blue colors that sparkled like diamonds.

"BC," I said, "This house reminds me of the beautiful house you used to live in—lake and all."

"Yes, I liked that house," said BC. "And I know Loretta will enjoy this house when she gets here. I have Annie living with me. She has a new friend that is moving in with us, so I'm adding an extra room."

Suddenly, a gorgeous young lady was standing in front of me, smiling, and I realized that it was BC and Loretta's daughter, Annie, who had been killed in a car accident when she was in her early teens. This is where my Disconnect Principle gets reversed. BC was disconnected from Annie when he was on planet Earth, but is now reconnected with her.

"Annie, you are beautiful," I said. "I love your spirit robe."

"Thank you," said Annie, as she reached out and touched me on the shoulder. I felt her wonderful loving energies run all through my body.

"I have invited several other people here for this building ceremony. So I need to call them in," said BC.

He didn't pick up a cell phone and call; just by sending out the thought, five people suddenly appeared on the spot.

"What a way to travel!" I thought.

BC motioned for us to follow him to one end of the house. He sent out the thought that they were going to add the extra room at that end. Ike had some plans in his hands that he handed to BC. Two other men were there who were going to help create this addition.

They all looked down to study the architectural design on the sheet. Then all four walked over, closed their eyes, and held out their hands. As they stood there with extended hands and closed eyes, in front of us a faint glow began to manifest, and became stronger and stronger. At first it was a smoky substance, which then began to manifest as a wall in front of us. Then a beam of light came down from above and seemed to be putting finishing touches on the wall.

The men stopped briefly, and BC stepped inside to see how the wall was forming from the inside. When he walked back from the manifesting form, he had a smile on his face and seemed pleased with the mental building that was taking place.

"Okay," said BC. "Let's take it on up."

The instant after he said that the room was in place, windows and all! It was beautiful and fit right in with the rest of the house. Everyone clapped, as did I.

BC and Ike turned to me and said, "Remember us when you get here. Have your home design in mind, and we'll be happy to build it."

I was very moved, not only because of their kindness and generous offer, but also by realizing that BC and Annie were reunited after a sad separation of several years. Annie was the apple of BC's eye, and it had been very, very hard on him when she suddenly "disconnected" from planet Earth.

I looked over at Radiant Lady and saw how much she, too, had enjoyed the event that had just taken place. Then she gave me the nod that it was time to descend.

"I'm ready, my friend of Light," I said gratefully. "I love you so much, and am so thankful for the tours you are taking me on. I'll never be the same again. Thank you. . . . Thank you!"

"It is my privilege, Rosalind," said Radiant Lady. "And I want you to know how much I love you, as well."

"And goodbye to you, Ike, BC, Annie, and the other friends at the creation of the new addition."

I could hear them all saying "Goodbye!" as the energy receded.

∞

I have to say that I smelled the smoke again just before the raising of the house. I got up and looked out my office door just to make sure my kitties weren't building a little bonfire or something to get my attention. I guess the new process of taking my spirit body up during a sleep session worked to an extent, but the increased energy must have worn off. Smelling the smoke is a strange experience—a very strong sensation that suddenly disappears.

It was almost five on Sunday morning, so it was good I took a nap before taking this tour. The tours were so much fun that I knew I was going to miss them tremendously when the manuscript was finished. But I was sure my little critters wouldn't miss them because they would like me to be with them out in the living room. They prefer that I sit or lie down on the couch so that they can curl up on my lap, or on me. Everyone and everything need love and attention. And I'm thankful for the love and attention I receive from them. As soon as my head hits the pillow, several of them crowd in around me.

When BC and Ike build my spirit house, I'm going to have to make sure there is plenty of room for all of my animals. Of course, when I have my house built in the next dimension, they will all be able to communicate their thoughts to me! So I'm going to have to know what I want before I get there, since all of them will be giving their opinions on what they will want in the house. Luckily, I won't have to feed them—or empty their litter boxes—when we get over there.

So we will all continue to be happy together in the next dimension. And I have several cats already over there, so they might even have our house built before I arrive! Of course, we don't have to live in houses because the weather is always perfect. It might be fun to live on a boat like Patrick does. It is great to have so many options . . . that are free!

12 Heavenly Conference Center

Again I relaxed deeply, my fingers touching my computer keyboard. And again, images from the Akashic record of my past, my Life Imprint, began to form in my mind.

Thank you, Radiant Lady, Ray, and Tash for projecting these scenes into my energy system.

I saw myself opening the door to the Sheraton Conference Hotel suite. I was overwhelmed with excitement. I had filled the whole hotel here in Fredericksburg, Virginia, close enough to Washington, D.C., to get limousine service. As the conference organizer, I had been given a free suite—the largest one in the hotel. Eight hundred people were already registered, and there would probably be a thousand conferees by the time walk-ins arrived over the weekend.

I anticipated this conference to be my largest ever. Jimmy Carter was president of the United States at that time, and his sister, Ruth Carter Stapleton, was a featured speaker. What a gathering it would be! A gathering of like-minded people looking for answers to some of life's most vital questions—those questions having to do with our spiritual lives!

This was the kind of conference I have always put on: personal growth conferences—the growth of body, mind, and spirit. They say we teach what we most want to learn, and I clearly organize conferences on the topic I most want to learn more about, the life of the spirit. I have always had a passion to understand more about spirit, who we really are. Not who we pretend to be here on planet Earth, but who we *really* are! The first thing I carried into my suite was a picture—not just a picture, but a picture of *The Laughing Jesus.*

A couple of weeks before I had gone with some friends to visit a friend of theirs. He was a young artist, and when we arrived at his house, there sitting on his easel was a portrait of Jesus. Jesus' face expressed the most wholesome heartfelt laugh I have ever seen. Nearly every picture I have seen of Jesus portrays him as *so* serious. I have always believed that joy and humor are two of the strongest traits of a highly evolved spiritual being. Therefore, Jesus, the Christ, being at the top of the spiritual ladder and living in the pure presence of God, would surely have a lot to be laughing about!

I was so awed by the portrait that I asked the artist about its history. He explained that he had seen a small picture entitled *The Laughing Jesus* in a magazine. It impressed him so much he cut it out and kept it in his wallet for years. Every time he looked at the picture, it made him feel *so* happy.

While he was in Vietnam, he always pulled the picture out and prayed during times when he and his unit were under heavy fire. Once, one of his buddies crouched beside him during an intense siege, saw the picture he was holding, and asked if he could hold it for a moment. He took the picture in his hand and prayed to Jesus to help get them home safely. Then he asked his friend to paint a copy of the picture for him when they arrived home. After arriving stateside, the artist began painting portraits of *The Laughing Jesus,* giving the first one to his Vietnam buddy.

I asked him how many of these pictures he had painted. He estimated at least a hundred. I told him that I would very much love to have such a portrait, wondered how much it would cost, and how long it would take to get it. He was selling them for $70 and said that the one on his easel would be finished in two weeks. I pulled out my checkbook and wrote a check immediately.

The picture was delivered to me on Friday evening of my weekend conference. The artist met me in the lobby of the Sheraton as I was checking into my suite. I thanked him for bringing it to me, walked into my room, and placed it carefully on a mantel, thinking it would keep me energized during the exciting and challenging weekend ahead. If the painting had been delivered to my house, I don't think I would have brought it to the conference, since I "thought" I had bought the picture for myself.

When I was lining up speakers for this conference, Ruth Carter Stapleton was receiving much publicity for her work, including a new book. For years she had been doing regression therapy sessions with clients. She would regress clients back to a place in their lives where Jesus would be waiting for them. Then the session would become a three-way counseling session among Jesus, the client, and Ruth. The basis of her counseling sessions was the "healing of memories" through the Love of Jesus, the Christ.

Ruth had done many sessions with women who had been sexually abused. She said in her talk at the conference that 65 percent of the women she worked with had had experiences of sexual abuse. Many remarkable healings had taken place over the 20 or so years of her spiritual ministry. Sometimes she did regression sessions with whole groups of people.

I was so impressed by the work she was doing that one day when I was reading an article about her, I thought how wonderful it would be if she could be a speaker at my conference. Wondering if she would accept my invitation, I reminded myself that she could give one of two answers, "yes" or "no," and I wouldn't know which answer she would give until I asked her. She wrote back with an affirmative response, and seemed thrilled to be invited to the conference.

The conference was an awesome event, and was topped by the fact that when I offered to drive Ruth to D.C. after the conference, she was happy to have me do so. That gave us a chance to get better acquainted, which then led to an invitation to visit her at her newly created spiritual conference center in Texas.

When we pulled up at the gate of the White House grounds, the guard looked through my window, saw Ruth, and said, "Mrs. Stapleton, hello, and welcome back to the White House"—not even asking me for identification or inquiring who I was. "President Carter just arrived back an hour ago from his trip abroad," continued the guard. "He and Rosalyn will be happy to see you. Go right on in."

It was dark and I just followed the drive that led right up to the back entrance of the White House. Two doormen were there to meet us and opened the door to let Ruth out of the car.

"Welcome, Mrs. Stapleton. We've been expecting you," said one of the doormen. "Do you have luggage we can assist you with?"

"Yes, George, I sure do," replied Ruth. "First, I would like you to take a picture out of the backseat for me. Be very careful with it because it's a very special picture."

"Yes, ma'am," replied George, as he carefully lifted the picture out of the backseat of my little Honda hatchback. I got out of the car and opened up the hatchback, showing the other doorman Ruth's luggage.

I walked around the car to Ruth as she was preparing to go into the White House. She gave me a big hug and a kiss on the cheek, and said, "I really do appreciate you giving the picture to me. I have never seen a picture of Jesus like this one before. I will cherish it for life!"

As I drove out of the gate of the White House grounds, I smiled as I remembered how overwhelmed she was when she first walked into my Sheraton suite and saw the picture of *The Laughing Jesus* on the mantel. After she said, "Oh! What a wonderful picture of Jesus!" I replied spontaneously, "It's yours."

I never regretted giving the picture to her. The next time I saw the picture, it was in an issue of *Parade* magazine that comes with the Sunday newspaper. I usually don't buy the newspaper, but something told me to pick up this particular issue. I was just casually looking through the paper when *The Laughing Jesus* jumped out at me. Right beside the portrait stood Larry Flynt, editor of *Hustler* magazine. Mr. Flynt had a big smile on his face as the proud owner of his new painting.

After being converted to Christianity through Ruth's ministry, Mr. Flynt became a special friend of hers, and was invited to visit her and her husband at their home in North Carolina. The picture had been hung in the guest cottage, and when Larry Flynt walked in the door and saw it, he exclaimed, "Oh, what a wonderful picture of Jesus!" at which point Ruth spontaneously replied, "It's yours."

I never saw the picture after that, or knew whether Larry Flynt passed it on to someone else who was overwhelmed by the magnificence of Jesus' laughing countenance.

After Larry Flynt was shot and became a paraplegic, his conversion by Ruth to Christianity took a turn downward. Ruth died of cancer shortly thereafter and I was never able to learn from her what happened in her relationship with him, and in turn with his relationship to Jesus. I did read an article later about the fact that Larry Flynt went from "born again" to "porn again." . . .

So who knows who the proud owner of *The Laughing Jesus* is now. It is to be hoped that it is still Larry Flynt. I feel blessed for having been the proud owner for even such a short time. But the joy of Jesus still resonates in my heart even if the picture is not hanging on my wall!

The pictures in my mind started to fade. . . .

∞

I sat, thinking jokingly, "So, Radiant Lady, I know you're here. Come out, come out, wherever you are. . . ."

"Of course I'm here," she said. "I'm always here. I'm alerted by the energy connection of your thoughts."

"I want to thank you for reminding me of *The Laughing Jesus* painting. And I do want to brag a little bit and say that I did once get invited to the White House for lunch."

"Did Ruth Stapleton invite you there?"

"No, a man named Milton Friedman, who was one of Gerald Ford's main speechwriters, invited me. We became friends after he attended several of my conferences. He said after one of my conferences that he wanted me to come to Washington and have lunch with him at the White House."

"Did you?" she asked.

"No, I was going through some major crises at the time and couldn't manage it. But the invitation was greatly appreciated. So what's on our agenda for today—lunch at the Heavenly Café?"

"As a matter of fact, it is. We have a big gathering planned. If people want to eat, they can. We always have lots of spiritually charged food available."

"I thought people didn't eat after arriving in your more refined dimension."

"Actually, there are quite a few people who cannot drop their old habits instantly after first arriving here, so they continue to create the foods that they liked while on Earth. They have no active digestive systems, of course, but the foods get absorbed into the intensified atmosphere. Gradually, such newly arrived souls eat less and less. When they get really involved in learning and growing here, they forget about food and don't eat anymore—other than a few of our luscious heavenly grapes now and then."

"So we are having a gathering with or without food—whichever one desires? And who will the featured speaker be?"

"Well, you're one of them! We're going to call you forward at the last minute to preach the sermon."

"I wouldn't really know what to say to such advanced souls," I responded. "But you must be kidding. I wouldn't think that sermons would be on the agenda in the afterlife."

"Anything your mind can think of is offered here."

"So if you have sermons, are you indicating that you have church services there?"

"Every kind of religious organization that exists on planet Earth exists here."

"That's a surprise to me. Who builds the religious structures?"

"It is a lot easier to build a church here than on your planet because there doesn't have to be building fund drives," Radiant Lady said. "Often, when a new group of past members of an organization get together, they simply design an edifice and manifest it with the group mind. Many of the religious groups that are tightly knit on Earth continue to worship together after arriving here, mainly out of habit, but also because there is a love connection between them. The main thing is that they love and worship God just as they did before dropping their physical bodies."

"So are the services the same as they are here on Earth?"

"Pretty much so."

"Are the buildings similar as well? And if you don't have time there, how do people know it is time for a service?" I asked.

"Yes, the places of worship look very similar to those on Earth. And as to timing of the services, the thought goes out that it is time for the service and the interested souls are there instantly," Radiant Lady explained.

"Do a lot of souls attend these services?"

"Many such religious groups gather regularly at first. But once the members are here for a while and realize that they are already in Heaven, they begin to check out other worship options and gradually lose interest in their old belief systems and ways of thinking."

"So if churches, synagogues, mosques, and temples are built and the attendance dwindles off, what then happens to them?"

"Oh, they often remain intact. And if you visited one, you would immediately notice some differences."

"And what would those be?"

"No cemeteries are surrounding the churches, obviously because no one dies here. And there are no signs anywhere outside of or in the structures that indicate topics and times."

"Oh, that makes sense. So when people realize they don't need their traditional worship structures anymore, do the buildings just get vacated?"

"Often, they are used for spirit gatherings when spirit teachers come from the higher realms to teach and inspire us. Remember the service you attended with BC and Ike?"

"Of course."

"That wonderful structure was built in the center of the town to be used for visitors from the higher realms. Some are elders and council members who help to oversee and manage the activities of each realm. Others come to help souls in their spiritual growth. And also we have many plays and musical events that take place there in the center square."

"From what you're telling me, it sounds like life in the Summer Realm is full of vim, vitality, and wonderful activities for everyone."

"Yes," said Radiant Lady. "And one of the major differences between our world and Earth is that we don't have crime, so we don't have to police our realm. And we also don't have 'terrorist alert warnings,' or fearful energies that keep souls from flying in and attending events. Our realms are filled with music instead of fear."

"That sounds wonderful. Since you obviously don't have radios, boom boxes, and CDs, how does the music get projected?" I asked.

"Actually, music and color are the two main energies that propel and energize our systems. Music and color are abundant in everything. As you remember, even the elevated spirit soil gives off melodious sounds when you hold it in your hands and drop it through your fingers. And it is edible, too, for those who want to be energized by the sounds and colors of the soil."

"I love it! So with music inherent in the spiritual atmosphere, do you tune into it just as you tune into each other's thoughts?"

"That is correct. Music and color are in the molecules of our atmosphere, and are the very life force of our existence. We also have the marvelous music events and concerts. I mentioned that many of the masters who once lived on Earth present special concerts for all to attend. We also have every kind of musical instrument here that exists on the planet—plus more. In fact, the instruments and music of your planet originated in our realm.

"The only music that doesn't fit into the vibrations of this realm is the slower vibratory sounds, like hard rock, that are actually harmful to the life force vibrations. Experiments done on Earth indicate that your plants can die when subjected to such low-vibratory sounds. The lower vibration sounds are not music in the real sense, but are generated from the slower vibrations of the dark realms."

"Radiant Lady, I'm amazed at what just happened."

"I saw it, too, Rosalind," she replied, "But do you want to express it so that your readers will know what just took place?"

"Absolutely," I replied. "I keep the door to my office closed while working on this manuscript. I had started out with my computer in my dining room, but had to move it back into the office to have better control over who strikes the keys on my keyboard. But I will still let certain cats in now and then when they ask to come in. Sabrina, one of my very special cats, was in my office for about an hour when she began to move around. So I picked her up while still at my computer to tell her I loved her, but that I would have to put her out, which I did. I came back to my computer to notice that while holding her above my computer, her little paws hit the following keys: 'QA'!!"

"She's giving you a message, Rosalind."

"So what is she telling me?"

"We're planning to have a QA session—that is, a Question/Answer session—and she's getting impatient for you to get on with it. Our plan is to have a Conference of Spirits, also known as a Spirit Gathering, with a roundtable discussion to get some questions answered. So thanks to Sabrina for keeping us on task."

"Maybe this is the time to mention Sabrina's story, Radiant Lady. She probably wanted us to tell her story before we moved on. I'm sure it's okay with her. But is it okay with you?"

"Certainly," replied Radiant Lady. "Sabrina is my special friend, and has been here with me on several occasions."

"Well, Sabrina was the first one to teach me about reincarnation. When I lived at the mobile home park, Sabrina was my all-white, fluffy, deaf, loveable cat. Living at the park was somewhat restrictive for my cats, to say the least. Therefore I broke the rules of 'no outside cats,' and would let them out late at night and on weekends when the management was off duty. I wanted them to get some open-air exercise.

"One Saturday evening, Sabrina was in my backyard and I decided it was time to bring her in. When I started out the door, she was rolling over to scratch her back on the gravel beside the road that ran behind my mobile home. As I started down the steps toward her, I was relieved that, since she was deaf, she was on the side of the road as a car approached. And I was pleased that the car seemed to slow down in order to pass her.

"Then all of a sudden, right in front of my eyes, the car swerved and ran over her tiny body—and quickly drove on. I screamed at the top of my voice, 'Oh, Michael, a car just ran over Sabrina on purpose!'

"Michael, a young friend from a neighboring mobile home, ran out the door, hoping to catch the speeding car's license number, as I ran over to pick up Sabrina's little bloodied body. Her eyes were popped out, and blood was gushing from her mouth as she did the death shiver in my arms.

"'Sabrina, Sabrina, please come back to me,' I cried, as I clutched her small, broken body close to my heart. 'And remember, you don't have to come back deaf—you can come back hearing. But please, please, Beanie, do come back to me,' I cried.

"Michael and I buried Sabrina in my backyard. At a memorial service we conducted for her, I thanked her for being with me for several years and I thanked God for sending this wonderful little soul to me. And I asked God to send her back to me. . . .

"About three months passed. I had a cleaning job for a beautician across town. One night I was in the salon late. It had just started raining and I looked out the back door. Just behind my car, a white cat came from out of the woods. I opened the door and said, 'Hi.' Instead of running, the cat—with oil all over its little back—ran up to me. There were major roads all around, and I had no idea where this beautiful little being had come from. I swooped her up in my arms and took her into the building. I carried her downstairs to the kitchen, took some baloney out of the refrigerator, and gave it to her. She gobbled it up.

"Her energies seemed very familiar to me. Then I thought, 'I wonder if this cat is Sabrina?' because she was white, fluffy and about Sabrina's size when she died.

"I was just getting ready to vacuum the downstairs, so I decided to do a 'vacuum cleaner' test on this night visitor who seemed so content to be in my presence. If she was deaf, she would probably climb onto the vacuum cleaner and ride it around. If she could hear, she would run, of course. I turned the vacuum on and she scampered quickly under a chair.

"When it was time to leave, I put her in my car, which was the same car Sabrina used to ride in with me. She walked all through my car, smelled everything, and then planted herself directly in the middle of the backseat, folded her front paws, and sent the message, 'I'm back and it's time to go home, Mom.'

"She looked just like Sabrina, and had all of her personality traits, right down to her enjoyment of eating salads. So Sabrina has been back with me now for more than six years and is very much enjoying her life here at Heavenly Acres. She loves to sit out in the woods by a large rock on my front property close to the road. I saw her cross the road once and she ran when she heard a car coming. I thanked God again for sending her back 'hearing' this time around."

"That is a touching story, Rosalind," said Radiant Lady. "Sabrina was with me when she crossed over. I missed her when she came back to you with a new body. But she comes back often to visit me in her sleeping state. And let me tell you, she was a little bossy when she was here with me, too. She likes things to keep moving. So her typing 'QA' was a good reminder of our mission for this session. Thank you again, Sabrina. I know you are eager for Rosalind to get this book finished, so that you can spend more quality time with her."

"Now, where will this spirit gathering be held?" I asked.

"Your dear friend, Robert Monroe, would like us to return to his Heavenly Conference Center for a group gathering of like-minded souls."

"Oh, I only saw his laboratory when we visited before. I wasn't aware that he had a larger facility."

"Besides his laboratory, he has built quite an elaborate facility for gatherings of all types. It has the same purpose as his Roberts Mountain Retreat back on the New Land in Virginia. People from all over the world gather there for conferences or Hemi-Sync programs. But here not only do spirit friends come in from many different dimensions, but they come in from the spirit realms of different galaxies. Bob met many of them through his prior travels through the galaxies even while living on the Earth plane, and has accumulated many friends.

"Where he now lives is a very plush place, and much more elegant than in some of the spirit worlds of other galaxies. He lived in another galaxy far, far from the Earth for many eons of time. But once he came to this realm he decided to stay, and to invite his friends to be here with him for special gatherings. So he has built quite an elaborate meeting facility, airstrip and all, for friends from many different spiritual dimensions and galaxies."

"After a session Bob and I had one time in his Earth lab, we were walking outside after dark and he looked up at the sky and said, 'Sometimes I get really homesick for the place where I used to live.' I just listened to him and wondered what he meant by that statement. Now I know. So you're going to bring me over to a large gathering?"

"Well, we can call it a 'Celebration of Life,' Rosalind, if you want to give it a title—like you used to give to all the many conferences you sponsored in the past."

"Whatever you call it is fine with me. Will there be anyone else there besides Bob that I will recognize?"

"Well, let's see—how about Larry?"

"Yessss!" I nearly shouted.

"And the two Patricks?"

"Yes, yes," I said enthusiastically.

"Ray and Tash will be there along with Ike and BC."

"Yes, yes, yes, yes!" I gleefully responded.

"And of course, AhSo, and your four Invisible Helpers who were always there to assist you in your research at the Monroe lab.

"Mr. Monroe is even inviting his daughter, Laurie, to be here for the celebration, though she will be here only as an invisible observer, rather than an active participant. He wants her to see the kinds of gatherings he is sponsoring at this point in his spiritual growth. He knows she will be pleased with his activities and spiritual progress."

"Wow, this is getting more and more awesome as we talk," I said. "And I'm sure my guardian angels will be there as well."

"Absolutely. So now is the time to send out the energy-connection call to all who are invited."

"Okay . . . I just received my call—and I'll be there if you, Ray, and Tash will help raise my vibrations to the occasion," I said excitedly.

"Just relax and your Life Imprint images will be directed to your present energy system."

∞

"I am *so* excited that I ask you to send some special energy to help me get relaxed, Radiant Lady," I said. And just as I was wondering what I should wear for the occasion, I looked down and realized that I had my Monroe Institute T-shirt on. I usually wear this shirt only for special occasions, but I had put it on that morning, intuiting this special occasion, I guessed. The shirt is dark blue and has the Monroe Institute (TMI) emblem on it, with the white imprint of the soul floating out from the middle of an energy vortex. "Well, then," I said. "I'm ready to take my TMI shirt on to the next level!"

I was finally getting relaxed and beginning to pick up the images of the higher vibratory dimension being projected to me by Ray and Tash.

Oh, what a beautiful scene! I could see a large field of velvety green, with rolling hills in the distance. There were lakes on either side of the field of grass. The lakes were deep blue and aqua, with sparkling diamondlike forms floating on them. I was looking at these tiny forms from higher up, and I realized they were small sailboats.

The field was circular, like the emblem on my T-shirt, with stunning little huts around the circumference, which I decided were guest cottages. They were in rainbow colors and resembled something from Disney World. It looked like a village made up of small living structures from different cultures around the world. Actually, some of them—gold and silver metallic structures—must have been replicas from other galaxies because their shapes were unfamiliar.

Right in the middle of the velvety green field was a large dome-shaped building, seemingly made of glass. It was absolutely stunning, with changing, brilliant colors of different hues, sending out celestial music with each changing ray. Since there was daylight at all times, with no central sun, a glass structure seemed appropriate. I sensed that this was the Heavenly Conference Center. It certainly was heavenly, and like nothing I'd ever seen before.

I next noticed what looked like a landing field for airplanes. I could see five unusually shaped airplanes on the landing strip, and two disc-shaped UFO-type craft. Evidently, Bob's friends from another dimension were going to join his airplane race with their circular flying discs.

I could see up on a hill, surrounded by trees, what I took to be Bob's laboratory, where I visited before. I spotted two figures coming out of the lab building and I went to meet them. I felt like I was floating, but I was actually moving quite rapidly. When I was closer, I saw that the figures were Bob and Radiant Lady.

"Hi," I called. "I finally made it."

I started to ask Bob if he liked my T-shirt when I realized he had one on just like it. Then I looked over at Radiant Lady, and her flowing, beautiful, blue robe had the same white emblem on it as we had on our shirts.

"We really have this conference together," said Bob. "Everyone will have their out-of-body T-shirts on since everyone is out of body. No physical bodies allowed here! They're all left back on planet Earth. Our motto at the Monroe Institute has always been, 'We are more than our physical bodies.' So we are in our 'more than' forms—our soul/spirits!"

"That sounds good to me, Bob," I said. "My body is in need of one of those extreme makeovers that are all the rage on planet Earth. But of course, those extreme makeovers are *free* when you get over here because you can drop the whole dang body. So I'm glad to leave my body behind, at least temporarily."

"Let's go on down to the airfield," said Bob. "We promised you an air show—and you won't be disappointed."

As we walked toward the air strip, I asked, "What are those saucerlike forms beside the airplanes, Bob?"

"Oh, they belong to my friends from my original galaxy. We all fly our air ships with our minds, of course, and we thought it would be fun to see how the saucer shapes move through this very refined atmosphere."

"So, are you going to be flying in the show?"

"Of course! This is mine, here," Bob replied, as he put on his goggles.

I looked, and he had a two-seater bi-plane with an open cockpit. Another plane looked much like Bob's and I asked who the two men were who were climbing into it.

"Oh, they are the Wright brothers," Bob said. "That's Orville at the front, and Wilbur in the back."

I was taken aback. "But how did you get Orville and Wilbur Wright to come to your air show?"

"I just sent out the energy invitations with my mind, just like you mailed invitations to your conference leaders back on planet Earth. They had the choice of coming or not coming—and here they are! Everyone is quite friendly over here with no Earth-like competition. We're all perfect here anyhow, so we don't have to compete to make ourselves look better."

"Who is going to fly with you, Bob?"

"You're welcome to climb in the back of my plane," he said, smiling.

"Well, since there's no death here in case of a crash, I have nothing to fear. Thanks, I'll take you up on your offer."

"And thanks for your confidence in my flying," replied Bob.

"Since you are flying this with your thoughts, I have a feeling that we will really shine, since I know you have an even more powerful mind in your new spirit body," I said, to make up for my last statement.

"And since you are riding in my plane, you can use your mind to help in propelling the plane."

All of a sudden there was a lot of commotion among the people standing around the airstrip. Then we heard people shouting and waving at something that was fast approaching us in the air. We all looked up and were amazed to see a flying ship—a ship with large wings and a propeller in front. The ship seemed to be flying itself and we could see two forms in the front of the ship hanging over and waving to all of us below. As the ship started in for the landing, I realized to my amazement that it was Patrick and Patty dressed in pilot's outfits, goggles and all.

Bob said, "That's a true airship because it can be propelled in the air and land on the water as well."

The airship pulled in right beside us and Patrick and Patty climbed out.

"I got your message that the show is ready to start," replied Patrick, "but I was putting some finishing touches on my airship creation. What do you think of it, Bob?"

"I'm impressed, Patrick. You told me that you were going to create something special for this show and I'm glad you brought it here to display your mental genius."

In his goggles and flying outfit, Patty pranced around among the guests, obviously expecting compliments on his latest costume.

"Patty, come on over here and give me a lick," I said. "You look great. . . ."

He came over and sat on my feet like he always did, as I looked toward Radiant Lady to see how she was enjoying the moment. One of the other pilots had taken her into his plane. It was a fancy Piper Cub composed of exceptionally bright colors.

The beings that were flying the saucers did in fact look like the little people with big heads that I had met on a mother ship while I was doing my work in the Monroe Institute lab (described in *Cosmic Journeys* in the chapter entitled "Alien Energy Systems").

"So Bob, who gives the signal to 'start the mental engines'?" I asked.

"I do," Bob replied. "I've given instructions to fly up to the hills on the horizon, and then back to the airstrip."

Finally, everyone was in their planes ready to go. I sat in the seat behind Bob, eagerly waiting to see what would happen next. I remembered seeing several flashes of light, and the next thing I knew, Bob was climbing out of the seat in front of me.

"What's happening, Bob?" I asked. "Did you call off the show?"

"We just finished it! We mentally moved our planes to the hills in the distance and back to the airfield," Bob replied.

"I don't remember the plane moving," I said quizzically.

"Well, just like when we project ourselves from one place to another, we don't remember moving, but there is a flash of light and we are where we desire ourselves to be," chuckled Bob.

"So who won?" I asked.

"Everyone, of course," said Bob. "But I want to admit that we did this as another demonstration to let you know how quickly and effortlessly we can move around in this dimension, and besides, that there really is no competition in this realm. We just have fun and have great respect for each other's creative mentalities."

"But how was Patrick able to move his big boat with wings through the air slowly instead of instantly?"

"Well, that's a special trick of the mind and it takes some unique energy concentration to slow the process down. But over here, everything is possible."

"Well, I'm impressed. The show all happened so fast. I didn't see anything but a few flashes of light."

Everyone got out of their flying machines with big smiles on their faces and headed toward Bob. The Wright brothers walked over and shook Bob's hand, thanking him for inviting them to his air show. They disappeared, along with their plane, as did all the other participants who were not staying for the conference.

"Where did they go?" I asked.

"Oh, they just left and dissolved their planes, which they created just for this air show," Bob said. "Actually, other than 'pretend' racing, most of the fun is in creating our perfect flying craft. Our minds, which are basically our soul/spirit bodies, are so highly developed that it is a great joy to use them in creative endeavors. And our memories are far beyond what our memories were while on the Earth. We remember everything in great detail."

"So is everyone highly developed when they take on their new mental bodies?"

"Soul/spirit bodies here are in varying stages of development. Many of the very young souls need to take classes to learn to develop their mental skills," said Bob.

"So you have classes here taught by qualified instructors?"

"We have instructors of classes here on every subject you can imagine—and even subjects you can't imagine."

"That is quite exciting. I'm interested in what's next!"

"I've just sent out the thought for us to meet in the Heavenly Conference Center for a question-and-answer period."

Since I was standing beside Bob and Radiant Lady, they must have included me in their energy projection. I found myself sitting between them in an awesome hall. The shades of light were as stunning inside as they had been outside the conference center. The colors were tremendously energizing, and yet somehow relaxing. There was a very large table in the center of the hall. The chairs were extremely comfortable—almost like sitting on clouds. Suddenly, just as we arrived, others started appearing.

Seated around the table were my friends. AhSo was there with my

Invisible Helpers. Larry, BC, and Ike were seated with them, along with a beautiful form that must be my guardian angel. Then suddenly Patrick appeared at the table, and beside him Patty, our dog.

It was so striking and even comical to see everyone with a Monroe Institute T-shirt on, including Patty, who had changed out of his flying outfit.

"Bob," I asked, "how did everyone get these shirts? And they seem to fit everyone so nicely, including Patty!"

"When I sent out the energy invitations to everyone, I also sent a mental pattern of the garb they were to wear, which happened to be my Monroe Institute T-shirt pattern."

"So did someone make the shirts for them before they arrived?"

"No, simply by thinking of the pattern as their attire for this gathering, the T-shirts were on them when they manifested here."

"I think Patty looks especially good in his T-shirt. You know, Patty attended Guidelines sessions with me several times at the institute and enjoyed every minute of his time there. Just a month before he came over here, he went to a program with me, going around to every participant in the room as I gave my talk. It was as if he were saying goodbye."

Suddenly, Radiant Lady stood up and the whole room changed color. She emitted such a glow that it seemed as though a spotlight had come down on her from the top of the dome.

"Some friends from the next dimension are directing some very special energies to us as we gather here for this wonderful meeting of the minds and spirits," Radiant Lady began.

As she spoke, she commanded great attention and I had the strong feeling that she held a high position in this realm. I didn't know what kind of position, but I knew that someday that would be revealed as she had promised.

"We have come together to discuss issues and answer questions that will be of interest to people on Earth. For those of you who have a question that you think would be pertinent on the Earth plane, please raise it and someone around this conference table with knowledge on the subject will answer it."

Tash stood up and said he knew there would be questions on the part of humans as to where the seven dimensions are in relation to each planet. So he wondered if someone could give a brief explanation of this.

Radiant Lady said, "The slower vibrational levels are closest to the Earth, and radiate out into the etheric and light dimensions. The higher the vibration, the less dense the dimension is. And all planets in Earth's galaxy or all physical galaxies have the same energy patterns.

"But the number of the dimensions varies according to the energy patterns of the planet. Planets are live entities and evolve just as humans do. So some highly evolved planets throughout the millions of galaxies in God's universe have more than the Earth's seven dimensions. They all have their slow vibratory physical center and the higher vibratory realms extending out from them. Planets in all galaxies that no longer have life forms existing on them have the soul/spirit beings in their own special spirit worlds."

I stood up and asked for someone to speak on the "color vibrations" of this Summerland, or Love, Dimension.

AhSo seemed eager to speak on this subject, as he stood and looked around at the magnificence of the color in the conference center.

"The colors are much more magnificent once we have dropped the Earth bodies," he began. "We have a brilliant spectrum of energies far beyond the normal array of colors that humans are accustomed to on the Earth plane. The Earth spectrums are at a slower vibrational rate and have a clinging effect on the soul/spirit body."

Radiant Lady, as the great chairspirit that she is, asked AhSo to clarify what he meant by "spectrums."

AhSo responded with the following explanation: "There is a special energy field that surrounds each physical body, including the celestial bodies, stars, and planets. This energy field is the energy that keeps the life-force functioning. We can see this spectrum energy within your bodies and outside your bodies. When a human dies, this spectrum field absorbs the soul/spirit of the person and moves it to another vibratory level, thus out of the physical plane."

My curiosity got aroused as to how those in the spirit world would view our "death process." So I asked that question.

AhSo continued with: "It is quite an amazing experience to view the 'death process' from our side. It is very clear from our perspective that death is a magnificent cycle of life. The energies of the physical body just go blank, like a light bulb that burns out. From our side, we view the physical body turning greyish and view the rainbow spectrums of the soul/spirit body as it enters our dimension magnify a thousandfold. This would be blinding to physical eyes, but it is awe inspiring to those who are here to greet this newborn soul/spirit."

"But what if the person vibrates to a grey zone?" I asked.

"When the physical body of such a being goes blank and turns grey, we can view a 'grey blob' floating into the grey zone. It is always a happy occasion as relatives on this side, spirit guides, and angels view this happening and thus send out a prayer of love and protection to that being. Sometimes the power of those prayers can instantly transform the 'grey blob' to a 'light form.' It is not a radiant form, but a 'light' form that can be 'floated' into a Hall of Rest in the Summerland, or Love, Dimension. The spirit/soul of this being will sleep and rest for perhaps even centuries of Earth time, and when it awakens will begin viewing the Life Imprints of its past incarnations on planet Earth."

"That is a testimony of the power of Love and Prayer," I said.

Larry, in all his radiance, stood and said, "I think it is important for humans to realize how important a positive, peaceful, and even joyful passing can impact a soul/spirit that is making their transition."

"Yes," said Patrick, who stood up, eager to respond to Larry's comment. "The happier the soul/spirit is when making the transition, the easier it is for the soul/spirit to enter this new vibratory level. Dropping fear and embracing joy and happiness instantly changes the vibrations of the soul/spirit. And happiness and joy in those surrounding their loved one helps greatly in the transition. Singing joyful songs or playing music loved by passing soul/spirits is the best way to send them to their new Home."

"Oh, I agree," I replied. "I would love to have a choir singing the Hallelujah Chorus when I pass over."

Then Radiant Lady stood and made the point that happiness and joy help the energy body of the deceased to disconnect from the physical body more readily, and said she thought it would be good for someone around the conference table to speak to the Earth plane about "grief" and its role in the ending of the "Earth Tour."

At this point, Robert Monroe stood. "Grief is a very important emotion in the Earth plane because it is an instant energy processor. Grief helps to restructure your energies at the cellular level by filling in the spaces of the energy field of the deceased as their energy moves into another dimension.

Of course, a part of your loved one's energy always remains within you, but it is different."

"In what way?" I asked.

"When grief goes beyond its normal processing period, it is a powerful energy that overtakes your cells and stagnates your energy field. When you grieve too long, your life essence becomes like a frozen frame."

"So what about the grieving loved ones?"

"Prolonged grief on the part of loved ones is like a glue that globs onto the deceased soul keeping it stuck in the spectrum energies. This is that clinging effect we referred to earlier."

"So Bob," I continued, "is that why souls seem to stay around for at least three days, or until after the funeral or memorial service? I have heard stories that people who have died often view their own funerals or memorial services."

"Absolutely!" Bob said. "If there is grief on the part of a lot of people, then the soul gets caught in that web of clinging energy until those thoughts change. This often happens when someone experiences a sudden or tragic death or is well known and well loved by many."

"So after a person is buried or cremated, and people quit grieving or thinking about the deceased as much, then that soul/spirit is free from this Earth cobweb to go on its way? Is that how it works?"

"Precisely," said Bob. "And that is why loved ones from this side come to help pull the deceased away from the magnetism of the Earth spectrums. Nancy was right there for me when I dropped my dilapidated body."

"Bob, I want to change the subject and ask you another question."

"I'm open to any question."

"Do you meet some of those participants who are taking your institute courses and 'flying' out of their bodies?"

"All the time," Bob replied with excitement. "I meet them at the Park, which is a special location in this dimension that I created for my program participants. It is actually located around my Heavenly Conference Center. There I give them special instructions that they don't receive from their Earth trainers. I'm the trainer from this side, and I work together with the participants and their spirit guides who we also call their ISH, meaning Inner Self Helpers."

"So how many bodies do you have, Bob, that you can do all this work?"

"It is amazing what happens to your energy body when you die. It can be separated into numerous forms. Everyone who takes the course at the institute is connected to my energy when they think of me or hear my voice on the tapes. So therefore my energy is at work in their energy bodies. Anyone who thinks of me is instantly in my energy field, and a part of my energy connects with them. We are one, instantly."

"Thank you, Bob," replied Radiant Lady, as she stood to keep the energy of the conference moving. "Are there further questions or topics to cover?"

"Yes," said AhSo. His spirit hands smoothed his beautiful beard as he spoke. "I would like to comment on the basic energy differences of the Earth versus the spirit dimensions."

"Certainly, AhSo," continued Radiant Lady. "Time is not an issue here, go right ahead and speak."

"The energies on the Earth plane are linear," said AhSo. "Everything that has a beginning always has an ending. Thus the linear Earth plane has a dual nature. It has two sides. After saying that, however, I want to say that the dual nature of the Earth is only a perception. It is not dual in nature."

"So is it different in your realm?" I asked.

"Yes. We view our dimension as a circumference, meaning that it has a boundary. We do not have the constant beginnings and endings that are the basic makeup of the Earth dimension."

"I don't quite understand that," I said. "Could you clarify what you are saying."

"Yes, I would be happy to. There is only one reality. Reality is circular, with no beginning and no end. In the Earth plane, you experience life as being linear because your boundaries go from one side of the circle to the other. Therefore, you perceive everything as having two sides because you do not allow yourselves to comprehend the entire picture."

"What is the entire picture?"

"Reality consists of an unending circular essence, and it is patterned after the trillions of cells in the human body. All knowledge is contained in each cell. Therefore, Spirit is encased in every form on the planet. The Spirit in each is the All That Is."

"So these forms you refer to are people, animals, insects, plants, and so on."

"Yes. Then there are planet formations that are circular. They are similar to all the bodies that inhabit them. This moves on into galaxies that encompass planets that consist of Spirit, the All That Is."

"Oh, so it keeps going on and on. But it is all basically the same. So you are saying that if you know what one cell consists of and absorb that knowledge, you know all that there is to know?"

"Exactly."

At that point, AhSo was really stretching my mind and I asked, "Astronomers can see planets and stars and many, many galaxies. Is this all circular? And where did the big bang come from? Did it come from some circle somewhere?" I stopped myself and thought, "Actually, that's a corny question."

AhSo, being able to read my mind, replied, "Actually, that is a good question. All That Is consists of a circumference essence. The big bang, as you perceive it on Planet Earth, was a circumference of energy patterns. It outgrew its boundaries, and a birth took place. New galaxies were born. Have you ever experienced a birth?"

I thought for a second and replied, "Other than my own, I did see a baby born once."

"Then you know what the big bang is all about: the birth of a new energy pattern that outgrew its original boundary. When a baby outgrows its space in the boundary of the womb, it feels somewhat like a big bang to the mother when its head first appears in its new environment."

"So you mean that all the galaxies that we view through telescopes are the result of a pregnant galaxy?"

"That is a good description," replied AhSo. "The pregnant galaxy had multiple births when its internal energy fields were ripe and ready to start all over in a different space. New forms were born. Are you getting the picture?"

"I'm trying to. So galaxies have births and deaths just like cells, people, plants, and animals?"

"Exactly. This is a regular pattern in the physical universe. There have been many big bangs over eons in the physical dimension. And it continues, just as birth and death take place on your planet."

"So if galaxies are born, then do they have to die—or at least appear to die?"

"Everything in the physical dimension expands and contracts," said

AhSo. "When the center of some universe dies out, it becomes more dense and pulls into itself everything in its path. This is what you call a 'black hole.' It just transports matter into a higher vibratory dimension. Everything comes out at another level, which would be unseen to the human eye or the telescope. It is just like a human that dies and then appears in another dimension."

"That is awesome. It is amazing that the same pattern is encompassed in All That Is. So the All That Is, as you call it, is a textured circumference ranging from physical matter to a finer substance that we would call Spirit. Right?"

"Well said. The universe is a patterned energy vortex that grows into the full extent of its pattern, and then it contracts. A human starts as a seed that contains a pattern. When the pattern reaches its maturity, thus old age, it contracts, drops its original shell—the body—and then starts all over in another dimension with a new energy body—its soul/spirit. It is merely transformed into another form."

Now I was really on a roll. I asked, "When our sun explodes and becomes a black hole, will it be like a birth canal from the cosmic womb we are now in into another world? And is that a nonphysical universe?"

"It is. When a star collapses, it is contracting and pulling all the energy forms around it into its density. Everything that comes into it comes out into a less dense dimension."

I was thinking this through as I responded. "I guess the same principle applies to humans when they die. All the millions of cells in the body are pulled into its 'black hole of death,' and come out transformed in another energy body."

"That is a good analogy. The Earth is a living entity, just like a person. When the Earth dies naturally, all of its inhabitants will be born into a less dense universe or dimension."

Right at this point, Radiant Lady looked directly at me and said, "We must go, Rosalind. This conference will continue at a later period of Earth time. As you well know, we can always pick up right where we left off in this no-time dimension."

"You're my tour guide, Radiant Lady," I replied, "and I will do whatever you say. I'm ready to leave if you say it is time to go."

∞

Suddenly I found myself back at my computer, wondering what in the heck had happened! I was not sure why this session had been ended so abruptly. But I was sure I would find out in due time.

So goodbye now, friends. We'll be together again soon.

PART V

New Beginnings

13 Preparations for Doing Time on Earth

Tash and Ray were sending me a mental picture from a tour I had led to Guatemala and Honduras. Our tour group was in a most magnificent rain forest in an unpopulated part of northern Guatemala. The town was Tikal, the location of remarkable ancient Mayan ruins. There are pyramid structures that seem to reach to the sky. Little is known about these structures that were built in 300 to 900 A.D. They had been abandoned when they were discovered and no historian knows why they were and what happened to the people who lived there at one time.

David and I awoke very early on our first morning at Tikal and decided to take a walk to the area where the ancient ruins were located. We climbed the steps of one of the pyramids. Then we decided to climb the one that was known as the Ceremonial Pyramid. It was a bit different from most of the large structures in that it was largely overgrown with jungle foliage that had climbed almost to the top of the pyramid. There were only a few upper steps remaining exposed, but we were able to make our way to the top and look out over the jungle where the early-morning sounds were gently comforting.

I sat down and lay back on a flat stone surface as David did some explorations around the top of the pyramid. I closed my eyes and, without even trying, began to see pictures of activities that were evidently taking place right on this very spot. What I saw in my mind's eye shocked me. I saw the image of a beautiful young olive-skinned virgin being sacrificed by a high priest. I saw her struggle as the priest put her in a position to throw her down from the top of the pyramid to her death. The image was so real, and I became such an integral part of the event that I realized I was the young girl and David was the High Priest.

It was such a profound emotional experience for me that I had to stand up and shake off the intense energy that ran through my entire body. But I couldn't shake off the tremendous anger I felt toward David for sacrificing me to the gods.

I had an instant feeling of wanting to get even with him, and push him off the top of the pyramid. As he walked toward me smiling over what he had discovered on the far side of the pyramid, he reached to give me an early-morning hug as I braced myself to shove him off the edge. By the time he touched me, I realized that if I did indeed push him, he would just tumble into some of the jungle brush that had overgrown the lower part of the pyramid, getting a few bruises and scratches. Then, luckily, I came to my senses.

I quickly said to David, "Let's leave now. We must get back to the group and have breakfast with them." I could not bring myself to tell him what I had experienced until we arrived safely at the bottom of the pyramid. I had no idea after so many centuries why I would have that much emotional attachment to the event. And maybe I just had the fear that if I told him the story, it might bring it all up in his mind again and he would have the urge to push me off again.

Oh, well, who knows. And it doesn't even matter. We evidently had the experience written into our Life Charts for those incarnations. But I must have not had much spiritual evolution from the experience since I still had so much anger attached to the Life Imprints I was viewing.

Then the pictures faded.

∞

Then I was sitting, anxiously awaiting the arrival of Radiant Lady. But something strange was in the air. I did not sense her presence, but that of another energy.

"Hello, Rosalind. You should recognize me by my voice, since I have talked with you over many years of Earth time while we worked together in Mr. Monroe's Lab."

"AhSo!" I exclaimed. "I do recognize your voice—and your energy. It is great to have you visit with me. What is the occasion?"

"Come with me. I have something very important to show you," he said, with an animation in his voice I had never quite heard before.

"I'm ready to go," I said somewhat breathlessly. "What should I do in preparation for going with you instead of with Radiant Lady?"

"Just relax, and Ray and Tash will send a Life Imprint into your mind that will help you experience what I have to reveal to you."

"Yes . . . I am relaxing," I replied, with a feeling of great anticipation of what was to happen to me.

Suddenly, I found myself on the steps of an incredible white marble building, the likes of which I had never seen on the Earth plane. I have been in Greece and this building had something of the appearance of ancient monuments still standing in Athens, like the Parthenon.

I was standing in the front of the building, and when I looked up I saw imprinted across the doorway of this magnificent edifice the words "Hall of Justice."

Then I noticed AhSo beside me, dressed in an awesome, ruby-colored robe, with gold embroidery around the neck and on the sleeves. He wore a wide golden belt around his waist with Chinese symbols on it, which must have represented something from his incarnation on Earth many centuries ago.

Our eyes met and I felt a tingle go entirely through my soul/spirit body. His depth of presence was so powerful that my energy was magnified by a mere glance from him, his eyes like pools of wisdom within his ancient energies. He stepped into my energy body, and suddenly we were inside the building in a very large hall holding a large U-shaped table.

Around the table were many highly dignified spirit beings. The men all had long silver-white hair and beards, and wore beautiful silver robes. Women were also around the table, dressed in flowing silver robes. Behind these beings stood a large array of stunningly beautiful large angels with elegant wings shimmering in the magnificently lighted room. It was an awesome sight.

I stood dazzled as I began to receive mental messages from AhSo, my spirit guide: "You are in the presence of God's Master Teachers, who are His spokespersons in this dimension. These are the elders who reside on this council for eternity. There are many councils like this; and there are always 18 members on each council. After you went through your orientation session to prepare you to return to Earth for your present incarnation, this council looked over the chart that your orientation team created with you to ready you for your descent back into the physical plane of existence."

"Fascinating!" I thought. "I can't believe I would receive this kind of attention—that this magnificent group of spirit beings and angels would take a personal interest in *me*."

"Every soul/spirit is important in the eyes of God," said AhSo. "And every human who exists on planet Earth gets this kind of attention from the council before going back to Earth for a new learning experience that will help them grow spiritually. But there is one exception, which I will tell you about shortly."

"This is amazing," I thought, as my eyes went around the table, looking at each elder. Then my eyes were drawn to one particularly beautiful lady elder, and I shouted out loud in my mind, "Oh, my goodness, that is Radiant Lady!"

"Yes," said AhSo. "I wondered when you would recognize her."

Just at that moment, Radiant Lady looked at me and sent an incredible ray of energy into my soul/spirit body. It seemed as if all activities in the room stopped, and all eyes were now on me. Not only were the elders looking toward me, but the angels as well. At first I thought that I was disturbing their activity. Then I knew from all the thoughts directed to me that I *was* the focus of their activity.

Radiant Lady, in all her splendor, rose from her seat and addressed the whole council. "I want to thank all of you for intervening in Rosalind's recent illness, and helping to keep her soul/spirit in the physical realm and on target in completing the task that many of us on this side are working on with her. When you, as her council, okayed the orientation chart before she entered the Earth plane, she had convinced you that she was capable of overcoming two illnesses of the heart—both congestive heart failure.

"Rosalind had planned these events to occur just before each of her books was published, as a demonstration of how powerful the help is from this dimension. However, she had a very difficult time staying in the body the second time around. We were able to help keep her in the body because that was not an option point of departure for her. Thanks to all of you for helping her stay in the Earth dimension. And I know that she sends her thanks as well."

"Oh, yes, yes!" I thought, as I directed my gratitude to all the elders and angels in this large and awesome council hall.

I received a thought from Radiant Lady that it would be appropriate for me to reveal what had taken place over the past month. The whole event was absolutely shocking and devastating to me, and it was still a little painful to think about reviewing it.

With no time in their dimension, the elders merely relaxed to listen to my own personal interpretation of the events that took place during my sudden illness and just-as-sudden healing.

A month before, I had turned the manuscript of this book over to David, my ex-husband, whom I have referred to throughout this book. With his brilliant mind (remember he graduated *magna cum laude* from Harvard), he has been given the gift of editing and proofreading. His present wife, Mary, and I agree that the books we each have written could not have been completed adequately without his masterful proofreading touch.

Since David was so generously helpful to me in getting this book ready for publication, I want to put in a commercial for Mary Morgan McKnight's book, which can be ordered through a "publishing-on-demand" company in Canada. (I love the book and highly recommend that you purchase it. You can go to any bookstore and order it by giving the ISBN number listed in the back of this book or you can order it over the Internet.) I learned as I looked at the cover of her book, *Jogging Through Space,* that we both have master of divinity degrees. And speaking of illnesses, Mary tells her amazing story of recovery from a life-threatening illness—a brain tumor—and features 60 pathways to feeling better.

One woman who read Mary's book had been contemplating suicide. The reader was amazed at the incredible odds that Mary had overcome on her journey toward healing. But Mary's awesome and positive attitude in the face of her struggles turned the reader's life around completely; she realized that her problems were nothing compared with what Mary had experienced.

The evening that I turned my manuscript over to David for proofing I suddenly got lung congestion without even a sore throat. Within a couple of hours, my lungs became so congested that I had trouble breathing. Whew! Speaking of a life-threatening illness, the congestion turned into a full-blown flu virus infection, which lasted for three weeks.

After two weeks of coughing myself to sleep each night, I went to my doctor's office, where I was seen by a nurse practitioner. She became concerned about my past history of congestive heart failure. So she took an X ray of my chest and checked my blood. Nothing after the second week of this virus pointed to congestive heart failure.

Three weeks after the onset of these symptoms, I felt I was getting better, but I was still very tired most of the time. On the fateful weekend before St. Patrick's Day, I drove to a health food store to look for something to give me more energy. On the way to the store, I put my foot on the clutch at a stoplight and my foot seemed detached from my body. Then I seemed to have no sensation in my left hand and arm. I couldn't imagine what was happening to me. I felt terrible but was able to drive.

I have hardly ever been sick in my life. I have always believed in positive and healthy attitudes that help to keep you well.

After I parked at the health food store, I had trouble walking and inside the store I stumbled like I was drunk. When I asked the clerk for something to give me energy, she showed me some pills and, as I took the bottle from her, I almost passed out. But I was able to pull some cash out of my purse to pay for the pills before I stumbled back to my car.

At this point, I knew I was too sick to drive, so I sat there in a reclined position for about an hour, waiting to feel better in order to drive home.

There was an Applebee's restaurant next door, so I drove my car through their take-out lane, thinking that perhaps I was weak because I needed some food. A young man came out to serve me and I told him how sick I felt. I ordered a sandwich and he kindly brought me the sandwich, along with some orange juice that I hadn't ordered, thinking it would help me. Then he even offered to call an ambulance to take me to the hospital, which I declined, still not realizing the seriousness of my condition. I took a couple of bites of the sandwich and decided that I should try to get home as soon as possible. It now seems a miracle that I was able to drive myself home in the condition I was in.

That night and all day Sunday I had so much difficulty breathing that I felt I would die. It's an awful, awful, awful feeling to try to take a breath and find that there is no air intake because the heart is too weak.

I was so sure I might die that I would think throughout the weekend something like, "I can't believe 'they' are going to 'take me out' to experience the afterlife firsthand before the book is even published." Of course, that was the victim attitude of "why are they doing this to me?" and I really don't believe we are victims.

By Monday morning, I realized that I needed an emergency visit with my cardiologist. I had such a "congested voice" from my flu virus that when I called the cardiologist, the receptionist who answered blew me off with "Oh, sweetie, you just have a cold. Just call your regular doctor."

So I called my regular doctor's office and they arranged for me to see the nurse practitioner that I had seen the week before. She checked me and I asked for an appointment to have an "echo" heart scan. She said she would have to get the approval of one of the doctors in their clinic. There were several doctors and one who didn't know my history might not have approved it.

However, the angels were at work. When we walked into the hall, I came face to face with my wonderful doctor (who, by the way, had taken most of my parapsychology classes at the local community college). Dr. Cannon was just coming out of a room after having seen a patient. He is such a popular and good doctor that an appointment with him must be booked a year in advance. He said, smiling, "Rosie, how are you doing?" And when I replied, "Not good!" he realized from my voice that there was something terribly wrong.

Then the nurse asked him to set up an appointment with my cardiologist to have the echo scan. It was ten o'clock in the morning and they were not able to get an appointment until 3:30 that afternoon. Having lost considerable sleep over the weekend and feeling very sick, I drove to the cardiologist's office, put my seat back, and slept soundly for the three hours.

For the echo heart scan, a nurse placed me on my side on a table and moved the scanning device over my heart. I could hear strange gurgling sounds, which didn't sound good to me.

When the nurse finished, I asked for the prognosis. She said, "Not good. The muscles in your heart are functioning at the rate of 10 to 15 percent compared to the normal 65 percent." Six years earlier, when I had had congestive heart failure, my heart had been functioning at 15 to 20 percent. With my heart pumping so slowly, I was literally smothering and I could have died within hours. A friend of mine with a similar condition had died overnight because they thought that she merely had a cold.

The doctor on duty at the cardiology facility called my doctor and gave him the prognosis and I was told to go immediately back to his office. My wonderful angel, Dr. Cannon, met me at his office door and gave me a choice of either going home and following his treatment schedule or going directly to the hospital, which was three blocks away. He strongly urged me to go to the hospital. Of course, I respected his opinion. I actually had no one at home to take care of me other than my supportive cats.

So by six that Monday evening, I was a patient in the cardiology division of our outstanding Lynchburg General Hospital. It is amazing that learning what is wrong makes one feel better, no matter how serious the situation is. So it was a comforting feeling to have all sorts of snaps stuck on my chest and wires attached to them so that the instruments at the nurses' desk could monitor my heart. Then they inserted an intravenous tube into my arm and injected me with something that would begin to take the fluid out of my body.

It seemed like I was up every 15 minutes all night with releasing the heart fluid into a container that kept tabs on how much fluid had accumulated in my overworked heart or lungs or wherever it accumulated. By morning, I had released two large containers of fluid and finally was able to breathe without gasping for breath.

Since I really couldn't sleep that first night in the hospital, I lay there being aware that there were lots of angels around my bed looking after me and helping me in the healing process. I would actually put my hand out and ask the angels to hold my hand. It was very comforting to feel their presence.

An article that had influenced my life strongly several years before was about a woman who loved God so completely that when she got cancer after having a baby, she was always radiantly happy, thinking, "Love God no matter what happens." The nurses and doctors would come into her room amazed at her positive and joyful attitude in the face of death.

Eventually, the woman died, leaving behind a husband and a newborn baby. Her husband and father were in the room when she left her body and the room was filled with such light and joy that it affected her husband and father dramatically. And she affected me dramatically as well.

I reread the article the weekend I felt so bad, just before entering the hospital. I kept thinking: "Love God, no matter what happens." And then I would feel good in spirit, even though I felt like I was slipping away.

The third day in the hospital was St. Patrick's Day. On that day I had the startling realization that I had been in the hospital exactly six years before during the same week. That was just before my first book, *Cosmic Journeys*, was published. And here I was, six years later, in the hospital with the same challenge just before my second book, *Soul Journeys*, was going to be published. I thought, "Something strange is going on here. But I'm not sure what."

When my cardiologist visited me on Tuesday morning, he walked up to my bed and said, "Déjà vu," and we both laughed. I grabbed him and hugged him, and said, "Oh, Dr. Moore, I am so happy to see you. You helped to heal my heart before, and I know you can do it again."

This wonderful cardiologist said, "The medicines miraculously healed your heart before, and I fully expect that to happen again."

I said, "I know you are right," and thought to myself, "The medicines along with all the prayers coming my way will help my heart to reset itself."

Then I got hugs every morning from my beloved Dr. Cannon, who always had a healing smile. One day, he even came in with his smiley-face tie on.

When I told him about my left foot and arm feeling "detached" from my body, he looked at me strangely, and said, "I think your heart was so weak that you had a minor stroke."

Then I realized what had been happening to me while I was in the health food store. I had been having a stroke due to a heart that was being overcome by fluid. It was as if my heart was crying. This condition had come on almost overnight. Dr. Cannon thought it might have been caused by the virus that had invaded my body. (And thank heavens, there are no viruses in the afterlife. . . .)

I had named my heart "Strongheart" six years earlier, and so I started talking to and thanking Strongheart again for keeping me alive all of 70 years.

After five days in the hospital—the same length of time I had been in six years before—I was released and drove myself home. A couple of people offered to drive me home, but my car was at the hospital and, also, I'm a stubborn Capricorn. (Elvis Presley and his twin brother, who didn't survive, were born on my birthday, January 8, a year after I was born.)

But the half-hour trip home took me five hours. I had to stop at the Wal-Mart pharmacy to get my prescriptions and to pick up some cat and dog food. I was so weak I had trouble walking through the store, so I asked for help in checking out. I was so glad to get home and into my own bed, where I could finally sleep without having my "vitals" taken. I was so weak that I had trouble getting out of bed. I slept almost continuously for five days.

But something amazing happened toward the end of that week. A friend named Neil called me from the Monroe Institute. He was taking the course entitled "MC²" (called MC-squared). He and his new bride, Wendy, wanted to come and visit me on Friday after the course was over. I told him that I had been in the hospital and didn't know if I would be well enough to accept visitors.

The MC² group works on moving energy—bending spoons, making plants grow faster, and so forth. So Neil asked me for permission to allow the group to send healing energy to me. Of course, I said, "Yes!"

I got a call back, saying that they would be working on me at exactly 11:45 A.M. the next day.

I was very weak when I got out of bed to feed my animals that next morning. I fed the cats, and then lay down and rested before feeding my dogs. I was sitting in a chair in my living room an hour before the healing session was to take place. I had planned to go back to my guest room and be stretched out on the bed when the invisible healing teams arrived. But I fell sound asleep in the living room chair.

Then at exactly 11:40 A.M., I head a voice loud and clear say, "Welcome," and I woke up startled.

"Oh," I thought, "the healers are here!" and went to the bedroom and lay on the bed.

Three cats immediately took positions around me. My very affectionate cat Lucinda lay right on my left by my heart. My white cat Angel lay at my feet. And my tabby cat Ronnie lay on my right. It was as if they positioned themselves to help in the healing.

I became wide-awake and alert during the healing session. I was clearly aware of energy beings surrounding me, and angels backing them up. It was a powerful session. I could actually feel pressure on my heart as they were working with me. At exactly 12:12 P.M., I felt they were finished and it seemed like someone "zipped up" my heart. (Later, I did indeed learn that the group healing ended at exactly 12:12 P.M.)

I lay there about 20 minutes longer, allowing the healing energy that was sent to me to be absorbed throughout my entire body. Then I got out of bed and started walking slowly into the living room. I realized immediately that I was more steady on my feet.

I had left my front door open, so that the glass door would let more light in. I looked toward the door as I walked into the living room and right inside sat the most gorgeous fruit basket I have ever seen. It had a large white ribbon on it, and a note attached: "Love, your friends from the Monroe Institute." Actually, the MC² group had nothing to do with this gift, but everything coordinated beautifully.

The more I walked around the house, the more I realized how much better I felt. My house was so dirty, since it hadn't had any attention for a full week, and I suddenly felt an urge to clean house as I realized the strong presence of angels helping to guide me.

Since angels don't talk, but communicate only by telepathy, one sent the message that there were angels present who are in charge of mental energy and also angels in charge of physical energy.

Then the mental energy angels began guiding me, telling me that mental energy is unlimited and comes from God. They said that if I would follow the guidance of my mental energy, and concentrate mindfully on only one thing at a time, I would overcome any awareness of any physical weakness.

So I started cleaning. I washed a large stack of dishes first, concentrating on one dish at a time, enjoying cleaning each one. Before I knew it, the dishes were done.

Then my physical energy angel suggested that I could rest a bit, which I did. Then I decided to scrub the kitchen floor. I moved all the furniture out of the kitchen and started scrubbing, enjoying each thing I did. The time seemed to pass quickly. Before I knew it, it was midnight and I had also scrubbed and cleaned my master bathroom. The longer I worked, the better I felt.

I then heard the thoughts from my communicating angel: "A body at rest remains at rest. A body in motion remains in motion." At midnight I wasn't even tired or sleepy, but decided I needed to rest anyway. So I lay down on the couch and watched TV for an hour and then decided to go to bed.

I woke up the next morning feeling so good that I decided to call the Monroe Institute and see if I could drive up that evening and have dinner with the MC² group. I wanted to hug each one of them and thank them personally for the marvelous energy they had sent me.

I was invited to join the group for dinner at six. I suggested that I wanted to surprise the MC² trainers and group. I did. They were thrilled to see me and learn the results of the energy they had sent me.

After dinner, I talked with the group and shared in detail what had happened to me the previous day. And many shared the experiences they had had as healers, which coordinated with what had happened to me.

As I left, I was surprised when they gave me a beautiful handmade card with $200 cash in it. They said that this was a donation to help feed my animals. They had collected this money, expecting Neil and Wendy to deliver it to me on Friday. Since I had missed a month and a half of work, this money helped tremendously. The next day, Neil and Wendy came to visit and brought another $100 from the group to help feed the animals.

Then the money continued coming to me to replace the income I was losing from not working. I realized how the angels were continually at work helping to heal me at all levels, physically and financially.

As I am writing this, another week has passed since my healing and I feel better daily. I know that my heart has "reset" itself. I have an appointment with my cardiologist next week, and I fully expect him to say that my heart function has returned to normal.

Life is good! God is good! I keep a sign in front of me at all times: Expect a Miracle. And miracles are an everyday occurrence in my life, as they are in yours!

I called David McKnight and told him what had happened to me from the day I gave him my manuscript. He replied, "I'm sure that Radiant Lady would *not* let you die," which indeed was correct.

A prayer that I have prayed daily for the last two years, which has helped create miracles in my life is "The Prayer of Jabez." It comes from I Chronicles 4:10:

And Jabez called on the God of Israel saying,
"Oh, that You would bless me indeed
And enlarge my territory
That Your hand would be with me,
And that You would keep me from evil,
That I may not cause pain."
So, God granted him what he requested.

I always end by saying "And keep me in the Light that I might express only Love and Joy. Thank you, God, thank you, God, thank you, God. . . ."

So there I was, still in the presence of the council of elders, telling my amazing story of recovery. This heart health challenge had been the most difficult thing I had experienced in this lifetime. And now I realized that it was in my "chart," and I planned for it to happen!

"But, Rosalind," said AhSo, "remember that you were in Paradise/Nirvana when you planned it. You had not a care in the world. You set it up as another challenge that would help you grow spiritually.

"We are not letting you stay too long," continued AhSo. "I brought you here to reveal to you one of the roles that Radiant Lady plays in the overall scheme of things in the afterlife and in your life as well. She is a very powerful spiritual being and one of God's very dedicated helpers. Besides being on the council as an elder, she is also the head of your orientation team. That is why you have always felt that she is an important part of you, because she is."

"AhSo, what is this orientation team you refer to?"

"Everyone that enters the Earth realm has an orientation team made up of their spirit guides, orientation team leaders, guardian angels, and many others whom you have chosen to help you decide the details of your Earth-Life College before you attend," AhSo explained. "You would never attend college without knowing where you are going, what you are going to major in, where you will live while there, who your roommates will be, and so forth."

"That is correct, AhSo. But when you say 'everyone,' you really mean that everyone who now exists on planet Earth has an orientation team?"

"Absolutely. Most souls/spirits have orientation teams, but those of the dark energies have teams of angels who have to send them back in and oversee their activities. Everyone is important in the eyes of God. *The concept that many people come back in certain roles to be punished for something they have done in a past life is not true.*

"Everything that is chosen to be a part of a Life Chart has an important role in helping the soul/spirit to evolve into a higher level of spirituality. God is not a vengeful God and punishes no one. God is pure Love energy and loves all of his children equally. In fact, God created all of you for Himself—to appreciate and enjoy you as His Beloved Children of Light."

"So how does the orientation team work to help create a chart?" I asked.

"Come with me," said AhSo. "I think the elders have finished their meeting, and Radiant Lady is now free to join us."

Radiant Lady rose from a beautiful marble chair with purple cushions and stood beside me. With her on one side and AhSo on the other, I was transported into another very large room.

"Are we still in the Hall of Justice?" I asked.

"Yes, we are," replied Radiant Lady. "We are now in the room where we set up your chart 70 years ago in Earth time, before you incarnated back to Earth."

∞

I suddenly realized that I was experiencing the Akashic record of my original orientation session. I was actually being projected back into the session to experience exactly what happened in planning for my current incarnation on Earth.

"This room that we are now in is our orientation room, located in the Hall of Justice," Radiant Lady explained.

The room was vast and made of white marble with white marble benches and tables arranged like a classroom. I looked around and noticed that the walls were lined with maps, charts, lists, and other visual tools to help us get our task done.

Radiant Lady, as the orientation leader, sat at the head of the table. AhSo, my spirit guide, sat beside me.

Much to my surprise, my brother Larry sat across from me, smiling. Now I realized why I always felt so close to him in life, even though he was born when I was 13; he was on my orientation team committee, thus very connected to my overall energy patterns. And there were several other souls there whom I recognized.

Radiant Lady stood up and pointed to a chart that had "Life Theme" written on it.

"So Julianna has chosen to have 'Spirituality' as her basic Life Theme," said Radiant Lady. "This is the force that will push her soul through life day by day."

I was surprised to hear her call me "Julianna." I have always loved that name, but never knew why. And it is interesting that my first name in this lifetime is Anna; I am Anna Rosalind. So JuliAnna must be the name I am known by in the spirit world. And my very intuitive mother tuned into at least part of my spiritual name by making Anna my first name. What a revelation!

"Now what will her Secondary Life Theme be?" asked Larry.

"That will be the conflict that she has to overcome to achieve her basic life theme," replied Radiant Lady. "That would be 'patience.' She has to overcome impatience, judgment of others, and fear of rejection in this upcoming life in order to fulfill her theme of spirituality."

"Now we have to add a challenge to her life," said AhSo, "that she will have to work hard to master. And that would be finances. She will have to concentrate at many levels to bring prosperity into her lifetime to come. She has been working toward this for many life experiences."

Suddenly, Tash and Ray appeared right behind Radiant Lady's chair. They indicated to her that they had collected information from all my lifetimes on Earth, and handed her a chart that would help us in choosing the details of my life experience—such as parents, brothers, and sisters, marriage partner, physical appearance, living locations on the planet, friends I would have throughout my lifetime, pets I would have, and so on.

Then Tash and Ray indicated that we would choose the exact date and time of my birth and several options for leaving the Earth and returning to my real Home in Paradise.

Two options went up on the board, and those were the times of my congestive heart failure experiences. But the committee decided that those would not be actual options because I would stay on the Earth after experiencing healing interventions by prayers, angels, guides, doctors, medicines, friends, and others.

We did look at one of the real options I had when I almost drowned as a child. We did not discuss the other options because they hadn't happened in my life as yet and the committee didn't want to influence my choices to come.

Then my suicide challenges came up.

"Suicide is never an option for exiting the Earth," stated Radiant Lady. "Individuals cannot break their Earth Contract, which is the most sacred contract any soul/spirit will ever make."

"Yes," continued AhSo. "The ceremony with the 'Earth-Resident-to-Be' and their orientation committee, council of elders, God, angels, and guides is one of the most powerful 'contractual experiences' any soul/spirit will ever have. That contract is witnessed by so many who helped to create it that if it is broken, the residue hangs on for eons of time and no-time. Many, many souls, spirits, humans, and even God are affected by the breaking of a sacred Earth Contract.

"Everything that God has created is set up, so that all of the soul/spirits who have wandered away from the Light into the shadows of a denser Earth can find their way back to where they originated. But God never judges or gives up on us. Nothing but Love is ever directed to us in our cosmic, soul journeys back to our original forms.

"The whole structure of God's creations is set up so that we will always have unlimited, unconditional assistance on the journey back to our original life forms of pure Spirit to live and exist blissfully in God's Realm. We will all eventually come face to face with our Father and Creator when we are back where we belong."

I looked over at AhSo as he finished his beautiful dissertation and, seeing tears of joy in his eyes, realized that the reason he chose to be a spirit guide for so many eons is his incredible Love of God.

Radiant Lady stood up and changed the energy in the orientation meeting. "We will continue with Julianna's chart. There are many reasons for suicide and sometimes it is because a soul has chosen a chart that is too difficult to fulfill. That is not the case with Julianna. She was just homesick for her physical home and her spiritual Home.

"In many cases, when suicide occurs the soul is sent right back to Earth without experiencing any time in Paradise/Nirvana—to deal again with issues that caused the break in the Earth Contract. In some cases, the soul who breaks their Earth Contract remains suspended between Earth and Heaven in a type of limbo until the time that they were supposed to leave according to their Contract.

"During this period, they review their Akashic records over and over from their Progressive or Collective Soul's perspective. There is only one soul/spirit with thousands of Earth-life experiences inherent in their energy. When some on Earth speak of a soul experiencing all of its lifetimes at once, it is that all of these Earth-life experiences are *always* there within the soul/spirit's Life Imprint files, their Akashic records to be drawn upon whenever necessary for positive and continued spiritual progression. But the only reality, as we have expressed before, is the Spirit—all else is fake and not real energy. Thus lifetimes are an illusion of the Soul, but important in the growth of the Spirit. . . .

"So most suicides experience the same life reviews that the dark energy souls experience, and all for the purpose of coming fully back into their own Light Essence. . . .

"The Life Imprint Reviews that the suicides and dark energies experience show all the progress they have made throughout thousands of life experiences on the Earth plane.

"This is a *rehabilitation* for the soul/spirit, helping it review all the positives of its previous journeys to help it continue on its one and only important journey back to the Godhead."

Larry intervened at this point to ask a question. "Radiant Lady, respected elder and orientation committee Chairspirit, I have a question."

"Yes, Larry," Radiant Lady responded. "Do ask your question now."

"Thank you," Larry replied. "Now what about the dark entities that are in the very slow vibrations. It was pointed out that they do not have the same kind of orientation committee and elder review that most soul/spirits have. So what is their story?"

"Well," replied Radiant Lady. "These very slow vibratory soul/spirits are overseen by God's very special legions of angels. When these rebellious souls are not cooperative with the Light Forces in making decisions in regard to returning to Earth, they are often *sent* back immediately after exiting the Earth. However, there are still many, many unenlightened souls remaining in the grey zones between earth and the afterlife as we discussed in an earlier chapter. Each soul living in darkness or light is extremely important in the eyes of God and is dealt with on an individual basis by the legions of Angels.

"Each of these soul/spirits has many, many angels that oversee it. They actually have some special work to do in helping some souls fulfill their Earth Contracts. Some souls actually agree to leave the Earth by being murdered by one of these dark entities. It is a very tough situation on the Earth plane, but forgiveness and unconditional love are usually the lessons learned by many."

Then Larry asks another question. "This has been my first time on an orientation committee. When we finish Julianna's projected lifetime, does the chart then go back to the elders for review for a stamp of approval?"

"Absolutely, Larry," Radiant Lady answered. "The elders, backed by the legion of angels who are all very tuned into life at all levels, will look over the prospective new Earth resident to determine whether the soul/spirit is capable of fulfilling that which is planned. Many times they will, from their higher perspective of knowledge of the soul/spirit, convince that soul/spirit not to take on challenges that are too difficult."

"Thank you. Also I want to know if souls/spirits can change their minds after going through the orientation, and decide to stay in Paradise or Nirvana a while longer."

"Absolutely. But only *before* the Contractual Ceremony. After the Ceremony has taken place, the potential Earth resident is destined to fulfill it and go back to Earth for another spiritual-evolutionary process."

"So then after the Contractual Ceremony, do the soul/spirits go right on back to Earth—and what is the process to get them there?"

"They go right over to the Towers, which is their departure location," replied AhSo. "There they meet with friends and loved ones who wish them the best for their lifetime to come, and then they leave them alone to contemplate their new beginnings back on Earth. Just before incarnating on Earth, each soul is anointed by a master. In some cases it is Jesus, or Buddha, for example. But in many cases, it is an evolved being from one of the higher dimensions."

"Then the soul goes into a room and stretches out on a table," said Radiant Lady. "It is put into a light sleep and sent to the womb of the mother it has chosen to be with. In some cases the soul does not enter the womb right away, but waits until the time that it *must* enter, which is the fifth month."

"And of course the many souls that come to Earth and are adopted for one reason or another definitely chose the *parents that adopted them*. There is the physical mother who offers her womb for the birth and then the mother and father who are contractually chosen before the soul/spirit enters the Earth dimension. It seems complicated, but where the soul/spirit ends up is exactly where it is supposed to be for that particular Earth experience.

"However, if the soul/spirit chooses to die in the womb before it is born, that might have been written into the contract for a spiritual growth lesson for the parents-to-be.

"Also, when a soul leaves its Earth body in the first year, that is usually in the Earth Contract and is only done for the spiritual growth of the parents and family of the potential new Earth resident. Also, in some cases the soul/spirit realizes that it forgot some very important spiritual issues that should have been considered before coming in and it leaves shortly after arriving on the planet only to come in at another specified time slot to the same family."

The scenes from the orientation committee meeting began to fade.

∞

"Thank you, Radiant Lady, for your Life Imprint review," I said. "As you took me back to review the preparations I made before coming in, I remembered what happened. And perhaps as others read this, they too will remember the things most important for their growth in this lifetime. It is to be hoped that most reading this book will remember what their Life Purpose is and it will help them to cope with challenges. And let me add an experience that happened to me that verifies what you just said."

"Yes, do feel free to share that information," replied Radiant Lady.

"Well, there is a man by the name of Raymond Moody who has written some important books about the afterlife. He lived in Charlottesville, Virginia, at one point in his life. I became friends with him and his wife, Louise, and offered to help him answer the many letters he had received from people. That was before e-mail became the popular form of communication.

"I would sort through the letters and then help him to answer them. One letter struck me at a very deep level and I never forgot it. The lady said that she had a four-year-old daughter who said to her one day that she had tried to come in before, but wasn't able to stay. And then the child replied very enthusiastically, 'But I got in, Mama. And I'm so happy that I made it this time. . . .'

"The mother was astounded by the child's story. The mother had lost an earlier fetus at around three months and the child had no conscious knowledge that this had happened to the mother."

"Yes," replied Radiant Lady. "When the fetus has to abort itself, this is a challenging spiritual lesson for the expectant mother and father. So the Earth child then comes in at a later time when it has a healthy fetus to enter. Life then continues as planned in the Earth Contract."

"Oh, Radiant Lady," I continued. "Thank you for sharing this very pertinent spiritual information. I know that it will be a lot of help to many on Earth who have gone through the pain of losing a child—you know, the Disconnect Principle."

"Yes, Rosalind, and in this case the Reconnect Principle does manifest on planet Earth."

"That is wonderful to hear. And I want to say that I am very impressed with who you *really* are and how our lives intertwine. I feel absolutely humbled by the knowledge that you, with your awesome spiritual energy, have chosen to work with me in my spiritual growth."

"Thank you for expressing your true feelings about me," Radiant Lady replied. "But, remember, you are also Radiant JuliAnna Rosalind, and the purpose of this book is to help souls/spirits remember who they really are, so as to give them more faith in God, and hope for the joys of returning to their real Home.

"Speaking of returning to one's real Home," said Radiant Lady, "please take my hand and I will escort you to the dimension where I reside when I am not doing my service work with souls/spirits, as I have done for eons."

"Certainly," I said, and reached out my hand for hers.

When she grasped my hand, we were instantly transported to a realm of light so intense that I found it difficult to absorb.

I realized that she was taking me into one of the higher realms of light that was beyond my normal vibrations.

I sensed that she lived in the sixth or seventh realm, the dimension of pure Light and Love in God's own backyard.

As we traveled through the incredibly invigorating atmosphere and I was able to see some scenes below, I realized that I had been taken here before by AhSo and my Invisible Helpers. (I tell about the journey in *Cosmic Journeys*.)

I could see in the distance the beautiful City of Light. Before, when I had been brought into this higher dimension, they had to put a type of filter on my eyes so that I could view the crystalline-type structures. They took me into the City of Light and into a courtyard where some highly developed spirit beings were viewing a type of crystal form in the middle of them, when suddenly a light being from an even higher realm appeared.

That was a demonstration of how beings from a higher realm come into the lower realms to bring messages and spiritual knowledge and truth. Of course, Jesus, the Christ, and Buddha are examples of these Light Beings who are sent directly from God's Realm to teach us the truths of unconditional Love and Light.

Before we returned to the Summer Realm, I received the thought to look down as we moved closer to the stunning landscape. I saw an incredibly beautiful home made of what seemed to be crystals. The flowers and gardens around were awesome. And I could see that she had many animals around her place of abode. I received the thought from her that she was taking care of some of my animals who had gone on before me. I knew that they would all be waiting for me when I was ready to return Home.

As Radiant Lady and I were moving back down to the Summer Realm, I realized that she is one of God's great messengers from one of the higher realms. And through this book, she is helping us all to realize who we really are. . . .

My basic Life Theme of "Spirituality," to which I committed before coming in this time, was chosen not only to help me grow, but also to help release more spiritual knowledge into the Earth realm. And it is a great privilege for me to help complete my life goals with the divine assistance of Radiant Lady.

Then I looked directly into Radiant Lady's eyes and said, "Thank you, Radiance, for revealing who you are, and for honoring me with a brief visit to your Home. I love you so much for guiding me closer to God. You have indeed transformed my life with our 'Guided Tours through the Afterlife.'"

"And now, JuliAnna Rosalind, it is time for you to return," Radiant Lady announced, with a tinge of humor in her voice. "It has been a great experience for me to work closely with you in your spiritual adventures growth. You are indeed fulfilling the Life Purpose that you, your orientation team, elders, guides, and angels contracted for this lifetime.

"When your wonderful ex-husband, David McKnight, said to you, 'Radiant Lady would never let you die right now,' he was indeed correct. And I must point out to you that the reason you had to share your husband—thus your divorce—was that two other soul/spirits chose him to be their spouse in this lifetime as well."

"Oh, thank you, Radiant Lady," I replied. "So all these divorces that are taking place here on this planet now have been in the Earth Contracts before arrival here. So then the last one who gets the 'shared spouse' has the option of keeping that spouse until the time of his or her departure from this dimension. There is sort of a Divine Comedy in all the human-relationship happenings as seen from a higher perspective."

We both laughed.

"And I do want to end by saying, Radiant Lady, that my near-death experience has been really good for me. I do feel in a sense that I have died and been reborn. Everything in life now means more to me. I am so happy to be back with my wonderful pets, friends, and family."

"You are not ready to leave this Earth yet. You have much work to do with regard to *our book*. (And I am letting you have my share of the royalties, by the way, since my wealth goes far beyond anything that the Earth plane could supply to me.)"

We laughed again.

"You are going to receive unlimited prosperity from this project and you deserve every bit of it. It is important for you to enjoy the last years of your time on Earth and to live fully in the moment."

"Yes, I am doing so," I replied. "I enjoyed life before, but I think I will enjoy it even more now that you have taken me on all of these incredible journeys. Thank you, thank you. . . ."

∞

Since the last journey, I have had checkups by both of my doctors and they are very pleased with my recovery. I am completely back to normal.

While I was in the hospital, I had an angioplasty, in which a scope was inserted through an artery to look at the inside of my heart. The doctor reported that my heart is "crystal clear." (Maybe my arteries and veins were cleared when Radiant Lady took me for a journey over her "crystal palace." . . .)

I am now ready to receive the prosperity that is mine, which will over-turn my financial challenge.

And, in turn, I hope this book has been a great help to all who are read-ing it. It has been a great challenge to write it and share it with you.

Let me also mention in closing this chapter that the trainer and developer of the MC² program, Joe Gallenberger, has created a Home Study Manifestation Course entitled SyncCreation. You can order this course off his website, www.RainbowVentures.net. His e-mail address is gammajo@BellSouth.net.

Blessings and peace . . .

14 Meeting the Angel of Light

I was getting an image of beautiful mountains. Radiant Lady wanted me to tell about the wonderful weekend in the clouds I had when I worked at the World Council of Churches in Geneva, Switzerland. I was sent there as a volunteer. It was a program similar to the Peace Corps, but run by a church agency rather than a government agency. In fact, it was in operation long before the Peace Corps was created.

I was still a teenager when I arrived at my volunteer destination in Switzerland. I had finished a one-year business degree at Miami-Jacobs Business College in Dayton, Ohio, right out of high school. My secretarial skills learned there qualified me for an office position, working for the head of our European volunteer program. Mr. Ziler, who has been in the afterlife for years, was my boss and was an amazing person to work for. He was quite elderly when I was working for him and had such a passion for life that it made a lasting impression on me.

Shortly after I arrived in Switzerland, Mr. Ziler decided to take his whole office staff on a tour of the famous Matterhorn for the weekend.

I began to get the Akashic Life Imprint of the experience.

∞

As we left Geneva and nosed our car southward, I practically sat on the edge of my seat to drink in the newness and beauty of my surroundings. It was fall and on this particular day the sky was especially clear. We followed Lake Geneva for many miles. The lake was dotted with birds and sailboats. On one side of the road, a farmer was turning over his fields with a hand plow, and following close behind him were seagulls, taking advantage of the freshly prepared meal of unearthed worms.

We passed through quaint little towns with cobblestone streets and overhanging buildings trimmed with clinging vines and colorful flowers. The southern region of Switzerland is a land of grape vineyards, and we passed miles and miles of rusted grapevines, touched with nature's brush of fall. We were stopped several times by herds of cows ringing their Swiss bells with great pride as they made their way to pasture.

The road began to narrow as we drew closer to our destination. As we wound around an unguarded road that spiraled upward, we could look directly into the deep, dark valley below. Finally, our road came to an end. We parked the car in a barnlike building and boarded a little red train to sit erect on hard wooden seats that held no comfort for the weary. I was too overcome with the excitement of this new adventure to be concerned with such trivial matters, however. After a couple of jerks, the train began its slow climb up the mountain. Gazing out into the darkness and seeing only my reflection prompted me to press my nose flat to the cold window to get a better look at the world of shadowed wonders beyond.

The moon was full above the mountains, and only their white nightcaps could be seen against the blanket of darkness. The journey ended all too soon as our electrified train came to a screeching halt. We grabbed our belongings and stepped out onto a quiet platform. The station was not set apart from the village of Zermatt, and as we rounded the corner of the station we were on the main street, the only street in town.

The time was only 8:30 P.M., and a blanket of quiet serenity hovered over the entire village. Many of the shutters of the buildings were closed, for it was off season for the tourists. We were lucky to have in our group of four a French-speaking German secretary who, upon asking a cobbler the best place to stay for the night, managed to find a cheap, choice set of rooms on the top floor of one of the Swiss chalets. Our Swiss hostess saw that we got everything we needed for a good night's rest, even a wine bottle filled with hot water for our feet—a true "hot water bottle."

The next morning my dreams were interrupted by the sweet peal of church bells resounding through the valleys. We opened the shutters, but the sunlight did not flow in, for the clouds hung low on the nearby mountains. I became mesmerized by the newness of this storybook land and my eyes scanned all portions of my surroundings, finally falling upon the spot where the famous Matterhorn lay. The clouds guarded this mountain as if it were a precious gem, their vigilance keeping us from getting a full view of its towering grandeur.

After filling our stomachs with a typical Swiss breakfast, we purchased tickets at the cog railroad station at the edge of town to take a trip to the top of the mountain opposite the Matterhorn to get a clear view. It was early and there were only ten people on this storybook train. It twisted and slithered like a snake through the fall wonderland of golden beauty, going up, up, up. At the same time, my ears were going pop, pop, pop, as I swallowed hard to keep them clear.

Finally, we reached the snow line and specks of cool, white fluff dotted the land about us. Before we knew it, this trip through a fall wonderland had turned into a winter wonderland. The big flakes of snow fell gently about us, and we knew that God had just covered the ground with a brand new white blanket. When the tracks were no more, the train stopped and I rambunctiously jumped off the train into a snowbank, which to my surprise came up to my knees. It was quite a thrill, though a cold one, to be suddenly flung from one season to another in less than a hundred turns of the train wheels. Our party walked around awhile, and after throwing some snowballs, taking pictures, and straining our eyes to see the Matterhorn, again boarded our faithful little train and headed back to our peaceful village.

We spent only one weekend in the clouds of this wonder-world, but in that short time got a taste of a peace that many peoples of the world struggle to gain. We carried back with us new insights on life, visions of the wonders of God's world, and inspirations to carry out our duties in the circle of daily routine.

Then the images faded away.

∞

I knew that Radiant Lady must be ready for our next experience.

"Yes, I am," replied Radiant Lady. "I'm so glad you got a good night's sleep and are now alive, awake, alert, and enthusiastic on this beautiful full-moon spring day."

"Oh, yes, yes. I feel so rested and ready to finish this manuscript with you at long last. I so enjoy my times with you, however, that I almost dread the end of this amazing experience. That's the only problem with time. It's linear and has beginnings and endings. I like the 'beginnings,' but I don't like the 'endings.' I always feel sad when anything ends.

"It's said that 'The most permanent thing in life is change'—and that certainly is true. It is one of the main things we have to get used to in this unreal world: change. And that in itself is a sign that it is not real because nothing in it lasts. Everything in the physical universe eventually disintegrates.

"The Disconnect Principle really is relevant here on planet Earth. We get disconnected from all that has meaning to us, and then we're left with just ourselves until we disconnect from our bodies. Even that makes me somewhat sad because I have gotten even more connected with my body and my wonderful Strongheart. God is so awesome in creating and loaning us these amazing bodies to walk around in on this challenging plane of existence."

"Rosalind, after 70 years on planet Earth, you should be so used to change that it shouldn't bother you anymore."

"Oh, no, it bothers me even more than when I was younger because I have become much more sensitive to the wonders of God's world. Everything in life has much more meaning to me than when I was young. I was always so confused about life and what it was all about then."

"Yes, I know, Rosalind and that is what we're going to talk about now."

"Oh, you're going to go back into my past when I was such a jerk."

"Now, Rosalind," Radiant Lady responded. "One thing you are learning is patience with everything and everyone, and judgment even of yourself should not be in your mind at this point in your life."

"I'm sorry, Radiant Lady. I do love myself. But I feel like a completely different person now than when I was younger. I guess that becoming a different person means that I have been following my purpose in life as I had planned it, and have overcome most of the obstacles that I put in my own way."

"That is certainly correct, Rosalind. And we want to share with all your readers the 'new beginning' that took place in your early life and changed your direction completely."

"Oh, yes, Radiant Lady. I'm ready now to review the most challenging time of my life, and how everything changed to put me on the road to a happier, more successful life."

"Your storybook life in Switzerland took a sudden downward turn after you were there for a while, and you started getting depressed."

"Yes," I responded. "I was only 18 when that happened. I had had such an active, exciting life as a teenager. I was part of a family of eight children and there was so much going on around me. I think perhaps I had never had a chance to take a good look at who I was. So when I went to Geneva and started working in an adult world with no young people, I began to feel very insecure and unsure of myself. My depression set in after about six months."

"Our orientation team was monitoring you very closely. We began to see something brewing that wasn't in your chart, so we wanted to keep close tabs on you when you started in a direction different from what we had planned together."

"Oh, oh," I said. "But you know what, Radiant Lady? I consider the experience I had in Europe my Dark Night of the Soul. I would never want to go through it again, but I cherish it as an amazing spiritual experience."

"With your main Life Theme being spirituality, you would indeed cherish the experience as it turned out. But we had to work very hard from this side to keep you from breaking your contract with God. When people commit suicide, they actually cut themselves off from God until they get back in line with their purpose for coming to planet Earth."

"It became *so* painful being in a physical body, at the emotional level, that all I could think of was to get rid of my body. As I became more and more depressed, I began to sink into a world that I was never aware of before. It was filled with darkness. I would even see a dark spot in front of me—literally; and I would reach out and try to pull that darkness away from my sight. But it wouldn't go away.

"I wrote in my spiritual diary, and prayed and prayed to God to help me. I wrote disturbed letters home to my mother. It was at that time that she said my spirit made a visitation to her. I was reaching in all directions for help, but I didn't feel I was getting any help at all. I was so young and sensitive about everything."

"Yes, Rosalind," said Radiant Lady, "and the turning point came when you got angry with God."

"Yes," I replied. "One night I was alone in our Geneva apartment. The family I lived with were gone on an overnight trip. So I sat down on the floor and began talking to God.

"I said something like, 'Okay, God, I have gone to church all my life.'" (My wonderful niece Patrice, with whom I am very close, recently pointed out that a spiritual teacher of hers said, "Sitting in church doesn't make you an authentic Christian, just as sitting in a garage doesn't make you a car. . . .") "'I sat in church most of my early life and I was taught that you exist, God. However, I never really called on you or prayed to you because things were going so well for me. Now, God, I really, really need you to help pull me out of this deep, dark pit that I am sinking into. I have been asking and asking for help, but you just haven't responded. So I think that I have been lied to, and that you really don't exist. I just took for granted that what I was taught in church and Sunday School was true. But now I think it is a bunch of bull.

"'So God, instead of asking you, I am going to *command* you.

"'I am giving you one last chance. I want you to send an angel right through the wall in front of me and have that angel take away the horrible emotional pain that I have been experiencing. I will give you *one hour* to respond. I am going to sit here and wait and watch. And if you don't send that angel to me to take away my pain, you are out of my life for good.'"

"Yes, Rosalind," replied Radiant Lady, "the whole orientation team was there with you. But you were *so* angry that we couldn't even begin to get your attention. You were so set on getting what *you* wanted and not what God wanted for you that you shut everything and everyone out of your life, including God."

"I know," I replied. "I was pissed at God for not granting my request to send an angel to take away the pain. So, as you well know, I just said, 'Okay, God, I gave you your chance to redeem yourself in my life. I just don't believe in you anymore. I've had it with you. So there!'"

"And that is when the Holy Spirit moved out of your life and left you to fend for yourself."

"Yes. It was so dramatically clear when I denounced God. I actually experienced the Holy Spirit leaving my body. That night I felt so abandoned, alone, and frightened—and even *more* depressed. I was aware of a dark entity coming into my room and standing beside my bed because I had released all of God's protective Love from my life in the form of the Holy Spirit. Perhaps it was that dark being that convinced me to go ahead and get rid of my body.

"I made the decision that night to go across the street the next day and buy some sleeping pills, which I did. It was so painful to be wearing this body that was now devoid of Spirit, that I felt compelled to take the pills that very night.

"After everyone in the household went to sleep, I snuck into the one and only bathroom of the small apartment, took the whole bottle of sleeping pills along with two aspirins. Then I went back to my bed and went to sleep—and slept for a *week* without even waking up!"

"Putting aspirins in with the sleeping pills was still your cry for some kind of help," replied Radiant Lady.

"The aspirins didn't help, of course," I replied. "My vision was completely blurred when I opened my eyes a week later to see two people bending over me discussing what they could do for me. After a couple more days I was better, and I survived the ordeal. I was very fortunate that I wasn't left with brain damage or blurred vision."

"And, yes, you were with us during that week that you were asleep, Rosalind," replied Radiant Lady with compassion in her voice. "We were working on you the entire time to help regenerate your body and keep your soul/spirit connected to your physical form. At times like that, your soul/spirit bodies get disconnected from you and, because you had put yourself in a limbo state between two worlds, we were there working with your soul/spirit bodies as well as with your physical body."

"Thank you, Radiant Lady," I replied gratefully. "I had no clue that I had such an incredible team of helpers working with me. I was so emotionally distressed that I shut out all inside and outside help. It is so amazing to me now that I was desperately asking for help and I was surrounded with mega-help the entire time—in fact I have been surrounded with unlimited help for my entire life while here on Earth!

"Then it got worse. They sent me to a psychiatrist who asked what was wrong. When I opened my mouth to start talking to him, he said, 'You're okay. Go on home.'

"So I left his office more depressed because my desire to have someone listen to my feelings about my pain—or merely to have someone to talk to—was squelched. There was no one who was interested in talking to me. I felt completely abandoned by everyone, including God. It is awful to be written off by adults as not even being important enough to listen to. That is why I take time to listen to any young person who wants to share his or her insights and feelings.

"Then the family I was living with, in their attempt to help me, did something that made me feel guilty for trying to take my life; things got even worse as a result.

"We all got together in a little circle in the living room and they made me promise that I would not tell anyone what had happened. They said that they would not tell anyone either. That made me feel *so* guilty because the bottom line was that I *wanted and needed help* and didn't care who knew what happened."

"It was your way of getting attention," replied Radiant Lady. "None of the adults around you were secure enough in their own lives to give you the attention you so desperately wanted.

"And, Rosalind, we saw at that time how your energies changed, and we became extremely concerned about you. The family decided, out of desperation, to send you to Kassel House in Germany, so that you would be with more young people like you, hoping that it would pull you out of the depression. They genuinely wanted to help you, but didn't know how."

"Well, when I got to Kassel House everyone seemed so happy—and that made me more depressed because I wasn't happy. So I just decided to get rid of my body once and for all by hanging myself.

"I was able to find a sturdy rope and carefully planned my demise. I stuck the rope under a heavy sweater and went down into the basement of Kassel House to a tiny bathroom that had some pipes to tie the rope to. It was dusk, and a stream of light was coming into the small bathroom near the top of the wall. I tied the rope up, and put the noose around my neck, and looked into the light as one last ray of hope.

"Suddenly, a voice, loud and clear, said, 'DON'T DO IT.'

"I was so *shocked* at hearing the commanding voice that I couldn't follow through with the hanging. I took the rope down from the pipes, put it under my sweater, and rushed out of the bathroom and back upstairs to my room."

"And that was when you had the first dramatic change in your life," said Radiant Lady. "Our orientation team worked hard to make sure you received the message. AhSo, your spirit guide, spoke it out loud and clear, and we were thrilled that it really got through to you."

"Well, I have to tell you, Radiant Lady," I said. "I had never had anything like that happen before, and it scared the shit out of me!"

"That was good," said Radiant Lady. "That was exactly what we had hoped for. Since that scared you so much, we wondered what would have happened if God had sent an angel to you as you originally requested. At that time you were so angry at God that you wouldn't have seen the angel if it had appeared to you. And I want to tell you that there were a *lot* of angels standing around ready to appear if the anger energies had dissolved to let their Light back into your life."

"Oh, Radiant Lady," I said, "I probably would have been freaked out by such a visitation because I *really* didn't believe that it would happen."

"There you go, Rosalind. Your lack of faith was the real reason the angel didn't appear. Having faith in God makes all the difference in the world. As you recall, when you shut the Light out of your life, you stepped over into the dark side. By shutting God out of our lives, we shut out the Light, and the dark side takes over."

"Oh, God, I'm sorry, I never really apologized to you. I love you so much, God. I can't believe that I shut you out of my life at the time I needed you most."

"God understands more than you can ever imagine, Rosalind."

"The next miracle happened a couple of days after hearing that wonderful male voice of my spirit guide AhSo, who gave me that command not to take my body from planet Earth.

"My parents knew that I was disturbed, so they called me home. The administrator at Kassel House drove me to Frankfurt and put me on a plane to New York City, where Mom, Dad, Larry, and Linda met me."

"Yes, and it was like being back in the womb when you got home. You lay on the living room couch in a fetal position for about two weeks before you began coming out of your depression."

"And, you know what, Radiant Lady? No one in the family *ever* asked me what happened or wanted to talk about my experiences in Europe. I was never able to process the experience adequately—until the next miracle occurred in my life."

"Yes, the angel visitation that you originally requested finally did take place."

"And did it ever. That was the *most* amazing experience I have ever had in my life, and I have never been able to talk to anyone about it until now—when I'm telling the world about it."

"So now is a good time to share the story."

"Well, I had been home from Europe about a month. I had slept a lot and my energies had become more balanced. I had a new appreciation for God after my dramatic rescue in that little bathroom in the basement in Kassel, Germany. I didn't really understand what had happened; but it saved my life and that was the important thing.

"I was sound asleep in my room late one night when suddenly I woke up and saw a large Angel of Light standing at the foot of my bed. I was astounded!

"I sat up in bed and stared at the Light that radiated from the angel and completely absorbed the darkness of the room into Itself. The amazing Light from the angel began circling around me, cleansing my entire body and lifting me into a higher level of vibration. I could feel the Holy Spirit dramatically move back into my entire system. It has never left me from that time when I embraced the Light of God and rejected the darkness.

"Then I lost all consciousness of being in my room. I felt that the wings of the angel wrapped around me and took me into a Heavenly Place where there was *only* Light. The angel moved me into the *presence of God.* I experienced Love and Joy so incredible that it filled every cell in my body and has never left me.

"Then a powerful message came from the center of the angelic Light form: '*Rosalind, you have been chosen to share my Light with others.*'

"I knew that it was God speaking to me through the angel. It seemed like I was in that special Light energy for an eternity. Now I know I was taken into the no-time level. The Angel of Light disappeared slowly, but the Light Energy that penetrated my soul/spirit has kept me since then in that *eternal presence of God.* I have *never* felt alone since that time and I have always felt connected. I knew I had a mission to accomplish in this lifetime and I was going to embark on it full speed and full Spirit!

"And this is where the concept of the 'unending circular essence' comes in, because that point was where the book begins, when I felt a compulsion to work with young people because of what I had experienced in my own life. And I might note that about 30 years after working with the young people I received calls from two of them who had to do a great deal of research to find me right here at Heavenly Acres, to say thanks for what I did to guide them in the right direction and for listening to them when no other adult ears were open to their inner thoughts.

"It was as if the Angel of Light plugged me into the Source of the All That Is . . . and helped me to realize who I really am: I am Light manifested in Love and expressed in Joy, Joy, Joy. . . .

"This book is one of the results of accepting the challenge put forth to me by the Angel of Light. On that night of transformation, I made the commitment that everything I did from that time on would be for the Glory of God. . . ."

"And, yes, Rosalind," said Radiant Lady. "You have helped to light up the lives of many. We want everyone who reads this book to know that the Angel of Light will be there for them when and if they call for help. And their spirit guides and guardian angels are always there with them, ready to help when called upon. And their Earth committee is also always there for them as well.

"And, of course, God is always there for them because it is God who has set this complete 'help line' in place. We want everyone to remember that all they have to do is 'Ask, and they will receive'—always. . . .

"The main premise of this book is to make people aware that there is so much help there for them at all times. We never sleep on this side. We are always with you, 24/7. Just call for assistance on your 911 Mental Help Line connected directly into God's Unconditional Love energies.

"So, Rosalind," concluded Radiant Lady, "this brings another chapter to a close, but it is not a 'close' but an 'opening' for many who are reading this book.

"Goodbye, and we will be together again soon."

15 How Did This Experience Change Your Life?

I could see myself walking. Yes, I was on my morning walk. I love my morning walks on this land surrounded by farmland and woods, and bounded by the James River. A railroad runs along the James River. I love it when the train comes by while I am walking. I wave to the conductor and he pulls the whistle. There are hills and mountains in the distance. And the birds—there are always birds.

Then a certain time of the year, the frogs come out, and do they sing! When I walk by the pond where they are singing so loudly, I say, "Hi, frogs." Then they all grow quiet, as if thinking, "Who is that interrupting our morning conversation?" Then I wait, and they all start croaking their animated conversations again. And when spring comes, the flowers bloom all along the road. I often stop and talk to the flowers to tell them how beautiful they are.

There are the cows and calves in Esthmus's pasture. Esthmus is the farmer who cut down some of the trees surrounding his pasture to keep his cattle alive and well so they can be sent to market for auction and eventually slaughter. It is a strange world we live in. We slaughter the trees to keep the cattle alive so that they can be sent to slaughter. Much of what happens on the Earth plane has to do with money and survival. Reverence for life is not usually first on the agenda here in this Earth dimension.

All the cattle have numbers, so I often stop to talk to 33, and then to

192, and so on. I frequently talk to Esthmus when he rides by. He slows his black pickup truck down to have a conversation with me. He tells me that he leaves the radio on in the barn for the cows that are going to the 4H meeting, which his granddaughter is involved with. They want the cattle to get used to human voices.

I have also gotten to know the families who live along the road where I walk. I enjoyed a talk with Bertha one day. She is a lady who has lived in the area since she was a little girl. She tells me how she lived in the house by the Galts Mill. The mill still stands but it is not functional. Then it was a mill along with a country store, and the train would slow down as it passed to pick up the mailbag, which was put on a pole beside the store. I love the stories of what life was like in the past.

Bertha told me about the nearby neighbor who had recently died, who lived in the now-empty house sitting on a high hill. As I pass that house, I wave to the lady who lived there. I always have the feeling that the past resident of the beautiful old empty house is still around. I look up at the house and feel that she is waving down at me, hoping that I will wave back, which I do. She was living alone when she died and now having someone recognize that she is still around I'm sure gives her a feeling that someone cares. Eventually, though, I didn't sense her waving anymore as I passed. That's good because I know that she has gone on to the no-time zone where she belongs. But I feel a sense of emptiness within me—you know, the Disconnect Principle—knowing that she is not there anymore to greet *me* on my morning walk.

Then there is the young man who drowned in the James River just beyond the railroad track. He drowned because he and his two buddies were drinking while fishing. The young man stepped into a deep hole in the river and never came back up. They finally found his body down the river. For a while after that, I always had the feeling that he was waving at me from the railroad track to get my attention to tell me that he was still alive. But he also went on after his Memorial Service at the little country church farther up Galts Mill Road.

As I have walked my two-mile morning walk for more than three years, I have waved to many other neighbors who passed me in their cars on their way to work every morning.

Then one beautiful morning I met Theresa. I had just crossed the wonderful bridge where I often stop and look down to see the snakes lying on the rocks sunning themselves in the summer sun. I was right at the corner where Theresa had stopped her car to make a turn. She had a cat in the backseat, and her passenger window was open a crack. We looked at each other and smiled, and she reached over and opened the window more.

I said, "Nice cat."

Theresa replied, "Oh, yes, I'm taking him to get him fixed. I took my trash to the dumpster one day and when I threw it in, this wonderful little kitten jumped out right into my arms."

I asked, "Then you are a cat person?"

"Yes," Theresa said. "I have several more at home. I live just down this road." She pointed back to where she had just come from.

"Well, I'm a cat person, too," I said. "I would love to visit you sometime and meet your animals. Do you have dogs, also?"

"Oh, yes," said Theresa. "I have dogs, and my dogs and cats are all good friends."

"I have dogs, too, Theresa. You'll have to come and visit my animals sometime," I said.

Theresa and I have become good friends. She is an avid reader and when I found that out, I gave her a copy of *Cosmic Journeys.* I wouldn't give my book to just anyone in this very conservative area. But I had a feeling that I should give a copy to Theresa, who is an open-minded person. She just loved it. She has read it more than once and is really looking forward to reading *Soul Journeys.* She'll be surprised to find herself mentioned in this book. I won't tell her. She was so thrilled to meet the live author of a book when I gave her a copy of *Cosmic Journeys.* So it will be fun for her to say, "I know this author and she wrote about *me* in her latest book."

I want to tell you a story she shared with me that I feel is relevant for what I am going to discuss in this chapter. A couple of years ago, she was a sitter for an elderly lady who had Alzheimer's. Theresa is a very sensitive and caring person and totally adored the lady she was sitting with. So she did very special things for her, like taking her for rides in the country. One day, after they had driven around for about two hours through a beautiful countryside with a lake and mountains in the background, they returned home and sat down to have a snack.

The lady looked at Theresa and asked, "Would you be willing to take me for a ride in the country sometime? I haven't gone for a ride in the country for a long time, and would just love to do so."

This story made me think that most of us here on planet Earth have memory loss of all the wonderful times we spent in Paradise between lives, where we went for many strolls (or flights) through absolutely breathtaking scenery. In fact, all of us "have been there and done that," and have forgotten that everything that exists in the afterlife, we have experienced.

Now the images of my walks are starting to fade, and I know that Radiant Lady is here to be with me for our final chapter. I'm really going to miss my tours and regular visits with her!

∞

"Hello there, Radiant Lady. Are you here? Are you here?" I asked.

"Of course I am, Rosalind. I think you are starting to get paranoid that I am abandoning you."

"I'm really not paranoid about your not being here. I think I'm just feeling sad that our regular sessions together are coming to an end."

"Just know, Rosalind, that I have been with you for many eons, and I will always be with you. I will be right here to meet you when you arrive in this dimension of Love."

"Oh, yes, thank you for reminding me. I have gotten so attached to your energies. And I will always remind myself that you are with me, no matter what happens."

"By the way," I continued, "as to the title of this chapter—'How Did This Experience Change *Your* Life?'—are you asking *me* that question, or the readers, or both?"

"I am asking both you and the person reading this book right now. Has the information through these journeys changed the way you look at your life as it relates to your journeys on planet Earth?"

"I can tell you that it has dramatically changed my outlook," I replied.

"In what way, Rosalind?"

"Well, when I look at people now, I have a completely different view of them. I can look at a drunk lying on the street or a multimillionaire like Donald Trump and realize that people have their own personal agenda, and are operating from their own detailed chart that they created along with their Earth committee before they came into this Earth experience. That fact in and of itself makes each individual unique."

"Yes, Rosalind, each person is unique and special in the eyes of God, and it is good that you can view them that way."

"Here on this planet," I said, "we have been programmed to judge people, and put them in categories of all types according to financial status, race, education, and so on. That means nothing to me now. In fact, this new information teaches me that I shouldn't waste my energy judging people because I have no knowledge of why they are here and what their Life Purpose and overall agenda are. I find myself being much more accepting of everyone. Now I look at people with curiosity instead of judgment, and wonder what their Life Chart might be like. Of course, we can tell that somewhat as we see people play out their life themes. But I don't want to get back into the judgment mode by trying to figure out how they are playing out their Life Chart information!"

"I'm glad that has made an impact on you because it is so important for humans to love and tolerate each other as fellow humans," Radiant Lady responded. "The fact that each human has the same orientation program before coming in makes everyone equal. You are all coming from the same place whether you are rich, poor, happy, sad, black, or white."

"We have just received a new resident in Lynchburg who is a past-life therapist," I said. "I'm fascinated by his brochure in which he indicated that in his own healing process he has experienced events from over 50 of his past lives. He has been a prostitute in New Orleans, an African shaman, a Shawnee Indian, an African-American slave, a Buddhist monk in Japan, a drug addict in Istanbul, a Bedouin desert nomad, a Druid priest, and a homeless beggar in London—just to name a few. And of course we usually have agendas running from lifetime to lifetime where we are probably working on some of the same challenges in each lifetime. He is absolutely fascinating in this lifetime, and has so many talents probably carried over from some of his other Earth lives. You can check out his website, www.leestone.net, and learn how interesting he is in this lifetime."

"Well, I don't think I'll check it out," replied Radiant Lady. "I am not too adept at using computers. But I am good at using my own mental computer."

"I'm sure you are, Radiant Lady," I replied. "I was actually suggesting to readers to check Lee out."

"It is well worth checking Lee Stone out," said Radiant Lady. "But remember, it is not who you were in a past incarnation, but what you accomplished with who you were and how you grew spiritually."

"Yes, I now understand that," I said. "Lee made it quite clear at a recent lecture that the lessons for all lifetimes are for spiritual growth. And there is another thing that has really made an impact on me—the quality of your life and the fact that you are interested in me and how I live my life."

"Well, if you think I'm interested, you should know that God's love for you extends far beyond my capacity to love," replied Radiant Lady.

"And you know, another thing that really, really impresses me is the fact that there is absolutely unlimited help from so many sources—and it is all free, with no strings attached. I get the impression that the afterlife exists mainly to help us Earth residents function more adequately. So much of what takes place over there has to do with helping people get back on the Earth to grow more spiritually, or helping people get adjusted back in that land of Paradise, or Nirvana, as it is also called. It's a win-win situation in your idyllic world."

"I find it such a joy to serve God and humanity, Rosalind," said Radiant Lady. "And I know you feel the same. You have truly become a service-oriented soul, and that is what life in our dimension, and your dimension, is all about."

"Radiant Lady, another thing I have learned from these journeys is that life in the afterworld is much, much better than I could ever have imagined. Just to think about what is in store for us when we return to our spiritual Home gives me so much hope and satisfaction.

"You know what, Radiant Lady? I'm going to have to shut down this conversation and get to bed. I have to get up early tomorrow, so I need to rest my heart and my mind."

"By all means, Rosalind, get your rest. As I always say, we have no time putting pressure on us here in the afterlife as you do on the Earth plane. Sleep and dreaming are vital to your health. And that is when everyone from the Earth plane makes nightly visits to go to school over here, visit loved ones, and so forth!"

∽

"I'm back, Radiant Lady," I said. "I was just thinking how amazing it is that each time I have written a book, I get a new heart!"

"Well, you know, Rosalind, the heart is the fourth chakra, which represents the fourth dimension, or Summerland, where most from the Earth plane come to retire after doing their 'time' on planet Earth."

"That's interesting," I replied. "So the opening up of our chakra levels represents where we will end up upon physical death. If I have opened my heart chakra through being loving while on Earth, I will migrate to the Love Dimension, where you took me on many of my visits."

"That is indeed so. Those who live in the lower, slower vibrations of their base chakras will end up in the lower, slower vibrations of the darker dimensions upon death."

"There is never an end to what you can teach me, Radiant Lady," I said. "Another thing that I have learned from your teachings and the journeys you have taken me on is the importance of clearing our energies before we leave the Earth plane. That is where the angels can be of help. There are many angels ready and waiting to help those who ask for clearance of their energy systems or a release from their addictions."

"That is indeed so," replied Radiant Lady. "And one of my favorite concepts is that if we ask for help, we will receive it. That is one of the most important lessons I have taught you because many of you on planet Earth are just not aware of all the help available to you."

"That has become so clear to me, and I am learning more and more to ask for help," I said. "In my earlier life, I had trouble asking for help because I either thought I didn't deserve help or didn't need any help because I was all-powerful, or something like that. They say that for many people it's harder to 'receive' than it is to 'give.' You know, we have always had so much emphasis on giving, giving, giving. But not much has been said about 'allowing'—allowing ourselves to receive love and help from others. It takes some releasing of our ego energies to admit that we need help."

"That is indeed so, Rosalind," replied Radiant Lady. "So often the souls that get locked into the stagnant energies, between dimensions, are those who are locked into themselves and are neither dead nor alive. And they remain so until they renew their stagnated lives, and begin to see that they need help to move into a higher light dimension."

"I realize that if I had died when I took the sleeping pills and was in my lower and slower chakra energy of doubt, anger, fear, and hatred, I would have gotten stuck somewhere in an energy space that was as painful as the one I was in while I was in my body. That emotional pain I was experiencing when I was in the Dark Night of my soul was as painful or more so than any physical pain I have ever experienced while in this body. So when souls go over with such intense emotional pain, getting out of the body probably allows the emotional pain to become even more intense."

"That's exactly right, Rosalind," responded Radiant Lady. "And that is why we were working so avidly to help you while you were still in your body. It is so important to do clearing of the addictions and emotions that are stuck in your physical body. It is much more difficult to clear them once the physical body has died. The physical body is a live entity, and it helps in clearing itself while it still has the Life Force in it."

"Well, I hope people reading this book will heed this advice and call upon the angels to help them clear their physical bodies of any or all of their addictions or lower emotions of anger, fear, doubt, hatred, and so forth. I remember that the Bible always indicated that you should never let the sun set on your wrath—meaning that if you have anything against anyone or anything bothering you, you should settle it before going to sleep. Just ask for help and forgiveness, and go to whoever is bothering you, tell them you love them, and apologize to them."

"That is very good advice, Rosalind."

"Well, Radiant Lady," I said, "I could just go on and on about what I have learned that has changed my life. The writing of this book with you has changed my life dramatically. I feel so much closer to God. When we are working with Ray and Tash, I become so aware of how close God is in our lives and in our own energy systems. I have also become so much more aware of my thoughts, and how every thought we have goes somewhere. So I have caught myself when I think negative thoughts about anything or anyone."

"That is the key to growing spiritually, Rosalind," replied Radiant Lady.

"The other thing that excites me and is helping me overcome my financial restrictions is the realization of how powerful our thoughts are in creating exactly what we desire to have happen in our life," I said. "Thoughts are powerful when we get into the afterlife, but just as powerful while we are in the physical bodies. I realize how much 'we are what we think.'"

"I have been with you throughout your present lifetime, and many lifetimes before. I can notice the difference in your energies, which is what your orientation team has hoped for. Therefore, we also hope that others reading this book have learned some of the same lessons that you have learned."

"I hope many others have gotten a lot out of this book, just as I have," I replied. "You have dedicated so much eternal energy to getting this book published on the Earth plane. The world itself is getting more and more difficult to live in because of all the intense energies that are pushing upon it from so many directions. I know that God is working from many different levels to help in the healing of Mother Earth herself. And I know that we help cleanse Mother Earth as we cleanse our own energy systems."

"Yes, you do, Rosalind," Radiant Lady replied, "If every soul in physical bodies on the Earth plane would clear their own energy systems with Light, Love, and Joy, the whole world would have a complete transformation. That is one reason why some souls chose to go back to Earth—not only to grow spiritually themselves, but also to help Mother Earth to grow spiritually."

"Again, it's getting time for me to retire, Radiant Lady," I said.

"Okay. Do have pleasant dreams."

"But before I go, I want to say that another very important thing I learned is the importance of living in the moment. That is all we have—this very moment."

"That is another thing that is hard for humans to accomplish because of fear of the future," Radiant Lady said.

"Well, when I found myself not able to breathe, realizing that I might die, it hit me so profoundly that appreciation for every second while in these physical bodies is vitally important. So I continually repeat my affirmation given to me directly from the spirit world: 'I am Light, manifested in Love and expressed in Joy, Joy, Joy. . . .'"

"Yes, JuliAnna Rosalind, that is the essence of everything we have taught in this book," replied Radiant Lady.

"And I would like to give a special thanks to all who are reading this book," I said, with a touch of sadness in my heart that this wonderful journey was coming to an end:

> May each of you enjoy your nightly tours of the afterlife that you take on a regular basis to visit love ones, take classes, and learn lessons about living life more fully on planet Earth.

I will see all of you on our journeys into the night skies of the cosmos.

I love you, Radiant Lady loves you, and God loves you.

I look forward to seeing you when we all return Home to God's eternal realm of Love from whence we came.

Goodnight . . . and pleasant journeys!

"Excuse me, Rosalind," replied Radiant Lady, "I don't like to interfere with your beautiful ending, but I need to have a last word."

"Oh, I'm sorry, Radiant Lady," I said. "You're the tour guide and should have the last word."

"I need to tell you why I so abruptly ended our session at the Heavenly Conference Center in the other dimension," said Radiant Lady.

"Yes, I *would* like to know," I said. "I was a bit surprised that you ended the Conference so quickly, just as it was beginning."

"My reason," explained Radiant Lady, "is that there is so much to learn and there are so many teachers available to help spiritually hungry souls on planet Earth that where we left off at the Conference Center is exactly where we will pick up in our next book. We don't want to overload you in this book, and want to give people time to absorb what has been presented before going more deeply into further lessons in spiritual growth."

"Oh, Radiant Lady!" I exclaimed. "I hope I haven't committed to getting another new heart before finishing the third book, like I did for *Cosmic Journeys* and *Soul Journeys.*"

"Relax, Rosalind," replied Radiant Lady in a firm, self-assured voice. "Remember, you said that one important thing you have learned from our experience together is to live fully in the present moment. Please *live* in the moment and hear me out.

"Our next book together is entitled *Earth Journeys: Spirit-World Guidance for Living in the Here and the Hereafter.*"

"That's a nice title," I exclaimed. "I wonder what we'll learn from that book?"

"Oh, yes, it is a wonderful book," replied Radiant Lady. "It is already written and we'll again drop it down to you as we have done with this book."

"Sounds good to me," I said. "But I hope I'll get a rest before starting another manuscript."

"We will give you time to enjoy the publication and promotion of this present book. When the time is right, I will appear again. But I won't wait for 40 years this time. You will be ready when I appear again," she said.

"Oh, thank you, Radiant Lady," I replied with great appreciation. "Thank you for helping me with this book, and for giving me a breather before the next one. I love you so much. Thank you—and goodbye!"

"And I love you too, JuliAnna Rosalind," replied Radiant Lady. "Our next journey will be a great spiritual experience for all involved. We will convene at the Heavenly Conference Center when the time is right to begin again.

"Goodbye, dear one. . . . And goodbye to all who are reading this book. We will be together again!"

Afterword

Before I close down for the night, I want to put in a special request for the animals of our planet.

I have recently acquired a new member of my animal family. The name of my handsome new orange and white male cat is Orson Osinga Welles. He came to my animal sanctuary here in Virginia all the way from Sedona, Arizona, thanks to Beatrice Welles, who rescued Osinga from a large community of starving, abandoned cats. Osinga found a new home through animal communicator Patty Summers (www.psanimal.com). Patty is an excellent animal communicator and a good friend of mine. She asked Osinga what type of home he would like to have and he told her he wanted to be with a "spiritual" person. Patty asked, "What about Rosie McKnight?" and Osinga answered, "Yes, yes, she would be a good person to live with." So, how could I turn down such a request when Patty approached me about allowing Osinga to join my animal community?

Osinga's cross-country journey was just like on Animal Planet. Beatrice had a friend transport Osinga in a nice carrier under his airplane seat to Baltimore, Maryland. Then Bernadette, another animal-lover and rescuer, met Osinga at the Baltimore airport and drove him down to Charlottesville, Virginia, where I picked him up.

Osinga is a very special and spiritual cat. One of the first things he did after arriving in his new home was to climb to the top of my house and, just as in Disney's *Lion King*, look all around the forest as if to say, "I am the new king of the cat jungle," which he is. He is now a very happy camper, thanks to all the wonderful and caring folks who helped get him here.

Osinga is the "grandcat" of Orson Welles (since Beatrice, Orson's daughter, was the one who sent him to me). Welles directed and acted in *Citizen Kane*, which is considered by the American Film Institute to be the greatest film ever made. As a child, Beatrice spent many hours with her parents helping to rescue animals, and her passion for helping animals continues to this day.

Now, Laurie Monroe, president of The Monroe Institute, also avidly works to rescue and help animals. Laurie and I are working to support a brand-new "no kill" facility in Nelson County where The Monroe Institute is located. Laurie has gone to the extent of installing Hemi-Sync tape equipment in all the rooms in which these animals reside to help them be more relaxed. (Can't you see all the animals with little headphones on? Just kidding! Hemi-Sync has to be projected through a stereo sound system, and that is what Laurie has installed.) The animals do not live in cages but together in beautifully designed rooms to help them feel more "at home" until they are adopted.

This facility has no state or county funding and depends strictly on donations from concerned animal-lovers to help meet its operational expanses. You can help by sending tax-exempt donations to The Humane Society/SPCA of Nelson County, P.O. Box 85, Arrington, VA 22922. You can visit their web site at www.nelsonspca.org. You can even mention that you are making your donation because of reading *Soul Journeys*. The animals, and Laurie Monroe (and Bob), Beatrice (and Orson), and I thank you for any help that you might give.

About the Author

Rosalind McKnight's life in and of itself has been a preparation for the writing of *Soul Journeys*.

She had a traditional religious background. However, having a voice speak to her several times, giving her guidance when she most needed help, and receiving visitations twice from nonphysical energies of light led her to seek answers to questions that she had not asked before. On her quest for more knowledge, she attended Union Theological Seminary in New York City and received a master of divinity degree in theology.

Over the next 11 years, her search for answers to life's mysteries took a completely different turn. She moved to Virginia and became an Explorer in a laboratory setting with Robert A. Monroe of the Monroe Institute. She worked on a regular basis with Invisible Helpers who took her on visitations into higher dimensions. These explorations are written up in her book *Cosmic Journeys*.

Soul Journeys is a follow-up to her first book and guides the reader into new levels of understanding of the "real" world that we all enter when we exit planet Earth.

Rosalind McKnight contact info:

P.O. Box 622

Monroe, VA 24574-0622

E-mail: SoulJourneysBook@aol.com

Website: SoulJourneys.info

Visit the site to share and explore your own journeys with others. Also visit my site to learn about special "Soul Gatherings" in the form of workshops and conferences. You can also learn where to order an autographed copy of *Soul Journeys*.

The Monroe Institute contacts:

The Monroe Institute offers training programs, tapes, and CDs using the Hemi-Sync process for achieving many goals, such as Changing Behavior Patterns (addictive behavior/anxiety/depression), Fitness and Sports, Financial Success, General Wellness, Learning and Memory, Meditation and Spiritual Development, Pain Management, Weight Control, and Stress Reduction.

The Monroe Institute

62 Roberts Mountain Road

Faber, VA 22938

Phone: 804-361-1252

Fax: 804-361-1237

E-mail: monroeinst@aol.com

Visit the Monroe Institute Website at: www.monroeinstitute.org

Those interested in Mary Morgan McKnight's book:

Jogging through Space

Order at any bookstore using ISBN 1-55369-669-7

Order online at: www.trafford.com/robots/02-0482.html

Order from Trafford Publishing in Canada by calling toll free: 888-232-4444 (Canada & USA only)

Hampton Roads Publishing Company

... for the evolving human spirit

Hampton Roads Publishing Company
publishes books on a variety of subjects,
including metaphysics, health,
visionary fiction, and other related topics.

For a copy of our latest catalog, call toll-free
(800) 766-8009, or send your name and address to:

Hampton Roads Publishing Company, Inc.
1125 Stoney Ridge Road
Charlottesville, VA 22902

e-mail: hrpc@hrpub.com
www.hrpub.com